missing marx

missing marx

A PERSONAL AND POLITICAL JOURNAL OF A YEAR IN EAST GERMANY, 1989 - 1990

PETER MARCUSE

MONTHLY REVIEW PRESS
NEW YORK

The photos on page 129 courtesy Ulrich Joho, Berlin; on pages 36, 64, 101, 113, 222, 250, 251, 252, courtesy Bauinformation, Berlin; on page 123, courtesy of Robert Grahn, Redaktion Neues Deutschland; on pages 79 and 144, courtesy Karl-Heinz Stana, Berlin; on pages 15, 31, 94, 185, 213, 230, by the author. The cartoons on pages 73, 165, and 171 are by Henry Büttner and are found in Rudi Geerts, ed., *Hier lacht das Volk: Witze aus der alten und neuen DDR* (Hamburg: Rowohlt Verlag, 1990), reprinted with permission.

Library of Congress Cataloging-in-Publication Data

Marcuse, Peter.
Missing Marx : a personal and political journal of a year in
East Germany, 1989-1990 / by Peter Marcuse.
p. cm.
Includes bibliographical references.
ISBN 0-85345-827-8 : $36.00. — ISBN 0-85345-828-6 (pbk.) : $16.00
1. Germany (East)—Politics and government—1989-1990.
2. Marcuse, Peter. I. Title.
DD289.M37 1991
943.1087'8—dc20   91-23063
                                        CIP

Monthly Review Press
122 West 27th Street
New York, NY 10001

Manufactured in the United States of America

10   9   8   7   6   5   4   3   2   1

For Bernd Grönwald—
who tried to work positively within a
contradictory system, supporting its structure
but encouraging its reform, and, finally,
succumbing to its demise

C O N T E N T S

preface

Events in East Germany in 1989 and 1990 were part of—and in some cases triggered—a wave of revolutions in state power in Hungary, Czechoslovakia, Poland, Bulgaria, Romania, now perhaps even Albania. It is a period of deep change such as one rarely encounters in a lifetime; a period in which what is happening at the level of a whole nation is so integrally connected with people's individual lives that individuals feel themselves part of history. And not just as victims, subordinated and carried away on tides not subject to their influence, but rather as actors, active participants, as when people feel that they are themselves making history, themselves influencing the circumstances that determine their own lives. We were lucky to have been in East Germany during the crucial eleven months from the first successful public break-out from the old system to the transaction with West Germany that effectively represented its end. This book is an account of what we saw, heard, thought, and felt during that time. We have also included some reflections on those experiences, some attempt to generalize, to analyze, to draw conclusions. We have called these reflections "Excurs," and there is one on how everyday life in East Germany differed from that in West Germany; one on whether "state" and "market" were appropriate descriptions of the differences between them; one on how the differences were manifested in city

7

living in the East, and whether the differences had to do with social-ism; one on what brought about the change from "socialism" that we witnessed; one on how that change might be expected to influence the future of the city of Berlin (and what that future, in our view, should be); and then, in a summing up, a discussion of why it all happened and what the implications for the future might be.

East Germany was considered dull, gray, and monotonous by most people when my wife Frances and I decided to go there for a year's study and lecturing, to see what "real existing socialism" was like. We arrived in August 1989, six weeks before anyone in the country had even begun to think that radical change was possible. We left in August 1990, after those unthinkable changes had taken place. We were ourselves caught up in those changes, and, although we tried to understand "objectively" what was going on, no description of such events (not even the type of bare-bones chronology that we have added as an appendix) can pretend to objectivity under such circum-stances. Thus this is both a political and a personal journal.

My background, and Fran's, of course influenced what we saw. For both of us, the events we lived through evoked echoes of the past. I was born in Berlin in 1928, to parents who emigrated to Switzerland, one step ahead of the Nazis, then France, then the United States (in 1933). My father, Herbert Marcuse, was a philosopher in the Marxist tradition, who achieved an international reputation in the late 1960s as the "father of the New Left" (which he regularly denied being). He was an active participant in the efforts to radically change society that swept through Europe in 1968. My wife, Frances, was born in the United States in 1930, to parents who had left their village in southern Germany in 1926, one step after the great inflation and one step ahead of the Great Depression. Frances was Catholic, went to parochial school as a child, stopped believing in her teens; my parents were Jewish atheists; we raised our children as (secular) Jews.

I practiced law in Waterbury, Connecticut, and was active in Democratic Party politics for twenty years before getting a Ph.D. in city planning, and now teach it as a professor of urban planning at Columbia University in New York. Frances began teaching school in Waterbury the same year I began practicing law, teaching first ele-mentary school and then science in high school, until her retirement the year we left for Germany. While this is clearly my journal, we have shared so much during almost forty years of living together, and experienced almost everything that was happening in East Germany after our arrival together, that it is hard for me to separate my reactions from Fran's, and I notice I tend to use "I" and "we" almost interchangeably in this journal. Frances has corrected it wherever it does not reflect the facts!

We came to East Germany in the expectation that the economic system there might have something to teach us in the United States about certain fields—particularly housing and urban development, my own area of work—but expecting to encounter severe limitations in the political system and to have many questions about the functioning of the economic system as well. Our initial experience, after our arrival in mid-August (three months before the opening of the Berlin Wall), suggested a schizophrenic society: no one we spoke to defended the political structure, yet almost everyone professed a continued commitment to socialism and took the prevailing political and social structure for granted, expecting, at best, small incremental changes here and there. Yet within three months that political structure had been radically changed and our initial questions took on an entirely new cast: our questions became not only at what the DDR had produced in its forty years, but also at how the transition from that product would go, and where it was likely to end.

On January 11, 1990, we received a letter from Andrée Fischer, a senior editor at Dietz Verlag in Berlin, asking us to consider writing an account of our stay in the German Democratic Republic (Deutsche Demokratische Republik, or DDR) for publication that fall. We debated it and agreed that the journal form was the only way a coherent and yet personal account could be prepared within the short time-frame she wanted for publication. We had kept some notes on our day-to-day doings up until then, and had collected lots of material; we were in any event interested in recording our observations and thoughts in more detail, as a way of understanding what was going on, of working out for ourselves what it meant. So we agreed to do it. The German edition was published in October 1990, under the title: *A German Way of Revolution: DDR-Tagebuch eines Amerikaners, September 1989 bis Juli 1990.* (Why that title was chosen is discussed below.)

This English edition has been reworked to expand those areas not familiar to non-German readers, to delete those that explain things well known to them, and to include the six Excurs. The introductory section to each of the two parts gives an overview of the political events of the entire year, with brief historical background and some highlighting of the main themes.

The "journal" part of the book remains, however, essentially a record of how we saw things at the time each entry was written. We have tried to keep out afterthoughts; where subsequent events so directly related to earlier occurrences, we have occasionally inserted a later comment or reference in square brackets. We have also inserted a number of political jokes in the journal, even if we heard some of them earlier or later, because jokes were in fact one of the ways those living in the DDR dealt with the contradictory realities of their lives. I suppose the same might be said for people everywhere, but it was particularly true in the DDR, where the contradictions were particularly obvious, but could not be addressed directly. There are even jokes about jokes:

> In the DDR, jokes are invented by The Class Enemy, passed on by word-of-mouth from comrade to comrade until they reach the Politburo, and are then put into effect.

> There must be, within the Politburo, a section for jokes; otherwise how could they be so prevalent in a socialist society?

We need to thank a handful of people in the DDR who became our close friends during the year, who provided us with much of the basis on which we came to understand and feel many of the events described in the book, and whom we consider among the salt of the earth. Bruno Flierl and Lili Leder in Berlin, and Fred and Ushi Staufenbiel in Berlin and Weimar, were among the closest to us, but there were many, many others. Since they appear in this book, we will not thank them by name here—they know who they are, and in any event they may well disagree with some of what we have written in these pages. But their friendship, and that of many other warm, decent, and courageous people in the DDR, was one of the permanent benefits of our year. We wish them the kind of peaceful, democratic, and prosperous future they have richly earned.

And we need to thank Susan Lowes, Director of Monthly Review Press, for innumerable helpful comments and suggestions, and Renee Pendergrass for her work on the book's interior design. *Monthly Review* and Monthly Review Press are unique institutions, not only as publishers but also as centers of critical intellectual activity and engagement on the major issues of our times. We are proud to have them as our publishers.

—*June 1991*

DENMARK

Rostock

Hamburg

Dahmen

NETHERLANDS

DDR

POLAND

Berlin

Potsdam

Frankfurt / Oder

BRD

Dessau

Quedlinburg

Torgau

Leipzig

Dresden

Bonn

Weimar

Ilmenau

Frankfurt / Main

CZECHOSLOVAKIA

FRANCE

AUSTRIA

part 1

THE WENDE—MISSING MARX?

Introduction: The Three Phases of the *Wende*

To put our daily journal in perspective, an overview of the major events of the year may be helpful. The chronology at the end of the book gives the exact dates; here I want to present the big picture.

The big picture has two quite separate parts, quite separate story lines. The first has to do with the attempts, at the beginning to reform, then to change from the bottom up, the forty-year-old system of the DDR. The second has to do with the attempts, politically to begin with, then economically, to integrate the territory of the DDR into the national systems of West Germany, from the top down.

In the first part, the questions centered around Marx. Was he there at all, in the old DDR, or was he missing? If he was missing, was he missed? The second part has to do with money or currency—specifically, with the mark—the West German mark, as a generally available hard currency that could buy whatever people wanted, was certainly missing in the DDR. Was it because people missed it so much that unification went so rapidly? In the end, as we shall see, both those who missed Marx and those who missed the West German mark missed the mark if they hoped to get what they missed through their actions during the year.

Wende is the term used in East Germany to describe the events between October 1989 and the spring of 1990. The literal translation is "turn," or "change," and it can mean a bend in the road as well as a complete turn-around. Just what it was that changed, how big the change was, whether there was not in fact more than one change—one newspaper headlined its summary of the second 100 days since the fall of Honecker as "The *Wende* in the *Wende*"—and why the changes came about, were all hotly debated questions at the inception of the Turn. Later, the results seemed the product of unstoppable forces. But certainly many imagined, in the midst of events, that there were alternatives to the final surrender to the West. What was imagined, how, by whom, and with what basis—these form part of the story told here. The events are relatively clear; the interpretation less so.

The DDR (we will call East Germany, as it existed until October 1990, what the people there themselves called it, however ironically: the German Democratic Republic, or, in German, the Deutsche Demokratische Republik, DDR) was *the* bastion of orthodoxy and leading model of a Stalinist "Marxist-Leninist" society after *perestroika* began in the Soviet Union. *(Photo on facing page shows statue of Lenin in Lenin Square, East Berlin.)* It had, during its forty years, always had the highest standard of living of any socialist state in the world; it had only required direct Soviet intervention to maintain party rule once in its history, in the workers' uprising of 1953, and the party had maintained an absolute control over almost all aspects of life, with a security apparatus involving over 2 million people in its orbit (in a country of 16 to 17 million), exiling and occasionally imprisoning all dissidents, co-opting the social democratic party, the Social Democratic Party (Sozialdemokratische Partei Deutschlands—SPD) within its Communist Party-dominated Socialist Unity Party (Sozialistische Einheitspartei Deutschland—SED), and bringing all other legal parties within the SED-dominated National Front. The only openings in this closed society lay in what people said and thought in the privacy of their own homes—East German humor produced some of the most biting sarcasm around, as many of the stories we heard in the course of our stay, and repeat below, illustrate, and in what people heard and saw from West German television, which could not be blacked out. The church was also given a little leeway, but in return for a basic commitment to support the regime. The construction of the Berlin Wall in 1961, the sealing of all borders with the West, the rigid censorship of the media, the ceaseless propaganda, the pervasive influence of the party, all contributed to creating what looked like an impregnable structure of rule by the party hierarchy. Yet it all collapsed, without any force being used on either side, within three months. So what happened?

If there are those who predicted the change, they have not surfaced. With hindsight, the process seems almost inevitable and its "causes" easy to list: a basic instability in the functioning of bureaucratic central-ized command economies, the exor-bitant price of competition with the West, a decision by the ruling strata in the Soviet Union to both change its system and abandon its enforce-ment of derivative systems in other countries, the discontent of people seeing promises betrayed by a stead-ily declining standard of living and increasing restrictions on personal and civil liberties. But no one, in  1988, thought that the East German regime was on the verge of collapse, that with a gentle push from the people and a hard yank from the West the entire leadership of the ruling party would resign, all borders would be opened, all state-owned enterprises put on the block, Marxism-Leninism publicly rejected and evicted from all edu-cational institutions, the East German mark replaced by the West German mark as the unit of currency, and Karl Marx replaced by the new German mark as the ideological touchstone of value.

Before the *Wende*, in the summer and early fall of 1989, while there were some signs that could later be understood as harbingers of change, everyday life went on very much as usual; a little more complaining, a little feeling that times had been better, but no striking difference. Economic and political protest was visible, but limited: economic protest as escape from the system to new opportunities across the partly opened borders to Hungary, and political protest as small groups forming and demonstrations of at most a few hundred people on the streets of Leipzig and other cities.

The first phase of the *Wende* began in earnest with the really large demonstrations in Leipzig in October. In the second phase, after the opening of the borders between East and West Germany in November, the direction became uncertain, as the appeals of nationalism and the economic prosperity of the West made themselves felt. In the new parliamentarianism on which almost all agreed in the third phase, at the end of the year, the original hopes of the early makers of the revolution were smothered under a blanket of West German manipulation. After the elections, in March 1990, the only question became what the terms of annexation by West Germany would be.

The three phases of the *Wende* in East Germany can be readily demarcated. The first, the democratic breakthrough, was made possible by Hungary's decision to open its borders to DDR citizens wanting to leave for the West. The exodus across the border was seen everywhere as a hemorrhage, a symptom of the state of affairs in the country:

> A party member is called in by the party secretary and asked why he had made an application for a visa to leave the country.
> "Well, I was afraid that if things changed here, we might be the first to be blamed for the old ways and would be punished."
> "Oh, don't worry," said the party secretary, "things around here won't change so quickly."
> "That's the other reason I want to leave!"

At the same time, small opposition groups—New Forum (Neues Forum), the Initiative for Human Rights and Peace (Initiative für Frieden und Menschenrechte), Democracy Now (Demokratie Jetzt), Democratic Opening (Democratischer Aufbruch)—already or newly formed, struggled for legality, their members hounded, activities suppressed. The critical moment came on the weekend of October 7, the fortieth anniversary celebration of the founding of the DDR, when Gorbachev, in his visit, asked to comment on the absence of *perestroika* or *glasnost* in the country, said: "He who comes too late, will be punished by life itself." The repression of the demonstrations in Berlin that weekend was the toughest in thirty-five years, but also the last reflex response of an antiquated regime entering rigor mortis. The decision not to repress the large church-sheltered street demonstration in Leipzig on Monday, October 9, was the first major success of the young opposition movement, primarily outside the party, primarily intellectuals, artists, professionals. It became the voice of generalized discontent, and an eloquent voice: the chants—"We are the people" and "We are staying here" (a reaction to the exodus across the borders via Hungary)—got international attention and became the slogans for the regular Monday night marches through the streets of Leipzig that followed.

The first phase of the *Wende*, from October 9, 1989, to November 9, 1989, was a period of mass euphoria. If "revolutionary" describes, among other things, a state of mind, a mass psychology in which people of all kinds become involved in events outside their own day-to-day existence, in which social questions become immediate and personal, in which awareness is heightened, energies liberated, creativity emerges from nowhere and is apparent everywhere, then the month between October 9 and November 9 was a revolutionary month. The high point was perhaps the November 4 rally in Berlin, sponsored by the associations of artists and writers, televised live, with speeches, banners, songs, poems, unthinkable in the public arena a month earlier. People everywhere seemed united in the name of DDR national pride and socialist ideals against the leadership of a bloated, rigid, thoughtless, and increasingly corrupt party apparatus.

The second phase of the *Wende* began on November 9, 1989, with the "opening" of the Wall, the provision for the granting of permission to travel to every citizen of the DDR. It brought a new kind of euphoria: once there was free travel back and forth across the borders to West Germany, the idea of all-German unity took hold and the wreath, compass, and hammer of the DDR emblem began to disappear from the red, gold, and black of the old German flag on which it had been superimposed. This second phase of the *Wende* was the phase of nationalist revival. The opening of the Wall opened the door to the allure of capitalist consumption and wealth, and the impact was profound.

Just why the Wall was opened remains a puzzle; the current assessment is that no one realized what the decision, read matter-of-factly at the end of a press conference after a meeting of the Central Committee of the party on November 9, meant. The reaction to it was clearly unanticipated: half of East Berlin streaming across to West Berlin in the middle of the night, and an international press sensation. The only doubt that I have come across that was expressed at the time as to whether such an opening was desirable came from Bärbel Bohley, one of the founders of New Forum, who said that, when she heard the news, she took a stiff drink, went to bed and pulled the covers up over her head for fear of the consequences. Few, even the most radical of the opposition, had suggested such an abrupt termination of all travel restrictions. With historical hindsight, there are still many on the left who believe that the construction of the Wall in 1961 might have provided the basis for a more solid construction of socialism in the DDR, free of interference from the West, had it been used properly. Of course it was not; but the legitimacy of the concern about external influence in the DDR's internal affairs has since been demonstrated.

If November 9 was the beginning of a transformation in the nature of the *Wende*, then December 31, when the Brandenburg Gate was opened for a giant New Year's Eve celebration, signalled the transition to the third phase, the phase of capitalist seduction coupled with massive public involvement by the West German leadership in East German affairs. All-German nationalism turned ugly. Neo-Nazis began to appear at the Leipzig Monday rallies, New Forum withdrew its sponsorship, the word "socialism" dropped out of sight. Witchhunts and oppression of former SED members were widely discussed. That these changes ran parallel with equally militant attacks by the progressive, often pro-socialist, opposition on the old Stasi, the state internal security service, and the formation of "citizens' committees" to search Stasi offices, go through Stasi files, take over functions formerly under the control of the Stasi, made matters more complicated; the antinationalist progressive opposition groups hardly distinguished themselves from the generally patriotic

German-unity-supporting citizens' committees. The upsurge of aggressive organized private action was taking place at both ends of the political spectrum.

For a period, at the end of December and through January and February, there were serious concerns about anarchy among both old and new political groups. No one any longer contended that the elections that had chosen the existing parliament were democratic; the government had questionable legitimacy at best. But neither did the citizens' committees that in many places exercised functions normally those of the police, particularly with regard to the state security apparatus. The regular civilian police, widely under attack for earlier handling of demonstrations and protests, restrained their law enforcement activities. In the vacuum of legitimacy thus created a new political institution developed, one which was thereafter utilized in other East European states: the Round Table.

Round Tables were first convened locally on the initiative of New Forum and other citizens' groups in various cities, and organized on the national level in December 1989. They were a coming together of all the oppositional forces, whether organized as political parties or as citizens' movements, sitting together with representatives of the old parties, chaired by competent and impartial church leaders. Originally views differed as to their precise role: some saw them as places where the opposition and the government would discuss/negotiate policy issues, others as super-parliaments. The national Round Table ended as virtually a second legislative body, passing proposals through to the "elected" parliament and effectively commenting on proposals coming from the government on their way to parliament. The Round Tables had elements of corporatism about them: interest groups were represented (although a limited range, and only "public" ones), and decisions were generally made by consensus. Not until shortly before the elections in March did classic party politics play a dominant role; indeed, it was the decision to move that election up from May, pushed through by the SPD, that changed the character of the national Round Table and lost it much of its legitimacy as a consensus-establishing forum. But by that time the government had invited the separate parties and movements represented at the Round Table into the government, they had taken positions as ministers without portfolio, the SED reform leader Hans Modrow had gained respect for his avowed effort to head a "government of national responsibility" rather than a party-based one, and that government was more and more transitional and caretaking. After the elections, the national Round Table dissolved itself. Local Round Tables continued, but most were dissolved after the local elections in May.

What happened in and to the SED seems almost peripheral now, but in the first two phases of the *Wende* it was absolutely central. The SED had been formed in 1946 by a pressured merger of the Communist Party with the SPD. Through the National Front, in which the Christian Democrats, Liberals, Farmers, and other minor parties and "mass organizations"—of women, youth, trade unions, etc.—were represented, the SED regulated every sphere of life in the DDR. Hero-worship of its leaders, first Walter Ulbricht and then Erich Honecker, was encouraged. But rumors of disaffection with Honecker within the Politburo were rife before the fortieth anniversary celebration. Almost ten years of economic stagnation, continual comparisons with West Germany made possible by omnipresent Western television, tight and often arbitrary restrictions on travel or contact with foreigners, a press and news services that were propaganda organs with no popular credibility, expulsion and censorship of writers, performers, artists— all these produced a groundswell of dissatisfaction. Honecker's lack of concern with the mounting number of citizens fleeing over the borders was the final straw, and the growing street demonstrations throughout the country provided the opportunity for the established second-string leadership of the party to dump him. Egon Krenz, considered Honecker's "crown prince," took over all of Honecker's posts, began campaigning for popularity, and obviously thought he could retain power in the existing party apparatus.

But the process begun by Honecker's ouster was soon out of control. Demonstrations of party members before the party's central headquarters in Berlin in early December demanded the resignation of the entire Central Committee and Politburo. Chants included "We are the party." The old guard capitulated and resigned *en masse*, including Krenz, who resigned both as party secretary and prime minister. Parliament now elected Hans Modrow prime minister; he was one of the few higher ranking SED officials (he was first secretary of the SED in Dresden) with a reputation as an honest reformer. Modrow remained through the March election the most popular political leader in the DDR, despite his party membership; most trusted his integrity in representing his administration as one of "national responsibility," rather than party politics. In the party itself, left leaderless, a "working group" of reformers took temporary control, called a special party conference, and in mid-December elected as chair Gregor Gysi, a lawyer with impeccable credentials in defending such major opponents of the Honecker regime as Rudolph Bahro, Robert Havemann, and New Forum co-founder Bärbel Bohley. Modrow and Wolfgang Berghofer, Dresden's personable, smart, and ambitious mayor, were elected vice-chairmen. The name of the party was changed from SED to SED-PDS; the SED was later dropped.

The new leadership appointed a commission to review all of the party's property and voluntarily surrendered major assets, from buildings to publishing houses to sales enterprises for imported goods, from office equipment to holiday facilities—that it found had not been acquired with its own members' funds. With some publicity it turned more than 3 billion marks from its coffers over to the state, to be used for health and educational purposes. Assets taken over from the old SPD at the time of its merger into the SED were returned to it. Old-line party officials resigned or were pressured out. Much of the party's central office building, in the heart of Berlin, was made available for public use (the rest was later turned into offices for the new parliament). Leaders of the old guard (from Honecker to Krenz and Mielke) were expelled from the party, and dozens of members expelled in previous years were "rehabilitated" and welcomed back. The media the party continued to own were encouraged to establish their own news and editorial policies.

But critics did not believe the party had really relinquished its control over the state apparatus. While prominent leaders at the top of the national and regional hierarchies had been replaced, at lower levels within both the state and the party apparatus many old Stalinists remained. One of Modrow's first pledges when he took office was to eliminate the Stasi. Under Honecker the Stasi had been built into a force of over 130,000, allegedly with over 1.2 million informants regularly supplying it with information; it opened and often confiscated mail, listened in on conversations, followed dissidents, spied on homes, kept files on every politically active citizen. Modrow decided to reform it by making major changes in its composition and purpose, transforming it into a "regular" internal security force, free of party control, similar to its West German or U.S. counterparts. That provoked a storm of opposition in December. The main Stasi office was stormed and many regional offices taken over by citizens' committees, files ransacked, equipment yanked out and destroyed. Modrow was finally forced to abandon his reform proposal and simply disband the Stasi outright: the DDR was for a time probably the only major country in the world today without a separate internal security force. But the fight over Stasi reform cost the party credibility.

When, in January, a war memorial was smeared with paint and right-wing slogans, the party helped organize a large rally against the threat of fascism, a rally in which many other groups, including the Christian Democratic Union (Christlich-Demokratische Union Deutschlands, CDU), under Lothar De Maizière, the future prime minister, took part. Some believed the vandalism was actually the work of ex-Stasi, done to show the need for their continued existence, and that the party at least cooperated in the effort. But later acts of vandalism were not used by the party for propaganda purposes, and the reform leadership of the party and the ex-Stasi had no love lost for each other. More likely, the party had no hand in the vandalism itself but used the opportunity it presented to try to recover some momentum for its own revival. It certainly flexed its muscles in the manner in which it went about it and in the conduct of many of its more vocal members at the rally, and left a bad taste in many mouths.

The acerbity of the debate over the vandalism resulted from a mix of strong anti-Stalinism on the left and old-fashioned red-baiting on the right. The two sometimes reinforced each other. The only thing all parties but the PDS agreed upon in the election campaign was that, if they won, they would consider coalitions with other parties with the exception of the PDS. The Greens and New Forum, as well as the SPD, said no coalition in the East. Even the Alternative List in West Berlin, a loose coalition of Greens and others, said it would not, in the event of an all-Berlin election, enter a coalition with the PDS. Wolfgang Ullman, of Democracy Now, one of the earliest of the opposition citizens' movements, said his group would not work with the PDS until it clarified "how it stood on the Leninist tradition." At the time, Lenin's picture still hung in the halls of party headquarters, although no one seriously saw the PDS as a traditional Leninist party. The wounds left by a consistently Stalinist policy were deep, and many were not willing to see in the PDS anything but a continuation of the SED.

Thus in early January, PDS election hopes were dim. The party had shrunk from 1.4 million to 700,000, and demoralization was prevalent. But at a jammed party conference Gysi presented a well-received new program to the predominantly youthful delegates. He showed himself a highly intelligent, dynamic, and popular speaker, and the mood was upbeat. Gysi became a very effective campaigner, tireless, imaginative, quick with repartee. When he parachuted from a plane to demonstrate his commitment to a sports club, he got his picture on every TV program in the country; when asked whether he would be willing to share a platform with West Germany's bulky Chancellor Helmut Kohl (Gysi is short), he said, sure, but there wouldn't be much of him to see, or much of Kohl worth hearing. Berghofer quit the party in February, but Modrow stayed and agreed to be the lead candidate in the March elections (although he spoke at only one political rally so that he could maintain the integrity of his multiparty government). The 16 percent of the vote that the PDS received in March made it the third-largest party in the country.

The election campaigns of the major parties were Western-style: placards and posters, leaflets, horse-drawn carriages with loudspeakers, mass rallies, balloons, shopping bags, pencils, whirly-gigs. Its protagonists were Western too: the "brother parties" in West Germany sent over their big guns, Kohl first and foremost for the CDU; Hans-Dietrich Genscher and Graf Lambsdorff from the Free Democrats (Freie Demokratische Partei—FDP); Willy Brandt, Helmut Schmidt (both coming out of retirement, but well known in the DDR as initiators of the "opening to the East") and Hans-Jochen Vogel for the SPD. The PDS had no opposite number in the West to provide help, but still had an ample treasury and used the professional competence of its members to campaign effectively in the new style. The Greens from the West sent over speakers on only a few occasions, since they had supported the concept, adopted by the national Round Table but not adopted by parliament and ignored by the major parties, that the campaign in the East should be waged without West money or interference.

New Forum, the Initiative for Human Rights and Peace, Democracy Now—the groups that were leaders of the first phase of the *Wende*—were hopelessly out-spent and out-"starred." The mathematical fairness of talk-show time allocation could hardly make up for the greater newsworthiness of the events of the major parties, and a little bus going from town to town with top campaigners was not in the same league as the hordes of advance men, press releases, news conferences, mass rallies, literature, and trinkets that money and an experienced political apparatus could provide. The election results were a stunning defeat for the groups and parties most responsible for the first phase of the *Wende* (5 percent of the vote—the revolution eats its children, many said), an upset victory for the CDU (46 percent), a poorer showing for the SPD than had been expected (22 percent), and a slightly better one than expected for the PDS (16.5 percent). With its conservative allies and the liberals, the CDU had an absolute majority; with the grand coalition into which it entered with the SPD, it had more than three-quarters of the seats in the new parliament, ample both to amend the constitution and to run the legislative show without regard to the opposition. Its problems lay more in achieving consensus within its own ranks, since some of its members, including many in the SPD were concerned about social issues, and others like Lothar De Maizière, the new CDU prime minister, still had allegiances to the identity of the DDR. But under Kohl's heavy-handed leadership, the coalition plunged forward toward complete German unity.

The victory of the West-allied parties in the March election represented the effective end of the *Wende* and the beginning of the express march to unification. The period between the national election in March and the local elections in May can be taken either as the fourth phase of the *Wende*, in which conservative forces achieved dominance, or the first phase of the drive to unification, in which forces in West Germany already clearly ran the show. Since after this time the dominance of the West can, with hindsight, scarcely be doubted, we pick up the broad picture again in the introduction to Part 2, where we begin to discuss the process of unification.

journal

BEFORE THE WENDE:
THE OLD SYSTEM

**From Mid-Summer 1989 to the
Fortieth Anniversary Celebration**

August 15

I didn't really want to go to Weimar. The title of the application I made to the Fulbright program in the fall of 1988 was "'Revitalization' of the Inner City." I proposed to look at whether the development of the "tertiary sector"—professional services, banking, real estate, finance, insurance, stock brokerage, legal services, international commerce—was producing the same kind of changes in a country with a purportedly socialist economy as it was in the advanced capitalist countries, in cities like New York, London, Paris, Milan, Tokyo, Hong Kong. One would hardly expect such a development in Weimar; in Berlin, most likely, or perhaps in Leipzig or Dresden, but not in what we from the outside thought of as essentially a small provincial town, cultural center though it might be.

Weimar has a very good school of architecture, true, in which urban planning is also taught, and a chair in sociology. But Weimar is in the south of Germany, in Thuringia, and while it was the home of Goethe, Schiller, Herder, and an intellectual center in the early nineteenth century, it has a population of under 60,000 and is far removed from the center of things. That's why it had been chosen as the place to write Germany's new constitution in 1919 (and why it was called the Weimar Republic): because it was removed from the hurly-burly of the politics of the big metropolises. Precisely why I *didn't* want to go there!

We never understood why we were sent to Weimar. There are two possible explanations. The Fulbright program, which started in the United States after World War II as a way of cementing international understanding (and reinforcing the United States' leading position in the world), sends a limited number of academics and professionals to various countries; a corresponding number from these countries are invited to the United States. It is administered by the Council for the International Exchange of Scholars in the United States and by the ministry of higher education in the DDR; it had only been in operation in the DDR for two years at the time of our arrival.

When we visited Weimar in the summer of 1988, the Hochschule für Architektur und Bauwesen (HAB; in English, the College of Architecture and Building) had just received a letter from the ministry in Berlin saying that A.K., a professor of architectural history, was arriving in September to teach, please arrange for his stay. The HAB in Weimar had not asked for him, did not know him, did not particularly need him; he was sent to Weimar because the HAB is one of the three major schools of architecture in the DDR, and presumably someone at the ministry in Berlin thought it was a good idea to send him there. No phone calls to Weimar to check, no consultation with A.K., no exploration of alternatives—the ministry just decided. It struck us as consistent with our image of the DDR: things were decided anonymously, bureaucratically, with no reasons given, that's just the way things were. The arrangement had in fact worked out well with A.K. because he adapted well, as did the people at the HAB. We surmise that we were sent to Weimar simply because last year A.K. had been sent there and the ministry had had no complaints. That was one possible explanation. You could call it the "big black box" explanation: a question is asked, a problem arises, it gets sent to Berlin where it goes in one end of a big black box in which all decisions are invisibly made according to unknown rules by faceless people, and the answer comes out a slot at the other end of the box. Kafka knew the system; Max Weber would have expected better.

The other explanation is more substantive: "they" didn't want me in Berlin. I had the reputation of being a critical activist in city planning and housing in the United States, although I had never written about the DDR and I doubt if anyone at the ministry had ever heard of me. (They may have had some contact with, and even political doubts about, the people in the DDR who I listed as references or possible hosts, but there were also "respectable" people among my references, and there is no evidence they ever checked.) But "they" may well have heard of my father; he, after all, was very well known in West Germany, particularly after 1968, had spoken at well-publicized meetings in West Berlin, and, as much as any other member of the Frankfurt School, had written and spoken critically and in detail against Stalinism and against the orthodoxies of East European "socialism." Conceivably someone in Berlin thought my application was too conventionally acceptable to make it possible for them to reject me without losing face with the U.S. authorities, but that it was better to have me out of the way in Weimar than in the center of things in Berlin. We later heard stories of others "exiled to the provinces," of academics steered to harmless locations for research, but more direct information never surfaced.

Frances felt differently about Weimar. She had taught public school for thirty-five years in Waterbury, a tough, sometimes thankless job. Waterbury is an industrial city with a population of about 110,000 lying ninety miles north of New York City. We had moved there in 1953 when I had my first job practicing law, and had stayed when I began teaching city planning at Columbia in 1975. We had postponed my sabbatical until Frances was ready to retire, and now that she had, she looked forward to a quiet year abroad, in a different and comfortable environment without the excess pressures or tensions of consumerism, of the drug culture, of homelessness and poverty that pervade life in the United States even if one is not directly affected. Weimar didn't seem such a bad place to spend a year in a society without our excesses and evils. In any event, we agreed to come, figuring that we could always try to change the arrangement once we arrived.

The train trip to Weimar from Hamburg, where we landed after the flight from New York, was uneventful. The border crossing business we had gotten used to from previous travel in Eastern Europe: the double passport control, from leaving jurisdiction and entering jurisdiction, the feeling of helplessness before authority that the situation engenders, what the border officials communicate with their body tone and stance, the "right" of those officials to ask questions and undertake searches at whim, the essential arbitrariness of the granting and denying travel permits, the lack of any form of due process or appeal if a decision goes against you, the ostentatious presence of armed force, guns, fences, and barriers if a decision is challenged. But we've had worse experiences: hearing the dogs under the train as it crosses the border to Berlin, searching to make sure no one is hiding underneath; being questioned about a little sketch of how to get to a friend's house in Leningrad that a border official found as we left on a Soviet train to Poland; having *Stern* and *Spiegel*, the *Life* and *Newsweek* of West Germany, as well as tapes for learning French, confiscated as we drove across the border from the West to Magdeburg in the DDR. For us, those events were just unpleasant hassles; for others, they could be much more threatening, and certainly dehumanizing.

After the crossing, when the guards have all left, there is always the feeling of relief, of tension lifting. No one talks to each other in the train compartment before the crossing; after the crossing, everyone relaxes, people smile at each other, even start talking. And it is a quite unpolitical feeling; whether you're an American presumably without political involvement in the DDR, an SED functionary with standing permission to travel, or a grandmother visiting her family for the first time, I think no one likes arbitrary authority, no one likes feeling powerless, and the solidarity against "them" or "it" is a pervasive human reaction.

The railroad station in Weimar was on the seedy side, but still quite functional, just like the trains: old, needing a thorough overhaul and modernization, or at least painting, grime covering the signs, trains arriving a little late but arriving, passages dimly lit but safe enough. We had decided not to have a car during our year, partly for ethical ecological reasons (Frances), partly to avoid the administrative complications (Peter); we figured trains and buses would be adequate, would show us more of the country and let us meet more people. Of course no one in the United States could tell us what the train arrival times in Weimar would be. We knew that Fred Staufenbiel, the professor at Weimar who was officially responsible for us, was supposed to have arranged to have us met. But the person with whom he had made the arrangement couldn't be reached by telephone from Hamburg, and we had no way of knowing whether the telegram we sent had arrived.

But met we were—by two young women, with flowers, who were standing at one end of the platform and recognized us right away from the quantity of our luggage (for a year's stay). Besides, Katya Remple, the older, had heard me when I had given a talk the previous summer at the old city tower (converted into a student center) in the middle of town. Neither of them had a car—many people don't in the DDR, reliance on public transportation is much greater. With all our luggage and several stops to make, a car would have been handy. So we looked for a taxi.

But there weren't any. Weimar has only five licensed taxis in the public taxi service, we were told. Nor were other private taxis licensed. The net result of course is a black market in taxi driving: anybody with a car picks up anyone looking for a ride, and expects to get paid. Prices have to be negotiated, and the driver has no formal legal recourse if the passenger refuses to pay, although that rarely happens. The dangers in the system are that safety isn't controlled, security isn't certain, knowledge of the town isn't reliable; but one gets where one is going most of the time. But neither Katya nor Ute were willing to use a black taxi on principle, to support socialist legality. They recognized the system to be inefficient, but didn't want to undermine its functioning. At least, not until almost half an hour had passed; then they negotiated with someone in a car, and we got going. I don't know how much they ended up paying him, but we privately slipped him five West marks (about $3.00) and he was overjoyed. West marks were trading at about 8 to 1 at the time, but, more important, DDR residents in a town like Weimar, unless they were directly in the tourist trade, didn't have access to them, yet there were many things they could only buy with West marks. Curiosities of the vernacular. East marks are referred to as "marks," West marks as "Deutsche marks," or DM—neither term acknowledges that there are two German currencies!

We had to stop at the international relations office of the HAB on the way to our apartment, not only to get the key but also to leave our passports so we could be registered with the police. I must say, the whole system of police registration still bothers me. It's actually German, rather than East German alone; other European countries have it too, to lesser degrees. But it's unknown to us in the United States; aliens must register with the Immigration and Naturalization Service, but the ordinary person would consider it an unconscionable invasion of privacy and an excrescence of bureaucracy to have to inform some official where he or she is living. I feel the same way. Funny how cultural attitudes differ: in West Germany, at the moment, they're arguing about whether telephone bills should list each call and the place called, because that opens the door to an invasion of privacy, yet that's something we take for granted, since its the way we know we're not being overcharged by the phone company. Yet Germans, East or West, allow police registration without visible objection.

August 16

Our first chance to look around. Our apartment is in a new housing development, at the top of a hill on the outskirts of the town. A typical prefabricated concrete panel development, Housing Construction Series 70 (Wohnbauserie 70, affectionately known as WBS 70), like those visible everywhere on the landscape—precisely the kind of housing we came here to study, the pride and joy of the system, stereotypical of the way a Westerner imagines life in the DDR: uniform, monotonous, solid, colorless, practical but totally unimaginative, decently providing the necessities of life but making the joys of life a little more difficult to experience.

In detail: a bathroom with sink, toilet, shower/bath, hot running water from a central remote heating plant—but no window in the bathroom, no towel rods (and no way to mount one without a drill that will work on concrete walls), a door that you can't open while any other door to the entrance hall is open because they swing against each other, plastic fixtures that are pretty fragile. A washing machine and spin-dryer—the washing machine mainly heats water, the spin-dryer needs a bucket to catch the water squeezed out of the clothes.

After one use of the machine Fran switched to washing clothes in the bathtub, reusing the soapy water for the dark fabrics. She found the spin-dryer quite useful, since it really extracted water, and by spraying the clothes in it with the hand shower she could get by with only one rinse. It took her about two hours to wash and hang up a week's worth of laundry. Her entry, in her notebook, is "Used the god-damn washing machine!" Thank goodness fresh bed linens were provided every two weeks as part of the furnishings of the apartment; on the advice of our predecessor we had brought our own towels, which would have been harder to come by.

The development had a heating system that worked well, with hot water radiators serviced from the central heating plant—but if we turned it off, it knocked and rattled throughout the house (the building superintendent, called a *Hausmeister*, "Master of the House," explained that the pump in the central plant was too big and pushed water through closed valves as well as open, noisily if closed, more quietly if open—so please leave it open!). The central heating plant was right outside our building, blowing soft coal smoke in our window whenever we had it open (*see photo*). Only four floors high, but of course we were on the fourth floor and forced to see how badly the stairs were finished off each time we climbed them, with gaps in the cement, plaster spilled and congealed over the treads, chips off the corners. And a slanted roof, although the technology contemplated a flat roof, so parts of each room were barely usable. [As a colleague told us later, people had objected to the appearance of the flat roofs because there was no detailing to suggest a top, "the buildings just end"; so the architects were very proud to have developed a slant panel system.]

The grounds were similar: not terrible, not even bad, just devoid of individuality or imagination. The four-story buildings were in a U-shape, six entrances per side, each identical to the other. The ends of the buildings were blank; the uniform room layouts called for blank walls between apartments, so there were blank walls at the ends too. Every apartment had a small balcony, even those on the ground floor; under the latter there was nothing, just a dead space where rubbish collected and nothing grew. In the center of the U between the buildings was a large circular sand pit, with a pleasantly curved walk leading to the corners of the U, and benches under trees; but the trees had just been planted, and no one was watering them, so some were already dead. Behind the development was a field that was farmed by a neighboring cooperative, and a nice view over the city; but the U did not open in that direction, but rather toward the farm barnyard next door, barely separated by some wild growth in the farmyard.

As Frances said, "No architect broke his balls over this one!" A little unfair; the system after all set the limits. But even so, more could have been done. The architects in the DDR aren't any worse than the architects anywhere else; from what we saw of their education in Weimar, they're just as rigorously trained as ours are, if differently. But the system provided no incentive to innovate, to improve, to experiment. It was much easier to do it the old way, and caused fewer problems. So that's what they did.

August 18

A knock on our door! We didn't know anyone, no one knew we were here, who would come unannounced? It turned out to be Thomas Simon, from the Liga für Völkerfreundschaft—the Society for Friendship among Peoples—with a visiting U.S. professor of Russian literature. The visitor wanted to see someone in Weimar, so they had driven down from Berlin for that purpose; they had no way of reaching us, they said, so they had just dropped by to say hello. We chatted briefly, and they left.

But the visit made us conscious of a social pattern we had not expected: dropping in on friends unannounced, expecting people to be home and in the mood to talk, an easiness and friendliness we associated more with the American character than with the German. Whether it had anything to do with either the German character or socialism we weren't sure, but it certainly had to do with the lack of decent telephone service. We had no telephone in our apartment; the development, of one hundred or so units, had one public phone in an outdoor booth. It often worked, we found. When it didn't, the postal service would dutifully come (once someone had found a way to notify them), look at the problem, then go away and come back to replace some part or other, which might or might not match. But no matter: a call only cost 20 pfennigs, 2 cents at the black market rate, there weren't that many people who had phones to call anyway, and even then the line was generally busy.

So telegrams were the main means of quick long distance communication. And they worked well; labor intensive but effective. What they meant, however, was one-way communication: "We will be in so-and-so on such-and-such a date, will come by to see you." It works with a more leisurely, relaxed life-style than ours. It's what I missed most living in Weimar: being cut off from instant communication with others, having to write instead of talk to communicate, having to wait for answers or messages. But the wait for a telephone to be installed could be three to five years, assuming one was entitled to one; no chance of our getting one in Weimar. Another reason to think about trying to move to Berlin, if and when it appeared possible.

August 20

Fran has been reading Stefan Heym's autobiography, *Nachruf*. They wouldn't publish it here and it's only available in the West. Heym was born in Germany in 1913, just before World War I. He left in 1933 after publishing a poem critical of the Nazis. Fleeing to Prague, he received a scholarship to study at the University of Chicago from a Jewish fraternity, and came to the United States in 1935. After getting a master's degree, he moved to New York to edit a left-wing German-language paper, married an American, and, when the United States entered the war, joined the army. His first big success, *Hostages*, a novel about the German occupation of Czechoslovakia, explained Nazi psychology in the course of a gripping story. Heym landed at Omaha Beach with an army psychological warfare unit that moved across France and into Germany by the war's end. He was part of the occupation of Germany until he became disillusioned about the possibility of working within the U.S. army to de-Nazify Germany. Back in the United States, he and his wife were active in left politics until a summons from the House Un-American Activities Committee seemed imminent, and then they fled, first to Czechoslovakia and then, reluctantly, to the DDR—reluctantly because he had had enough of Germany and did not want to live there, like most Jews having direct experience of the Nazi era.

In the DDR Heym continued to write and publish his novels, as well as a popular newspaper column, "Offen Gesagt" ("Openly Said"), but because he refused to limit himself to the official line he had increasing difficulties with the authorities, and by 1977 he had been kicked out of the Writers' Union and could no longer publish in the DDR. He continued to live in the same house he had been given in the 1950s and to publish and give interviews. He remained a dedicated socialist who proclaimed his loyalty to the DDR and his wish to remain a citizen.

Fran found his narration and discussion of American life perceptive and penetrating, and was prepared to accept him as a guide to the realities and contradictions of the DDR. But as she read the last third of the book, in which Heym describes his life in the DDR, her eyes got bigger and bigger, and she kept stopping to read passages aloud, unable to believe that it could have been so bad. We had heard about the circumstances that Heym describes: the censorship, the arbitrary decisions, the personal vendettas, the tentacles of the party. But he gives details, names, dates, meetings, threats, interviews; he makes the story vivid, and yet tells only the facts as he himself experienced them. These were the real existing contradictions of real existing socialism. The fact that people like him, or like Robert Havemann, or Walter Janka, or Wolf Biermann, who were supporters of socialism and principled, intelligent, creative people, whose support any really socialist regime should have been anxious to have, nevertheless had such problems, made it all the worse.

August 21

Off to Dessau, and the Bauhaus. For many years after the war, modernism and the progressive traditions of the 1920s were out, "German national traditions" in; West Berlin obtained masses of material for its Bauhaus archive that the East wasn't interested in at the time. Then slowly, partly under pressure from foreign interests, the modern traditions peculiar to the territory of the DDR were accorded recognition. That meant the Bauhaus model house in Weimar, and above all the Bauhaus central building that Gropius designed in Dessau (*see photo next page*). Funds were allocated to its restoration, and Bernd Grönwald, who had good credentials from SED party activity—he had been secretary of his party youth organization, for instance, and had the confidence of the party hierarchy—but who was an architect who had done research on issues of the built environment and had a broad and open vision of what the Bauhaus could be, built the Bauhaus up into an important institution in Dessau and the DDR, welcoming to foreigners, permitting independent research, playing a constructive role in the city of Dessau and the architectural and building establishment in the DDR. When Grönwald went on to head the institute for urban development at the Academy of Building (Bauakademie) in Berlin, he brought in as his successor a progressive named Rolf Kuhn (a Weimar graduate, so ties with Weimar were good), and the Bauhaus continued to be supported as a symbol of progressiveness in DDR architecture.

The Weimar HAB had a studio project planned for Dessau, and I had agreed to participate. Each year, in a program started by Fred Staufenbiel, the second-year class, about forty-five strong, together with a professor of sociology, several research assistants and graduate students, undertake a sociological/planning study of a different city in the DDR, for one month in the late summer before the fall semester begins. We could never get away with that in the United States; the students would protest, either they want their summer vacation or they have to work to earn enough money for tuition and living expenses. That's not a problem here; there's no tuition, students get a regular stipend while they're studying, sufficient to cover their expenses. Housing, although of minimal quality (four to a dormitory room), costs something like 10 marks per month. School cafeterias also are heavily subsidized. The deal for the summer studios is that the city being studied has to provide the housing and cover the meals for students and staff and give a party at the end. The staff, including professors, are expected to be working eleven months a year anyway (again, unlike us; we consider the three months off in the summer as

partial compensation for low salaries, and need it to meet the pressure for research and publication). So Dessau was the studio this year. I had gone for the opening presentations by city officials and had agreed to come back for the students' interim and final presentations.

For Dessau, the Bauhaus was very important. Dessau is an industrial city, the biggest industry before the war being the Junker aircraft plant and its related producers, and it is now in the middle of a heavy and very polluted industrial belt. As a place to live it really has little to recommend it, apart from some older parks and green open spaces; the rebuilding of the inner city was never completed, essentially because the overblown plans produced under the prevailing approaches were too expensive to realize and more moderate plans were taboo. It has problems of pollution, traffic, housing, culture and community facilities, identity. If the students can do something with this, they're good!

We were put up at what the students fondly called the "Mohrüben," the "Carrot," a reddish high-rise of prefabricated concrete panels not quite in the center of town, a residence for students and other visitors; basic, but adequate, accommodations. Meals were at a small bar/restaurant nearby, again basic but adequate, and dirt cheap. We usually came a little late for breakfast, after the students were gone; then the construction workers for a renovation project down the street came in for their coffee break, which was really a beer break; they were usually still there when we left for the Bauhaus. A somewhat leisurely approach to work, it seemed to us.

August 23

Our first direct discussion of DDR politics. It was late at night, and Fred Staufenbiel and Bernd Hunger had gathered in our apartment for a glass of wine (we had two rooms, they each had one, so ours was the most comfortable for talking). Fred Staufenbiel is our official *Betreuer*, hard to translate both as a word and as a concept: "attendant," "caretaker," "guardian," are the dictionary meanings; in practice, he's responsible for us, both to us and, we assume, to the powers that be. But he's an unusual person, large and round and hearty, with a real gruff working-class manner and accent, a great deal of charm and a little glibness. He sees things clearly and calls them by their right names, in private. Bernd Hunger is quite different: younger, sophisticated, full of life, plays the guitar, speaks and writes well, with some polish; also clear-thinking, critical. Fred has the chair in sociology at the HAB; Bernd was his teaching assistant and still has an appointment there, but is on "detached assignment" to the Academy of Building in Berlin. We've had enough discussions for them to trust us, or at least to believe that there's no danger if they talk openly in front of us.

The conversation turns to the exodus across the Hungarian border and the growing rumors of dissident activity in the DDR. Fred tends to pooh-pooh it; things have been like this before, it will blow over, nothing radical will happen. Bernd disagrees strongly. Not only is the reform movement more active than ever and the international situation quite different, but the government is preparing to treat it differently. The police are putting down demonstrations with force, the army is being readied for use, the Stasi are everywhere, tensions are building up: there's going to be an explosion. Bernd is urging Fred to say something, do something, tell the party that they can't deal with these protests with force; otherwise there'll be bloodshed. Fred is concerned,but thinks Bernd is exaggerating, going off half-cocked; there have been greater expressions of discontent before, and nothing major, either good or bad, happened. Bernd is visibly distressed at the reaction; but he has no concrete proposals.

August 28

Back in Weimar. Our first full experience shopping for the daily necessities of life. Our little development—in the United States we would call it a project, but the term has quite different connotations here, almost all new housing being in projects, project residents being very heterogenous, and there being no stigma attached to them—is at the edge of town, at the top of a hill, and schlepping groceries all the way home is no fun. The bus comes by once an hour, so that you have to plan your trips; anything we can buy within convenient walking distance is a blessing. There is one little store as close as the nearest bus stop, but we can't quite figure out what it is: it sells beer, soap, clothes pins, bread, a little fresh meat and sausages, canned but not fresh vegetables, house plants, dish towels. The items seem arbitrarily chosen, and the selection for any one thing is minimal. As Frances says, the store carries a little bit of everything, but not much of anything.

Then there is a fruit and vegetable store further down the hill. They carry mostly local produce: always cabbages and apples and potatoes, and, depending on the season, tomatoes, carrots, turnips, cauliflower, broccoli. All apparently come directly from the farms, and are in any event only moderately processed before arrival. The carrots, although hardly straight and narrow or wrapped in plastic as in New York, taste good. Our friends in Weimar consider them a threat to DDR agriculture, however, because they have so much dirt on them that they're afraid the fields will shortly be depleted of soil!

There's certainly enough to eat in the stores, even if one does have to search to find some things and give up even thinking about others. Hard currency is the reason we are told fruit from Greece or Italy or Spain can't be imported; but we aren't told why their equivalents from

Bulgaria or Hungary aren't available either. I would suppose the Bulgarians would rather sell to hard currency countries, but there must be some solidarity, and some *quid pro quos* the DDR could offer. Then there are opening and closing times to get used to. Hardware stores are, not inappropriately, called *1,000 kleine Dinge*, "one thousand little things," and there are, as far as we know, two in Weimar. One is conveniently located next to the old marketplace near the center of town. We need a new tea kettle, so we go. There is a scaffolding over the building and planks in front of the door, so it's closed. The next day the planks are removed—they weren't actually working on the storefront, only the facade upstairs—but there's a sign: "Closed for inventory"; not that they have that much to count, or couldn't do it during the slow hours. We come back the next day. No luck: "Closed for intake of goods." Of course, other stores are closed for quite different reasons: for instance, for lunch, or for vacation, or because of illness or a death in the family. In each case, a little certificate is posted in the window giving the reason, duly approved by the city council. The one we like the most, though, is: "Closed for technical reasons." That seems to cover it!

Jokes about shopping in the DDR are legion:

> A woman comes into a butcher shop and asks for a pound of veal cutlet.
> "We don't have any," says the person behind the counter.
> "Then let me have a pound of steak."
> "We don't have any," says the person behind the counter.
> "How about some lean chopped meat?"
> "We don't have any," says the person behind the counter.
> The woman leaves in dismay.
> "She's not quite with it," says the woman behind the counter to her co-worker, shaking her head. "No, but what a memory she has!" her co-worker responds.

> A man comes into a store to buy a tea kettle.
> "We don't handle tea kettles," says the salesperson. "We sell coffeepots, and we don't have any. The store where they don't have tea kettles is down the street."

The truth is, as the saying goes, one can get almost everything one really needs in the DDR, but not quite everything, not all the time, and not all over!

A man asks a policeman in Leipzig where the department store called Principle is. The policeman looks at his map and says, "We've got the big store called Center, and there's Consume, but I don't see any store called Principle. What makes you think there is such a store?"

"Well, whenever we're looking for something we can't find, our party leadership tells us that, in Principle, we have everything."

August 29

We came back by train to Dessau for a mid-studio session arriving at the railroad station the city is reconstructing: a new modernistic mural on the walls (muscular workers, heroically portrayed, of course, but at least with flair!), a new entrance hall, a new restaurant (serving the same monotonous food, but at least with light and a view). It is hard to see how they put up with the old station for so long, and you'd think renovation would be in the ordinary course of things, but not so. When the Bauhaus started to put Dessau on the national and international map, those concerned, from the Bauhaus director to the city administration, thought the station through which visitors would arrive, just down the road from the Bauhaus itself, should give a foretaste of something interesting and stylish, not of neglect and ugliness. But the DDR railroad system, to which the railroad station belonged, had no money in its budget for renovations. So (we were told) the SED party secretary called a meeting of party leaders in the various industries and offices and told them that they all had to put in so and so much in money, or material, or time from their construction crews, to get the station rebuilt. And of course they did. It wasn't in the plan, but it got done. Somehow there are priorities in every human system, no matter how rigid; here the SED served essentially as an escape hatch from its own policies and regulations.

I spoke to a group of visitors and students at the Bauhaus about citizen participation in planning in the United States; a lot of interest and sympathy, but little sense that it was directly relevant to what they were doing.

September 1

Back to Weimar for some serious work on housing and urban development: conferences, interviews, reading, seeing. Being in a small town has its advantages if you want to work peacefully. Occasional interruptions to attend student dissertation defenses, eat out, etc. We became friendly with two Syrian students who lived in our development, had been here for several years working on their doctorates; Syria is one of the countries with which the DDR has standing support agreements, for reasons of international policy. Both warm, friendly, open, people; the mix of cultures: Syrian, German, socialist, United States, meant almost everything—cooking, eating, home furnishing, attitude toward time, attitude toward teachers—was worth discussing, comparing. Syria would be much more of a culture shock for us than the DDR.

Seeing how much less the DDR is an auto-culture than, say, West Germany or the United States makes us think we were very right not to get a car. There are very few gas stations, repairs take a long time, parts are seldom available (as our first taxi-driver told us!), roads are narrow and bumpy once you get off the main drags. On the other hand, there isn't much congestion, and the smog is the result of industrial activities and burning brown coal for heating and energy, not car exhaust.

Public transportation is dirt cheap at the local level: all bus fares in Weimar are 10 pfennigs (four cents) at the official rate, and obviously have nothing whatsoever to do with costs. Beyond that, it's strictly an honor system: you buy tickets at newspaper kiosks or some stores, and you cancel them when you get on the bus by putting them in a gadget that stamps a pattern of holes in them. Theoretically, when a conductor comes around, you have to show him/her your ticket, and if yours is not properly canceled, you pay a fine; but apparently there aren't any conductors in Weimar. On some buses you can buy tickets as you enter: there is a metal box with a slit in the top where you put the money, and a roll of tickets next to it from which you tear off however many you've paid for. But there's no connection between the box and the tickets; in fact, you could take as many tickets as you want without putting any money in the box, and you can put any amount in the box, since there's no way to tell what you've put in. The system is at least internally consistent: since fares are so cheap, why go to the expense of seeing that they're paid? And it makes good transportation planning sense, if you want to encourage people to use public transportation instead of private cars. Very few people are likely to "waste" public transportation (unlike electricity or hot water, for instance) if it's free, and the social savings from its use are great.

September 2

The office I was assigned was very different from what I have at Columbia, and from what I had in West Germany eight years earlier. At Columbia, my office is small, comfortable (if crowded), adapted to my own needs, bookshelves, pictures, plants accumulated over the years, and arranged to suit my own tastes. In West Germany, I was assigned a largish office in a new glass and concrete university highrise, steel furniture like that in every other office, totally anonymous but relatively efficient. In Weimar, the HAB—and schools of architecture usually pride themselves on their own built environment—was in a dingy but spacious old four-story building with long corridors, large lobbies, and substantial rooms, but with ancient furniture (bolted-down chairs in the lecture rooms, old wooden desks, minimal clamp-on lamps); kept quite clean on the inside, but with peeling stucco on the outside and covered with the soot that is a hallmark of the DDR's cities. In the offices, each large enough for at least six good-sized desks, people tried to humanize their spaces, but without much involvement. Students worked four to a room; most professors shared offices; a few smaller rooms, on the upper floors and under the roof, were for one person only. They all looked clean, shabby, cared for but not loved. Administrators' offices were generally larger and had antechambers, but otherwise had the same air of seedy stolidness. My office had my desk, a desk for a regular full-time lecturer, and a conference table. We shared a telephone, which would have been a real nuisance if it had been easy to make phone calls; since all long-distance calls had to go through an overworked central switchboard and lines were constantly busy or unanswered, the phone wasn't very useful anyway. Computers were all in a single room in the data processing division: they were overused, aged but operational, and had they had amenities like ribbons for their printers, I might have used them more often; as it was, I was glad I had brought my own lap-top and mini-printer. But there were all the basics, and one could certainly work there.

The coffee-break was what took me most by surprise. At ten o'clock on the nose three or four people came in, spread out a table cloth on the conference table, put a kettle of water on a little electric heater, got out silverware, china teacups and saucers and teapot, and prepared tea. Someone usually brought cakes or cookies; all the secretaries, teaching assistants, professors (if around) came, either to our coffee-break or another one. No one was able to work during the coffee-break; nor did anyone want to. The telephone went unanswered, visitors were asked to wait, business was not discussed. I made the mistake a couple of times of asking people I wanted to see if we could talk over lunch; they were always glad to have lunch, but then our appointment would be after lunch; one did not eat and talk business at the same time. The lunch room in the basement was as free from the pressures of work as the coffee-breaks.

We meditated a good bit on the implications of this—see Excurs 1 below.

September 7

A filling came out at breakfast, a gold filling probably put in twenty years ago. Where to go, what to do? We are fully insured for medical treatment under the Fulbright program, and in addition I'm covered under Frances's Health Maintenance Organization back home (it pays for care elsewhere if you can't get to their facility). But is dental treatment covered under either? We don't think so.

I call up the international relations office at the HAB, and the person responsible for us tells us to go to the school clinic; they usually handle emergencies from 7:30 to 8:30 a.m., but I should see if they could arrange to see me immediately. When I got there, I explained the problem to the nurse behind the window, who took down my name and told me I'd be called. No questions about who I was, insurance, financial ability, or anything. After a twenty-minute wait,

I was called in, a young dentist looked, saw the problem, put in a temporary filling, and told me to get an X-ray and come back. The X-rays are taken in clinic eight blocks away. They were already closed for the day (they take X-rays from 10:00 to 12:00), but I could get one the next day, which I did. A cumbersome arrangement, and reflecting a shortage of equipment, but I suppose not inefficient. And still nothing on who I was, payment, etc.

September 8

We have a decent television set, but as an aid to understanding everyday life in the DDR it's about as useful as "Dallas" is for understanding the United States. The soap operas idealize what we see around us: not by showing everyone swimming in wealth and power, but by making everything seem rational: higher-ups make decisions and may make mistakes but are ultimately persuaded to do right, the petty tribulations of everyday life disappear, love and death and career choices play their roles against a backdrop of a socialist society that doesn't seem to make their development in any way different from elsewhere.

News programs are hopeless; they are simply propaganda, as is the daily press, particularly *Neues Deutschland*, the organ of the Central Committee of the SED and the biggest selling daily paper in the DDR, delivered by the postal system as part of its newspaper and magazine delivery service—subscriptions are entered directly at and with the post office, and only papers get delivered by post. Headlines tell how such and such a factory has overfulfilled its production quota, how Erich Honecker received the head of the brother-party from Czechoslovakia, how they exchanged greetings and pledged the support of the peoples of their countries for the enduring bonds of peace and friendship between them, and so forth. Because West German television is also received here, the East German channels have, as a regular feature, what's called the "Black Channel," in which Eduard von Schnitzler, aptly named it seemed to us, with a paunch and a sharp little van Dyke beard, responds with ponderous sarcasm to the major Western TV stories of the week. East German television doesn't seem to cover controversial stories at all, or it reports them only via the comments from party leaders; rather, the standard fare is extracts from some dignitary's congratulations to the faithful and committed workers of X for finishing the construction of a factory for the ever increasing production of ever higher quality widgets in the town of Y, as he cut the ribbon opening the plant. A story has it:

> A producer of a television news show on DDR Channel 1 was indicted for anti-state activity and inciting disrespect for the elected leaders of the country because he proposed to carry live and in full a speech Honecker was scheduled to give at a party congress.

September 10

Back to the dentist. This time when I presented myself at the window, I was asked for my *Ausweis*—the identification card issued by the government to every citizen, in which essential information is listed: birthplace, residence (changes to be entered when people move), occupation, next of kin, etc. It's the standard form of identification, much as a driver's license is in the United States, although with other control functions too. I said I didn't have one, but showed my official letter from the Ministry of Education showing my status, and said I thought I had insurance coverage at home as well. The lady said fine, the doctor would be with me in a minute. I asked her, out of curiosity, what would have happened if I didn't have the letter. Oh, she said, we need to know whether you're in the right place; our clinic handles those affiliated with the HAB; if you work elsewhere you go to your employer's clinic, or you can go to the clinic in the neighborhood nearest you, or to the general clinic at the hospital; we just want you to be in the right place. Do you want my insurance information? I asked. Oh no, she said, that doesn't mean anything to us.

The doctor handled me quite competently, I thought, drilling to replace the temporary filling with a permanent one. He gave me the gold filling and told me to keep it; he didn't think it best to do a new gold filling, rather a silver one, but if I ever wanted a gold one I'd have to provide the gold myself—they had none. [When I came back several weeks later, he put in the new filling and everything seemed fine. I asked him for a bill, explaining that we had looked at the Fulbright program description and thought we had insurance. He said he couldn't give us a bill, they didn't have any way of charging, maybe they could get an accounting for the cost of the silver and I could pay that. I asked about his services, the X-ray, etc.; no, there was simply no procedure by which they could make out a bill, it wouldn't be right, everybody was entitled to care, they didn't charge for it, nothing he could do about it.]

Mind-boggling!

September 11

To Berlin for several days visiting. Saw Mayakovsky's *Der Schwitzbad*. Certainly things get said and unequivocally implied in the theater that would never be permitted anywhere else. It's an early Soviet satire on bureaucracy (among other things). But the company can get away with it partly because it's Soviet, partly because theater still has a prestige and an aura and international resonance that makes the local bureaucracy leery of attacking it directly. And theater folk exercise *some* restraint, in return for being allowed to produce—always a delicate ethical/political bargain, which I think in most cases the theater people get the better of.

September 14

Back to Dessau for the students' interim presentations. I came a day early because I wanted to do some interviews on housing policy and inner-city development. My major appointment was with several people from the city building administration, the *Hauptauftraggeber*—almost untranslatable: the "chief assignment-giver"—along with the *Auftragnehmer*, or "assignment-taker," the city architect, someone from the plan commission (not to be confused with a planning commission, in the U.S. sense of city planning; the plan commission administers the national plan at the local level and is responsible for virtually all spheres of economic activity, including construction). I wonder how many people in the DDR understand these bureaucratic structures?

Two things left an impression of life in Dessau. One was of lower level bureaucracy: getting in the door of city hall. You have to be announced, and get permission, before you can enter; there's a desk in a glassed-in booth in the entrance lobby for that purpose. We had an appointment, but the person who set it up wasn't at his telephone when we arrived. Fred Staufenbiel, who had come with me, showed his identity card and convinced the woman at the desk that he was legitimate. But all I had was a document showing I had permission to be in the DDR, and, even worse, a U.S. passport. No dice! No authorization, no entry. It took us about ten minutes to convince the woman that it was okay, and then only after someone else who worked there intervened and overruled her. And even then she scolded us and the world at large for another five minutes for telling her she had a job to do and then not letting her do it in accordance with the rules.

The other impression was of high-level bureaucracy. The relations among the seven or eight officials present were complicated enough; several, at various times, drew me organization charts and no two were the same. Yet they all knew how the system worked as it affected themselves, what they each had to clear with whom, who made the decisions that affected them, whose orders he or she had to execute. Maybe that's to be expected in a complex bureaucracy. What surprised me was their attitude. All of them shook their heads at the stupidity of the system, complained how long it took to get things done, saw no purpose in most of it; yet not one had ever even thought of suggesting changes, of trying to streamline the system. And not one of them knew the system as a whole; the focus was on how it affected each person as an individual, and any overall concern was simply nonexistent, except as complaint. And not complaint in the sense of, damn it, something has to be done, but complaint in the sense of grumbling, carping, expressing irritation. Understandable, indeed, given the way things were, but hardly either socially constructive or personally satisfying.

The student presentations at the Bauhaus were methodologically sound: the interviews were solidly done, the tabulations useful, the maps good, the data relevant; but the questions they addressed were, to my mind, simply naive—so general as to be almost meaningless. My assessment must have been close to the mark, because the questions I asked after the presentation seemed to bring out their own unstated concerns. The city's center should be more socially alive, more "communicative" (a favorite word, and actually a good one if not so tattered with constant and ultimately unthinking use), more encouraging of social interaction. How could it be, I asked, if you couldn't even get into city hall without a fifteen-minute struggle and if no one wanted to discuss politics in public? Residents should have more of a feeling of living in "their" neighborhood, more of an identity with "their" city. What control did they have over their neighborhood or their city, I asked, that would justify such a feeling, what decisions could they participate in, what did they actually control for themselves? Dessau had great promise as a city, from its location in the center of the DDR to its green spaces to its history. Why hadn't its promise been fulfilled, I asked, and what would have to be changed, politically, economically, administratively, to bring about change? They all agreed those were good questions. But no answers came. Not surprising, I suppose; it's easy for me, a foreigner, a visitor, a secure American professor, to ask such questions; it's different for them, young, vulnerable, living in the DDR, their futures still in the balance, to deal with them.

Basic facts about the housing system in the DDR are sometimes so taken for granted that no one bothers to explain them to a stranger, but they are indispensable for understanding the whole system. The matter of choice is one. We are used to choice being exercised in the market: to the extent you have money, you can choose from the range of goods and services offered you. In housing, your choices increase as your income increases; everyone above a certain level has some choice, exercised through the market. Not so here; there is a general scarcity of housing, and (with exceptions for those with "special needs," which includes party leaders, artists, officials, some others with influence, exceptions nevertheless limited in number) people are simply assigned housing based on the composition of their family and the units available, and take what they are given. The matter of distributional equity rarely arises; everyone complains about the limited quality and quantity, but not about who gets what there is. There is some limited opportunity for choice, primarily by trading: someone with a larger apartment on the outskirts puts up an ad, or lists their unit with a central housing office, offering to exchange with someone with a smaller apartment downtown. Number of rooms, central heating, number of floors to climb, location, are the factors that prompt exchanges. Rent or cost hardly enters into it; almost all rents are affordable, and they are generally uniform per square meter, so money doesn't enter into the process. The same system exists in most real existing socialist economies; in many, a black market develops and money may be exchanged to even out a trade, but the German orderliness and discipline apparently make that much rarer.

Of course, the system doesn't work perfectly:

> A woman tells her friend, "My husband finally got assigned a new unit in Marzahn [one of the largest prefabricated concrete-panel developments in Berlin], but it's so terrible, I had to trade."
>
> "Oh, you were able to find someone who wanted to move to Marzahn?"
>
> "No, I decided it was easier to trade husbands than apartments, so I did."

September 15

Fran had to make a special trip to Berlin today to pick up our visas for the Soviet Union. At the Czechoslovakian consulate, you apply in the morning, either wait or come back that afternoon. To get a DDR visa in the United States, needless to say, you have to send the application to Washington and it takes a month or more; ours, despite all the official auspices under which we were going and six weeks lead time, had to be sent by express mail to reach us on time. The Hungarian policy is almost free market: normally, you wait three days and come back in person; for expedited one-day service, they simply charge twice as much. But the Soviet Union is something else again; everyone we know has gotten their visas at the very last minute, regardless of when they applied. Never think all the "socialist" countries are alike; they vary immensely. Anyway, our Soviet visas did arrive in the nick of time.

September 16

Fred Staufenbiel came by with a suitcase he had picked up for us, and brought with him a Cuban student, in Weimar to finish his dissertation. At least at the graduate level, the foreign students are well integrated into the everyday life of the school. That hardly seems the case with those from other countries who come (or are brought) to work; one day last week we thought we'd stop for lunch at what showed as a hotel on our map. But there were no hotel signs on the building and it appeared to be a residence for young black men, presumably from Africa. We went in and asked: our guess was right, we were told by a young man who was very surprised to see a stranger coming in the door. We chatted briefly and left. We have also seen an all-black soccer team playing on a field nearby, with only black men on both sides. Integration does not seem to have progressed very far here; nor have we encountered any visible efforts to foster it.

September 17 - 23

By train to Prague: sleeping car not available, but we had double seats in a first-class compartment and could stretch out and snooze. A business-like conference on housing policy, scheduled for three days, some sight-seeing, long talks with friends depressed by the situation in Czechoslovakia, but seeing little hope for change.

September 24 - October 6

To Moscow for a combined conference of the sociological association's research committees on urban and regional development and on work, and for some discussions on joint Columbia University-Soviet research. At the opening session of the sociological conference, our Soviet host, in the new spirit of open participation, suggested to the fifty or so attendees that they should decide what to discuss at that first session. No one being prepared for the question, there was complete silence; he then said, well, he had three theses that might serve as a basis for discussion. Sure, we all said, what are they? The first was: "Democracy and the state are incompatible." Dead silence. The discussion on it, and the other two similar formulations, never got off the ground. [With hindsight, I now take the thesis to reflect a profound skepticism about any form of state, and a search for a concept of democracy that would not involve a governmental apparatus of any nature; if the discussion had come at the end of the conference, when people understood each other a little better, it might have gotten further.]

The incident from the whole stay that we found most striking happened on the middle weekend. Our prospective research colleagues invited us to spend the day on a boat their institute had on a lake thirty kilometers or so from Moscow. It was a delightful day, great weather, warm people, a brisk refreshing breeze on the boat, lunch cooked over an open fire on the lake shore (actually an artificial lake built by prison labor under Stalin), and so forth. But the mechanics of such arrangements were what struck us the most. How did they get the boat? Someone at the institute knew someone in Leningrad who knew someone in Estonia who knew a fishing crew that was getting a new boat; no one cared what happened to the old one, so the institute got it for nothing. And how did they get the boat house on the lake? The local coast guard (as we understood the description) had their station nearby, and it had burned down just as the institute was building its new offices in Moscow. Comrades, the institute people said, we can let you have some building materials we happen to have if you'll give us a spot for a little boat house. No sooner said than done. And who cared for the boat, paid for the fuel, etc.? Those who wanted to use the boat worked on its upkeep, those who didn't, didn't. Fuel? No problem. The lake was on a canal connecting Moscow with the Volga, and long-distance barges passed up and down it. If the institute boat needed fuel, they'd pull up to a barge, and say, "Comrades, would you like some vodka?" "Sure," the bargemen would say. "Comrades, have you any fuel you could spare?" "Sure," the bargemen would answer. So they'd pump gas from the barge to their boat. And that was that.

October 7

The flight back from Moscow was uneventful. On the way we had a chance to reflect on what we were going back to, in the DDR. Moscow was a strange experience for us, with cultural and language differences adding to a largely foreign history and system. The DDR was much closer to our experience: we knew the language, we knew more of the history (and had lived through a little of it, as children, and been involved in it through our parents). And, above all, we had lived in West Germany on my last sabbatical. So we had a known standard of comparison. Somehow, after almost two months' exposure to its different way of life, the DDR felt more comfortable to us, more like a place we'd like to live and work in (although with severe disadvantages) than West Germany. Why? Our attempt to figure that out is the subject of the Excurs that follows.

excurs 1

OF COFFEE-BREAKS AND ELBOWS:
WHAT WAS DIFFERENT
IN EVERYDAY LIFE IN THE DDR

What positive features did everyday life in the DDR offer its citizens? What distinguished life in the DDR from that in West Germany or the United States? How did the good compare to the bad, in terms of everyday life?

The answer is simple in some ways, complex in others. The simple part runs through, on the positive side, an encompassing social net, including health and child care for all, generally egalitarian conditions of life, comprehensive social and personal security, support for a rich and diverse culture, lack of commercialization and "commodification" of individual desires and preferences, and lack of violence as a presence in everyday life. The simple, if profound, negatives, run from bureaucratic domination and inefficiency and a restricted range of material goods and services to the pervasive official propaganda, censorship, hierarchical decision-making, obsessive restrictions on personal freedom, specifically the right to travel, and pervasive if generally unobtrusive surveillance by a vast state security apparatus.

The coffee-break and the elbow symbolized for us the more complex and ambivalent side of the pros and cons of life in the DDR. It has to do with *the role of work*. The coffee-break was at the same time a humane attribute of working life and an interference with efficiency. The elbow, as a symbol of life in West Germany (and the United States), comes from a slogan that subsequently became part of the political debate about unification. The reference is to an *Ellenbogengesellschaft*, an "elbowing society": one in which people relate to others by elbowing them aside—elbowing as a symbol of selfishness, alienation, inhumanity in people's relations with one another. Of course, coffee-breaks exist in the West and people elbow each other in the East, but the nature and importance of the interactions seemed to us to differ significantly.

Both symbols are double-edged. As a positive symbol, the coffee-break is a limitation on the "performance principle," on the overwhelming pressure to compete and produce. Performance is necessary and competition is often productive, but performance is not the only purpose of life; it is only one of many means to realize a good life. And when the purpose of the performance is just "to make a buck," as a leading entrepreneur from the West expressed it, then there is not much that can be said for the "freedom to perform and achieve" that the West so often boasts about. The pressure to perform better and better can destroy people, whether taken to the point of suicide for the failure to perform successfully, as in Japan, or simply psychological insecurity and loss of perspective and values, as one business scandal after another in the West suggests. These are extreme examples: the "publish or perish" aspect of a young academic's situation suggests the same undesired but inescapable pressures in academia, and the inability of "busy" people to take the time to visit, to talk at leisure, to pursue simple curiosity, to enjoy their own physical existence outside of "fitness" programs, attests to the same phenomena. The coffee-break in the DDR was not simply an escape from such a pattern for a few minutes every day, but a self-evident priority, as much a purpose of the working day as on the job "performance." You could call this "bourgeois" (*Biedermeierlich*) when practiced by the upper classes; but for working people it has much to do with humane attitudes in the workplace.

The opposite side of the coin, of course, is inefficiency, lack of production. Sometimes elbowing people aside is necessary to get things done; even in the DDR, as we learned later, the successful building crews produced because, when they ran out of materials, they literally elbowed others aside to take bricks or cement or fixtures allocated elsewhere.

But why must humane relationships in the workplace contradict productive performance? Is the pressure of competition the only way to get people to perform and achieve? Must the fear of failure to the extent of suicide exist in order to make people work creatively? The coffee-break in the DDR probably developed into such a ritual as a protest against irrational working conditions. But even if working conditions are good, a civilized coffee-break seems to me a desirable part of a civilized working day.

The absence of elbowing-aside, of pushiness, of hostile competitiveness, was also noticeable in everyday life. We have waited on lines at airline counters in the United States, at banks in Italy, at train stations in West Germany, at restaurants in Paris. You have to guard your place in line; it's considered clever to figure out how to jump the queue, to get ahead of your place, to avoid the wait others have to undergo. Usually money can help: whether it's an outright bribe or a no-wait service for first-class passengers or knowing the headwaiter in a fancy eatery, the idea that people should act fairly occurs only to the people who aren't unfairly getting ahead of the line. It was different in the DDR. There people spent a fair amount of time waiting on line, and certainly some privileged people had ways of getting around the waiting; but as a matter of everyday experience, people respected each other's rights, kept their positions in line, were friendly and supportive of each other.

The attitude toward work that I'm using the coffee-break to symbolize is also explicitly represented in attitudes toward the shortening of the workday or week and the treatment of unemployment. In an exaggerated performance-achievement society, the length of the workday is a question of the efficiency of production. Whether or not work-times are shortened is a question of conflicting interests. In the DDR, although the work week is longer than elsewhere, the goal of shortening it is a general social goal. It was difficult for people in the

DDR to accept the idea that some should be working overtime while others are unemployed and seeking work—that seemed a societal failure to them. In West Germany, as in the rest of the West, it is taken as a natural result of free competition. In the East, reasonable work was a part of a reasonable life, not the means to higher production. Cynics spoke about the fact that the DDR, which claimed to have no unemployment at all, had many unemployed, but they all held jobs. There was truth to the claim; but is it such a bad solution to fluctuations in the need for work?

The most negative side of the coffee-break, however, seems to me not to be the interference with performance at work, but the absence of the possibilities of converting work into something other than itself, something done for the pride of creative achievement rather than because one is paid for it or gains other benefits from it, whether wealth or power or prestige. In classic Marxist philosophy, socially necessary work is distinguished from efforts that are more akin to play, undertaken for the joy of doing, although they may be as, or more, "productive" and socially useful. As "work" is reduced in scope, through shorter working hours and technological advances, the opportunity for creative activities undertaken for their own sake, producing a pride of achievement related both to the joy of the effort and the social usefulness of the outcome, should be expanded. That never happened in the DDR. For many, bureaucratic inefficiencies and hierarchical decision-making rendered daily work inefficient and frustrating; the possibilities for creative alternatives were equally limited.

The *ideal of the just society* was a second aspect of life in the DDR that impressed us, as positive as the different role of work but less ambiguous. As a pattern for everyday morality, it is deeply ingrained in most DDR citizens that society should be "just," that the purpose of a society, of a state, should be to provide a better life for all of its citizens—and not just to improve the opportunities for individuals to succeed. Not wanting to get ahead of others in line is a part of it, but only a small part.

The concept of a just society is not so much about expectations regarding the social role of the state, which one can find elsewhere, if not spread as widely. Rather, it's about the concept of a way of life in which each person should care about others, and where the society encourages and supports such caring. People's Solidarity (*Volkssolidarität*—the organization of and for the retired and elderly) is quite different from charity precisely because it ensures solidarity among equals and not donations from the wealthy to the less fortunate. This kind of solidarity ethos was an outgrowth of the workers' culture, and also of the workers' parties (the social democratic as well as the communist); in the DDR this ethos of solidarity encompassed all of society. To be sure, not always followed, but at least acknowledged as a goal.

Four people in a one-room apartment is both unjust and asocial. It is even more unjust, when, at the same time, someone with inherited wealth lives in a mansion. That many must walk while others ride in limousines is unjust. A social market economy distinguishes itself from a socially just society in that the former only places a lower limit on the injustice while the latter holds out a model in which all can expect just treatment from each other and from their society and government. Such ideals and expectations are eminently desirable. It was in part the contradictions between these ideals and the special privileges of a small elite that led to the peaceful revolution in the DDR.

That *social security*, and especially health care, is taken for granted struck us as a third enviable part of life in the DDR. Despite the many weaknesses of the health-care system, caused in part by lack of supplies and out-migration of nurses and specialists, our experiences were heartening. There are few other societies in which it is so ordinary and taken-for-granted that *everyone*, without question, without regard for status, responsibility, or means should be treated and protected. In the DDR such treatment is not an exception from market-oriented relationships, not a compromise between individual capacity and public duty, not something that is supervised and limited, that must be protected against abuse by the needy, the socially weak. Social security or the social net isn't only for the socially weak, and therefore not a sign of weakness but a natural part of the society. Not to stigmatize a substantial minority as socially weak and "other" was an aspect of the DDR that struck us as very positive.

The *perspective on consumption* and shopping was a fourth aspect of DDR life quite different from that in the West. In the DDR shopping was not an addiction but a necessary activity. Often there was not enough, and often there could have been a greater selection, but the purpose of the purchase was not to display status or power or wealth. Erich Honecker and the others who lived in Wandlitz wanted a wall so that other people could not see their privileges, unjust in the egalitarian DDR—although modest enough compared to the country homes, luxury apartments, and yachts of capitalist elites. Conspicuous consumption was unknown in the DDR.

This is hardly coincidental. Western economies need a continually increasing demand for goods and continually growing opportunities for investment. The more goods sold, the greater the profit. Therefore the greater the drive to consume, the better it is for the economy—regardless of whether what is consumed fulfills human needs or not; regardless of whether the demand must first be manipulated or not; regardless of whether advertising costs double the price or not; regardless of whether such consumption hurts the environment or not. Entering a store in the DDR, one doesn't have in the back of one's mind the suspicion that the salesperson will try to sell a product only because it will make a profit for the business. Indeed, in the DDR, with its price subsidies, a sale could well mean a net *loss* for the state. And the relationship between buyer and seller is not a conflict of interest. This is certainly positive; selling and buying should serve human needs and not the need for ever increasing profits.

Equality, indeed *egalitarianism*, characterized life in the DDR from near the top to the bottom, a fifth positive characteristic of everyday life. The difference in income between a factory manager and a factory worker was slight; production workers often made more than technicians or foreman. But as with other positive elements in the DDR, the principle was sometimes taken to an extreme, as was generally recognized: one old joke has it:

> An alcoholic worker's family goes to the head of the factory where he works and says, "We're worried about our Willie, he spends all the money he gets on drink, please give him a promotion so he'll have less money and won't drink so much!"

Famous artists and top sports figures earned significantly above the general scale; below them (and with the exception of party figures, whose privileges ran much more to direct benefits than high salaries) the range between the top and the bottom earners was probably on the order of 10 to 1.

Likewise with social status: no one was considered to be of a higher status than anyone else because of their incomes or jobs (party officials, artists, and sports figures again excepted). They all had comparable housing, shopped in the same shops, rode the same trains and buses, and drove comparable cars—the top leadership drove, or were driven in, Volvos, Ladas from a plant Fiat built in the Soviet Union; these were the top of the line and were considered somewhat superior to the DDR Wartburg, which in turn was better than the legendary Trabant, but the differences were gradations on a narrower scale than that between a BMW or a Mercedes and a Chevrolet or a Ford, and nowhere near the difference between a stretch limo and a compact. You couldn't tell, driving through a given section of any town in the DDR, who lived there: students lived next to police, teachers next to mayors, engineers next to cafeteria workers, researchers next to bus drivers. Segregation, both economic and racial, is one of the banes of life in the United States, and part of an increasing polarization of society. The DDR looked very different in this respect, and much better. To extremes, perhaps, and at the cost of limited expression of personal preferences, but, to our minds, a more desirable net result.

Those were the five major positive features we found in DDR society. The major negatives are easy to list: a lower standard of living than we were accustomed to, a rigid and all-pervasive official orthodoxy, and limited freedoms. The standard of living issue (apart from the decrepit telephone service!) was hardly intolerable; by comparison with what was shown on *Dallas*, it was spartan, but nobody really believed life was like *Dallas*, there was no direct experience of the West to compare it with because of travel restrictions, and everything one really needed was available: not everywhere and not always, went the joke, but always some where, some time.

What probably bothered us most about the economic backwardness was the feeling of restricted possibilities of improvement in the future. Through the beginning of the 1980s things were getting better, year after year, even if far behind progress in other countries. That changed in the 1980s; things that had been available in previous years became harder to get, repairs were made less frequently, the sense of progress disappeared. That was particularly hard for young people because it also meant that job opportunities, career advancement, challenge, exploration of alternatives, became more and more restricted. If people were fleeing across the borders of Hungary to the West and gave economic conditions as their reason, it was not so much shortages as restricted opportunities for personal betterment that moved them to act.

What hurt as much as the restricted standard of living was the restricted freedom. For intellectuals, the censorship, the limitations on publication or presentation, were often intolerable; many simply fled as soon as they could. Most people, though, adapted to it, one way or the other. For those millions who could not leave, for family reasons, or who didn't want to, because after all it was their home, or because they thought they could change things from the inside, the rules for expression (or nonexpression) were clear. If one obeyed them, one could say what one wanted at home, to one's friends, even at work. The sharp wit that so delighted us, that came out of the *Volksmund*— the "people's mouth" ("folk expressions" doesn't quite capture it), was certainly uncensored. If one behaved by the rules, one was let alone, and most people had learned to make that compromise.

The inability to travel was much harder to live with. There were plenty of places to go on vacation in the East: Lake Balaton in Hungary, the spas of Czechoslovakia, the Black Sea coast of Bulgaria, the Crimea, Georgia, Moscow, Leningrad, Prague, Budapest. But at the resorts it was always hard currency that was given priority, and the Ossies, those from the East Germany, always felt they were second class. And why not be able to go West? If it was really so terrible, why didn't the government trust them to see for themselves? Why couldn't they visit their relatives in West Germany except with special permission and for special occasions? Weren't they old enough to be trusted to talk to foreigners? As the flight over the Hungarian border increased and restrictions on travel even in the East tightened, people in the DDR felt themselves more and more cooped up, imprisoned, treated like children having to ask permission to go outside and even then not getting it. Even for us, U.S. citizens coming to the DDR under an official exchange program, crossing the border into the DDR made us feel as if a door had shut behind us, as if we were entering into a severely restricted society; how much more must life-long residents have felt their society was closed, chokingly oppressive.

That they did was clear. And the events of the following months showed how bitterly they resented it.

journal

THE FIRST PHASE: EUPHORIA

**From the Fortieth Anniversary
to the Openiing of the Wall**

October 7

A big day for the DDR—and for us. The fortieth anniversary of the founding of the DDR. The big parade, with bands, reviewing stands, speeches, all in the old style. Gorbachev's visit: he was asked whether *perestroika* and *glasnost* might not also be needed in the DDR. He had full confidence in the comrades in the DDR, he replied, and it was their decision, but: "He who comes too late, will be punished by life itself." The comment spread like wildfire throughout the country, taken as support by Gorbachev for change in the DDR. "Help us, Gorby," on a few signs held up by protestors along the parade route. There was even a mild protest demonstration, quickly suppressed by the police. All this we learned from friends the following day.

We had returned by plane from Moscow to East Berlin and landed at Schönefeld Airport at about 5:00 p.m. Fran was tired and wanted to lie down at Bruno Flier's, where we were staying. I wanted to see the action downtown, and at about 9:00 p.m., went to Alexanderplatz, the large plaza at the center of the city. *(See photo page 64, which shows Alexanderplatz with the Hotel Berlin and the Central Department Store.)* Groups of people were standing around talking; I eavesdropped. People from New Forum, the leading independent opposition group, were talking over events of the afternoon, demands for rights to travel, political pluralism, the merits of socialism, in amazingly open and honest terms. About 10:00 p.m., people began a march uptown toward the Gethsemane Church, which had often sheltered oppositional meetings. I walked along with the group, talking to people on the way, then walking alongside a West Berliner who had also come along to see what was going on. Suddenly the police blocked off the front and rear of the street we were on, and swept everyone in their path into army trucks—including me. I protested mildly that I was a foreigner on my way home, but no one listened; besides, I wasn't reluctant to go along, wanting to see how such things were handled here. I've been to enough marches and demonstrations in the United States, and as a lawyer have represented enough people arrested in them, to have a decent standard of comparison. And I was certain enough of my probable "innocence" that I didn't have any real concern for my own welfare. We sat jammed in the back of the army truck for three hours. Those being arrested were pushed in with us, urged on by blows from billy clubs; silence was enforced by more blows.

The psychology of such situations is interesting. "Quiet," the young policeman barks from the rear of the bench in the truck. And everyone is quiet. At one point a woman says something to her neighbor; the policeman swings his club, indiscriminately, in the direction of the voice, and there is silence again. But he couldn't reach the front half of the van, he would have had trouble preventing group conversation; yet no one says anything.The back of the truck is really jampacked; the wood benches along the side, where I'm sitting, are full, and the entire space in the middle is packed with those pushed in and forced to stand. After a while I figure I have the least to fear and I begin speaking to my neighbor; the policeman barks, and my neighbor says "hush," but in a whisper he tells me to tell his friend where he is if he's not out by the time I am. Later I suggest out loud that those sitting should get up and let those standing and stooped over sit; several people (but only a few) do, and silence descends again. Everybody thinks about their own situation. It takes preparation, collective prior discussion maybe, to undertake the kind of resistance that could have moderated the situation.

The trucks—ours and, from what we could see, several dozen others—drove into a courtyard through heavy iron gates and then into a large garage-like structure where they all stopped and were unloaded, one by one, ten minutes or so apart—some people stayed cramped in the trucks for another hour or so. Then two hours in what turned out to be the old "interrogation prison" at Rummelsberg,

 waiting, being searched, led through corridors with steel doors, short passages, guards, coldness. Then into a small room with a senior police official, a captain perhaps, being searched, handing over my U.S. passport, getting a special look because of it and being accompanied to a special room; where the others were taken, I couldn't see. Waiting in the small room for another hour with two awkward young guards and three other foreigners—a Czech journalist, a West Berlin student, and a young West Berlin worker who had been waiting for a street car and was panicstricken that he would lose his job for overstaying his one-day visa. The student was given the hardest time; he was stripsearched, told to turn his socks inside out, treated with the greatest hostility; they obviously were hoping to be able to pin the demonstration on "Western agitators." I was taken out, handcuffed (the only point at which I got angry, but to no avail), put in the back of a regular police van, and taken to a different building, about fifteen minutes away—what I later learned was the Stasi's Lichtenberg prison.

Then followed a three-hour interrogation. It was conducted by a business-like and rather pleasant young man, a desk type rather than

a police type. I'm a lawyer and have taken many statements myself; I was interested in his approach, and saw it as, for me personally, almost a harmless game, as soon as I figured out what he was after: evidence that the march was a planned "assembly" (hence illegal, without a permit), rather than, as I suggested, a spontaneous movement of people with no previous plan. Almost harmless, I felt; the only danger that seemed to me to come out of my willingness to give a statement, one that countered what he wanted to hear, was to anyone whose name I might mention, so I studiously avoided the names of others. Finally, about 6:00 a.m., out of concern for Frances, who would have no idea where I was and would presumably wake up fairly soon and be upset, I told the young man questioning me that I would not answer another question, nor sign anything at all, unless I was thereafter, and promptly, given a ride home. He said something noncommittal but not negative, and continued asking questions. Two minutes later I simply stopped answering; after a minute he got up, walked out, came back two minutes later, and said all right, I'd get taken home. He showed me the statement he had written, I made various changes and corrections, signed it when it appeared to me thoroughly harmless, and we were through.

Ten minutes later he asked me to come with him and we walked to what turned out to be his own car, a newish blue Lada, and he drove me to where Fran and I were staying. I tried to break through the formal situation and talk with him, without much luck. He wouldn't, for instance, tell me his name—"Not a good idea, considering his job," he said. Why did he go into this line of work, I asked? He had considered alternatives, he said, but this was a good job and he felt he was doing something for his country; wouldn't I feel the same way, under similar circumstances? It depended what my country was doing, I said, for a short answer. Sure, he said. Then we got to where we were going, I got out, saw Fran standing on the balcony looking down at me getting out of the car, and went in. It was 7:00 in the morning.

Will my actions have any adverse impact on my hosts, on the Fulbright program, on my friends here? Surely the Stasi know who our friends are. A few hours later, a telephone call from West Berlin (monitored, no doubt): the student arrested with me had given my name and address to a newspaper there, would I give them a statement? I said I'd call back. Fran and I discussed it; I couldn't really add anything to what the student knew (and had no doubt already said), I was not personally manhandled, and the publicity might make life significantly more awkward for our friends here, who had already had their share of problems with the state. We decided no statement until we could get their reactions, and I told the newspaper that. They had the full story the next day, including my name, but coming from the student; fine, we thought, let it be that way.

I don't think one can really appreciate what impact such a situation can have on people unless one is oneself vulnerable. I wasn't; the worst they could have done was to throw me out of the country, and that was pretty unlikely. But for those who could have been exiled with no place to go, separated from family, job, home, roots, it was very different. And for those who could have been kept in jail—I had a small taste of Rummelsburg, but it was enough. Cold bare cells, complete helplessness and subjection to others' commands, isolation from all normal contact, dignity only at a high price and with no visible benefit—one has to have enormous respect for those who took such a risk. I wasn't taking them. The closest I had come to anything similar was during work in Mississippi for the civil rights movement in 1964, and that was quite different.

What was scary here was not so much what I had to fear personally, but what the behavior of the young policeman with the club and of the Stasi questioner implied: how easily brutality can be aroused, how widely it can be organized, how "civilized" its defense can appear.

October 9

A big protest march in Leipzig, by far the largest yet; covered on the television, and no police intervention. "We are the people," "We're staying here"—i.e., we're not going to leave and cross the border into Hungary, we want to stay here and be heard. Clearly a new stage in the struggle. Watching television, reading the paper, gets more exciting every day. [We didn't learn until later how there nearly was intervention by the police, including the militia in Leipzig, how central the roles of Kurt Mazur, leader of the Gewandthaus orchestra, and a few top party leaders and prominent individuals were in heading it off. Egon Krenz later took credit for avoiding a show of force, but no one believed him. Whatever happened, it was a crucial choice, which enabled the *Wende* to proceed without violence.]

October 12 - 16

An affair in commemoration of the tenth anniversary of my father's death was being held in Frankfurt/Main, and we went. A lively, informal, often argumentative event; the left political culture of Frankfurt/Main has always struck us as particularly abrasive and not particularly constructive. I had just reread *Soviet Marxism*, which has never been available in the DDR; a pity, because it strikes me as holding up very well after more than thirty years, and is directly to the point in dealing with the deformations of Marxist thought in the evolution of Soviet "Marxism-Leninism-Stalinism." In the evening they showed films, including clips of the 1967-1968 events in Berlin, the meetings at the Free University where my father spoke and Rudi Dutschke was a dominating figure. I wonder how much of those events and debates are known in the East.

I spoke at the plenary on the second day, giving some of our reactions to the recent changes in the DDR and raising the question of how far the process of internalization of social relations, of changes in the structure of thought and feeling, which my father had dealt with in terms of Western capitalist development, had proceeded in the DDR; whether any of what he described had been uprooted, whether something different had replaced it, what would be emergent now that the Stalinist regime seemed on the way out. I didn't have any conclusions to offer.

On the way back to Weimar, the same tension and then easing off as we crossed the border. We were prepared to fight had there been any hassle about the books or magazines we were bringing back, but they never even looked.

October 17

Erich Honecker resigns as general secretary of the SED and chairman of the Council of State—a triumph for the protest movement! Egon Krenz, a Politburo member and close to Honecker, is elected to succeed him.

Honecker was hardly a popular leader, ever:

> "What's the difference between Honecker and a plumber?"
> "The plumber never comes, and Honecker never goes."

or:

> "Why doesn't Honecker ever play hide and seek?"
> "Who would look for him?"

October 20

A phone call from someone I didn't know, a Werner K., in the Marxism-Leninism section of the HAB, who wants to talk to me about my father. Sure; we arrange to have lunch. It turns out his field is philosophy; the part of the university he teaches in would, in any Western country, simply be called social science, or some such, but here, since Marxism-Leninism is supposed to inform all the social sciences, that's what the section is called. Thus there is no philosophy department, no sociology department, no department of economics or political science; those are all parts of what's familiarly known as M-L. What people actually teach varies a great deal; some pretty much ignore Marx and Lenin, others do a formal obeisance to the classical writings, some present them dogmatically (although we haven't met any such—a self-selection process, I suppose), but very few seem to deal with it as a live method of inquiry or a controversial analysis of society. The story goes:

> A high-school teacher asks his class:
> "Who wrote the *Communist Manifesto*?"
> "Not I, not I, I didn't do it," all the pupils quickly respond.
> Aggravated at how little of Marxism-Leninism they know, he tells the story at home to his wife that evening, and she says, "I don't know why you're so upset, maybe it really wasn't any of them."
> Now really upset, the teacher storms out of the house and goes

down to the neighborhood bar for a drink. He meets a stranger and
tells him the story.

"Don't worry," says the stranger, "I'm from the Stasi. Don't
worry, we'll get to the bottom of it, we'll find out quickly enough
who wrote it!"

Whatever the level of knowledge about Marx may have been, it
was quite clear that very few people in the DDR had ever read Herbert
Marcuse or knew much about the Frankfurt School. Their writings
were not available in the bookstores and only a few libraries had
anything at all, and then it was only available to those with special
authorization. Yet Werner K. was determined to write his dissertation
on Herbert Marcuse. He had not found anyone in Weimar who would
be willing to sponsor it, nor in Halle or Leipzig; but a professor in
Berlin had shown some openness to the suggestion. As we talked, it
turned out that Werner K. had only read one book by my father and
was only just beginning to explore the matter. I offered what help I
could, told him of our efforts to open an archive of his unpublished
writings in Frankfurt/Main, but also suggested that there was a huge
amount of material already written that he might want to sample
before embarking on his venture. He owned as how he was really not
that optimistic about it anyway, he was too much of a nonconformist
ever to get far in philosophy in the DDR, he was also looking around
for other things to do with his life.

October 23

Attended an SED unit meeting at the HAB Weimar; an unusual
thing for an outsider, a non-party-member, to be allowed to do. But I
asked if I could sit in, no one really minded, everyone had other things
to worry about. A well-attended meeting, students, professors, staff,
research assistants, about twenty-five in this particular section. They
followed a prepared agenda dealing with national positions, but had
issues of their own to discuss. One was the *Sputnik* incident. *Sputnik*,
a glossy little popular magazine published in various foreign lan-
guages in the Soviet Union for circulation in other countries, was
banned in the DDR by order of Honecker after it carried an article
discussing the Hitler-Stalin pact that suggested that Stalin had erred

in his assessment of Hitler's strategy and had his own fish to fry in signing the pact. A student in Weimar distributed a leaflet criticizing the ban; he was interrogated by the Stasi, and although they decided not to prosecute him for the crime of distributing an unauthorized leaflet, they turned the matter over to the HAB to handle. The HAB set up a disciplinary commission, and as a result of their deliberations the student was expelled. Several of those in the room were on the disciplinary commission. A month or so earlier the HAB had decided to limit the suspension to one year and readmit the student. But several of the younger members wanted to know if anything had been done to make amends to the student. Had they at least apologized to him? There was a half-hearted defense: the expulsion was after all according to the law at the time, they had taken it back, why make an issue of it when there were more important things to talk about. The younger folk were clearly dissatisfied with these answers, but didn't have either the skill or the organization to push the question further; their political past has not trained them to be constructively obstreperous.

Then someone, I think innocently, asked whether party members should, or even could, belong to citizens' groups like New Forum, which had been organized in Weimar and was now holding public meetings. The youngish but bureaucratic secretary of the section said he thought not, and proceeded to read a long statement from the party central office criticizing New Forum: it was not a legally recognized group, democratic discussions should take place within the party and its affiliates in the National Front, subversive elements were using New Forum, and so forth. I was shocked; even from a self-interested point of view, it seemed to me that the party should be anxious to have its members in every political group it could, to defend its position and stay in touch, and, from a principled position, it had much to learn from New Forum. But by the time the secretary got through reading the long and pompous statement, no one had any further desire to debate the issue.

On the party hierarchy's attitude toward *Sputnik,* and toward Gorbachev's reforms in general, a joke is told:

God looks over the earth and decides it's all gone wrong, he has to put an end to it. He calls in Reagan, Gorbachev, and Honecker, and tells them he intends to end the world in fourteen days.

Reagan goes back to Washington and tells Congress: "I have some good news and some bad news. The good news is, there is a God and I just spoke with him. The bad news is, we won't be able to finish our Star Wars program."

Gorbachev calls the Supreme Soviet together and tells them: "I have two pieces of bad news: there is a God, and we won't be able to finish putting *perestroika* into effect."

Honecker calls the Politburo together and tells them: "I have two pieces of good news. The first is: there is a God, so it's good we tolerated the church in the DDR. The second is: we won't have to introduce *perestroika* into the DDR."

In the evening our doorbell rings: a pleasant-looking woman in her early fifties comes up the stairs. She's from the post office and has come to collect for our newspaper subscription. She tried to get us on her regular rounds, but we were never home. If she doesn't turn the money in soon, our subscription might (her word—not "will"!) stop, and she didn't want us to go without if we wanted it. She doesn't mind giving up an evening to chase us down; she often has to do the same for the students, and considers it part of her job.

We invite her in and get into a conversation. She wants to know where we're from; a high point in her life was a trip to Cuba but it takes ten years' savings and she doubts if she'll travel that far again. She tells us what to do with our mail if we're away for a few days, in painstaking and concerned detail, and leaves. The newspaper only costs 15 pfennigs a day, less by subscription; that probably doesn't even cover the cost of printing, let alone this system of distribution and payment. It really has nothing to do with economic principles; it's a set of human and even friendly personal relationships that gets built up to deal with an everyday situation.

October 24

Leipzig has its protest marches every Monday; Weimar is trying to have them every Tuesday, and seems to be succeeding. They start at the center of town, follow quite a long route across the middle of town and back around the edge back to the Platz der Demokratie (Democracy Square), then have a relatively brief rally. At least that was what happened today. We saw the front of the march, under a banner calling for a public hearing on the general plan for Weimar (I was of course enormously pleased to see city planning issues playing such a forward role in the movement!), and we went to the rally at the end. There was a broad range of short speeches, focusing on environmental problems. People who identified themselves as from New Forum spoke, as well as people who said they were ecologically concerned, and some who were clearly in the SED. Impressive, in a situation where such a meeting would have been banned and broken up by the police just three weeks ago.

In front of the National Theater, where we went to see a performance of Schiller's *The Robbers* after the rally, there is a statue of Goethe and Schiller proudly overlooking the square. Someone had hung a sign on it: "Wir bleiben hier!"—"We're staying here!"

October 26

The first big public rally called by New Forum and other smaller groups to be held in Weimar. All the major city officials were invited, from the Christian Democratic (CDU) mayor to the leadership of the SED to church leaders and HAB representatives. The meeting had at first been called for a large auditorium in the Fachschule für Staat und Recht (Technical College of Public Administration), but it became evident that it would be an overflow crowd, and with huge effort and surprising cooperation from the city it was moved to the Weimar Hall, the largest public auditorium in the city, and loudspeakers were set up outside.

We got there a little early and it was already impossible to get inside; the crowd outside was spilling out of the large courtyard and into the adjacent park. There was apparently a podium inside, and everyone got to speak briefly. Content was what was to be expected, the mayor defending his administration and getting repeatedly booed, New Forum and the ecology folk getting applauded, the HAB representative pussy-footing; we couldn't catch many of the innuendos and local references in the speeches and even fewer in the catcalls. A representative of the SED had also been invited to speak, an older man who was initially roundly booed, then made an impassioned and touching speech about how he had worked in the party to build the country up from the ashes of war, was proud of what he had accomplished, there might have been some mistakes, but they had worked hard and selflessly for the good of the country and the party, it was his party and he thought it was entitled to respect. Our sense was that most of the audience was moved, but also felt that the speaker was out of touch, talking of the past; he had nothing to do with current events.

The speakers from the floor were also what was to be expected: teachers and parents alike complaining about the school system, others airing particular problems, some discussion of the city's investment in building a luxury hotel, many criticisms of the run-down condition of the inner city and the lack of attention to housing rehabilitation. Not too much by way of positive ideas or next steps, but then, even in an experienced democracy, big public meetings are not where people are most likely to go into

*Please, may I politely
suggest free elections!*

practical detail. We walked home convinced that there was indeed a national mass movement at work here, if even little conservative backwater Weimar could produce such a meeting.

October 28

A long talk with Fred Staufenbiel over dinner. I don't know if such a conversation would have been possible before October 7; probably not. A tremendous amount runs under the surface in the DDR, is assumed without being stated, is known without being acknowledged, is communicated without being said. DDR literature raises this form of implicit communication to the level of art; that is why the theater, for example, is so important. The authorities are helpless to forbid it without looking foolish (and there is probably much they simply don't understand), yet its message gets across to a wide audience. In any event, over the course of the evening Staufenbiel told us his life story, and it was fascinating.

Fred Staufenbiel's is the story of how a person with a strong independent, anti-authoritarian character, with principles and innovative ideas, survived and made a way for himself in the DDR. The independence and the necessary self-assurance to go with it came out of the war: Staufenbiel was drafted in his mid-teens (in the last year of the war), got out of the army by simply walking away in 1945, found work for himself (making up the appropriate background as he went along), found his way back to familiar territory, made friends with all kinds of people, from local Soviet commanders to discharged veterans to older people in small villages and cities. The jobs he could get were in construction, as a mason; he learned the trade as he worked. Then he got himself further education in building technology, worked some more, went back to school to learn public administration, didn't like the jobs the *Einsatzkommission* (the "placement office," with the power to assign students to jobs) at the school thought were most suitable for him—he was considered too impulsive to make good party material and he refused to go into administration. So he simply turned them down and found work on his own, heard of a new school for building and construction and got a job there, met and married his wife, got into mild arguments with the hierarchy but remained able to assert himself (i.e., not go to training schools he thought were a waste of time), got sent for further study to a research institute in Berlin that he thought looked promising, got an advanced degree there, did research on working conditions in the DDR that got him into trouble with the hierarchy (read: party) at the institute, found an opening at the HAB in Weimar and took it, and since then has been doing solid work, critical in substance but formulated in terms just acceptable enough to permit it to be published and circulated.

Life at the HAB has not been all smooth sailing for him, however: between pressure from above to conform, to conduct himself more in keeping with accepted academic procedures and expectations, and pressure from below, from students and research assistants, for more concrete and bolder statements and challenges to the way things were (and are), it has taken all the force of his personal charm and integrity to maintain a position where he can be effective and maintain any kind of long-term personal equilibrium.

I suspect that there are countless people like Fred in the DDR, people who do not accept the system as a whole but who have grown up in it, consider it their country, speak its multiple-level language, find enough in its expressed ideology for them to be able to adhere to their own principles and work toward their implementation while rejecting the authoritarian structures and empty displays of the hierarchy; people who have made their peace with the decent bureaucrats in the system, had their fights with the indecent ones, are willing to put up with a certain amount of shit as long as they feel they are accomplishing something or able to help others. Some, almost by chance, reach their limits, and/or get thrown out; others get old and defeated and give up, grumbling only at home and doing the least possible at work. But many do their best within the system, improving things as much as they can along the way, knowing the limits and keeping their disappointments within bounds.

There's a saying among many in ordinary jobs in the DDR: "They pretend to pay us, and we pretend to work." But there are many other, more active forms of resistance to be found within the system.

October 31

To Quedlinburg, on a bus chartered by the HAB for students and faculty to look at the successes and failures of historic preservation in the old towns of the DDR. Wernigerode is the showpiece; Quedlinburg is a very similar town, also located on the northern edges of the Harz mountains, but here the process is more typical.

We were taken around by the town planner, a HAB graduate. On first look, it is a beautiful old town, with well-preserved or restored half-timbered houses, small streets and lanes, a very pleasing town square. But the town planner was very critical indeed. He took us, after the formal tour, to some adjacent streets and alleys: crumbling buildings, piles of rubble, roofs with gaping holes, streets dug up (or eroded) and unrepaired, crude sanitary facilities. Some of the worst of what he showed us were in fact the backs of the houses whose facades were show places on the formal tour. And he complained: no money, no support, no understanding, even the local people would rather have new modern industrialized concrete panel apartments than restored old houses, the city council didn't care, Berlin was only interested in show, deterioration was proceeding faster than repair, nothing could be done.

But the whole account was passive; he described what was happening that was bad, but said nothing of any effort to change things. I asked him, as politely as I could, what he was trying to do about it: organizing, petitions, complaints, newspaper articles, committees, presentations to the council. No, he said, it was all useless. Weren't things different now, I asked, weren't there new possibilities, with all the changes going on? Not that he could see, he said.

Very depressing; there is a deeply inculcated passivity that hasn't blocked an ability to see things as they are, but has affected any conception of what can be done about them. Forty years is a long time.

November 1

I find myself writing and talking more and more about the United States to colleagues and students and groups here, responding to an open upsurge of interest that was probably always latent. The United States looks, from afar, like a wonderland; young people think of it as a place with streets paved with gold. I've brought slides that show both the successes and failures of urban life—the skyscrapers, the wealth, the cars, the shopping, the natural beauty, but also the slums, the poverty, the pollution, the overvaluation of consumption, the environmental degradation. People are disturbed; they don't want to believe it, they desperately want something different from what they have and see the private market as the way out. Not all; we have no way of judging, but certainly many are suspicious of the market, yet don't defend the system the way it is. Is there something other than state domination or market domination? This is the underlying question I keep wanting to address: is there something that avoids the failures of the DDR but also avoids the failures of the United States, something that combines that which is good in the DDR with that which is good in the United States? It's a debate to which I can perhaps contribute something from the U.S. experience, and I'm writing a good bit on current policy issues to try to bring that experience to bear. Hans Reichling, my office mate, has offered to correct my German, so I'm trying to write in that language.

November 2

Harry Tisch, the old head of the FDGB, the Free German Trade Unions, has stepped down and for the first time a woman, Annelis Kimmel, is elected chair. Tisch was one of the inner circle around Honecker, and the FDGB was tightly controlled by the SED. And Margot Honecker, Honecker's wife, who has been minister of education, steps down too.

November 3

Another series of resignations from the Politburo: Kurt Hager, Erich Mielke, Hermann Axen, and others: the hard-liners responsible for "cultural policy" and for the Stasi! The old guard inner circle seems to have surrendered completely; but the younger guard inner circle (i.e., people like Krenz—he's only 52) seem still to be in somewhat precarious control.

November 4

I don't recall ever sitting in front of a television set for so long and paying such rapt attention as we did today watching the giant rally at Alexanderplatz in Berlin. The attendance was overwhelming; it must have been the biggest independent rally ever held in the DDR (*see photo on page 79*). Commentators reported from 500,000 to 1 million; whatever the true figure, there were masses of people. The slogans were wild: witty, uninhibited, trenchant, memorable—so much so that the person chairing the rally called on all those with banners to bring them up after the rally so that they could be saved for a future exhibition [which was in fact held at the Museum der

Deutschen Geschichte in March 1990—and was tremendously effective].

Samples:

> AGAINST MONOPOLY SOCIALISM—FOR DEMOCRATIC SOCIALISM

> REVOLUTIONS ARE HOLIDAYS FOR THE PEOPLE!

> THOSE WHO ACTED BLACK YESTERDAY AND TALK WHITE TODAY WILL BE GRAY TOMORROW, MR. KRENZ!

> A 360-DEGREE TURN IN THE STATE SECURITY SYSTEM?

> SKEPTICISM IS A CITIZEN'S FIRST OBLIGATION

> STEPPING DOWN IS A STEP FORWARD

> I'M A GRANDMOTHER AND LOVE MY COUNTRY

> REFORMS, BUT UNLIMITED ("UNBEKRENZT," A PUN ON EGON KRENZ)

> THOSE WHO DON'T MOVE, DON'T FEEL THEIR CHAINS

> PROPOSAL FOR THE NEXT MAY DAY PARADE: LET THE LEADERS MARCH IN A PARADE IN FRONT OF THE PEOPLE

> CUT DOWN THE BUREAUCRATS, SAVE THE TREES

> LONG LIVE THE OCTOBER REVOLUTION OF 1989!

> TO GO IS SILVER, TO STAY IS GOLD

> NO VISA REQUIREMENTS AS FAR AS HAWAII!

> SEND THE SECURITY POLICE TO WORK IN THE FACTORIES, PAY THEM ONLY FOR WHAT THEY PRODUCE!

> ASTERIX BELONGS IN THE POLITBURO!

and, my two favorites:

> NO POWER FOR ANYBODY!

> PRIVILEGES FOR ALL!

[Only later did what was *not* among the slogans strike us as significant: nothing anti-socialist, and only one in the whole bunch that called for a united Germany.]

It was not so much the text of the speeches but the tone of the event that was thrilling. All the speakers said it in one way or another: it was as if a new world had opened. There was still much to do to get rid of the old, to disempower the SED, to eliminate the Stasi, to rid the system of its old bosses; but there was equally much to do, and it was much more challenging, to build a new society, to try something new and exciting and different and better. The slogan that captured it best: "Forward, but never forget the past!" The atmosphere was infectious.

Even sitting in front of the television in our little concrete pre-fab in Weimar, we felt it.

Many of the names of the speakers were unknown to us, so we could only draw general conclusions. Clearly the old guard of the SED was not represented, with the exception of Günther Schabowski, the SED secretary for Berlin, who was mercilessly booed. In terms of staging, it was good he was there, so that the crowd would keep its enemy in sight, not forget it. Markus Wolf we had heard of; he had been in charge of foreign activities for the Stasi until he had stepped down several years earlier. He tried to present himself as a reformer within the SED, but he got nowhere. The other speakers we could place were largely dissidents, with a record of opposing SED oppression either within or without the party. Almost all spoke of socialism, or in one way or another of building on what existed in the DDR; there was no reference to the West in the pointed speeches.

The demonstration was arranged by the artists: from the Berlin Theater originally, then with the Association of Visual Artists, the Association of Film and Television Workers, and the Committee for the Entertainment Arts. They were the official sponsors of the rally because they happened to have taken the initiative in obtaining a permit for a rally several weeks earlier. It was a happy coincidence that the country was ready for it when it happened. The demonstration was simply lifted up on the tide of history. The entire DDR was ready for it, wanted it: not just artists or even intellectuals (there aren't that many of them), but everyone. That was the sense we got from watching the rally, from the media comments (East and West alike), and from talking with people.

November 6

Despite all the complaints and protests, the government has come out with a proposal for revising travel regulations under which granting permission remains discretionary, overall restrictions remain in force (although "in general" thirty days a year out of the country are to be permitted), and bureaucratic controls seem hardly diminished.

November 7

Wonder of wonders, the committee of the Volkskammer, to which the proposal on travel has been referred, rejects it! And the remaining ministers, forty-four of them, step down in concert, although they will remain until their successors are appointed.

November 8

A meeting of the Politburo, and the entire membership resigns. The ZK, the Central Committee, thereupon elects a new Politburo, which looks like a compromise slate, some reformers, like Hans Modrow, some *Wende-Hälze*, literally "neck-turners" (maybe "turncoats" would be the American slang equivalent), people like Krenz, and a few old guard remnants. Wolfgang Schuman, a sociologist at the Humboldt University with whom I've been working and whom I trust, tells us it is not an acceptable compromise. There's going to be, for the first time in history, a mass demonstration of party members outside the ZK building that evening, demanding thoroughgoing reform. Their slogan, building on the Leipzig demonstration chants, ("We Are the People!"), will be: "We Are the Party!"

November 9

The day the Wall came down. We weren't there when it happened, we were in Prague (more on that below). The stories about what happened are contradictory; the one thing that seems clear is that no one in authority anticipated events. The most believable story is that the ZK, which had met that day, decided it had to make some concession to the demand for freer travel and would ease restrictions as of the next day. But while Günter Schabowski, then press spokesman for the ZK, was giving a press conference on other points in front of the building where they were meeting, someone walked up to him and handed him a note with the decision scrawled on it. He read it to the reporters as it was handed to him (accurately or not, no one knows), and the reporters interpreted it as the immediate lifting of all restrictions on travel across the Wall. That is what went on the radio. People heard it and started moving toward the crossing points and over into West Berlin. The stunned border guards tried to stop them, but the people shouted, "Haven't you heard, the Wall is open!" The guards were nonplussed, gave up and let them through. No one knows what orders they finally got (or indeed if anything at all was communicated to them that day), but the word spread like wildfire and there was nothing anyone could do to stop the mass of people. The exhilaration, and the frenetic welcome on the other side, are all matters of history; it was certainly a night like no other in the postwar history of the two Germanies.

Whether the story is true in detail or not, it has the ring of truth: the rapid pace of events, the mounting expectations, the panic that seemed to color much of the Politburo's actions, the growing public emboldenment, the declining authority and self-confidence of the authorities. Many people, including leaders of the early opposition like Bärbel Bohley, later considered the opening of the Wall a terrible mistake, as delivering a vulnerable and unprepared East German public to the seductive attractions of West German capitalism, but then no one, then or later, considered the actions of the Politburo in

October or November to be well considered or smart, even in their own self-interest.

The juxtaposition of the two events—the November 4 demonstration at the Alexanderplatz and the November 9 mass celebration in West Berlin—symbolizes the two possible directions of the *Wende*: toward the reform of socialism or toward the West German model of capitalism. If the alternative is only between socialism as it is in the DDR and capitalism as it is in West Germany, the choice will be clear; the West will triumph. But it seems to me that those are not the only alternatives, that the question is poorly phrased. The question should instead be: What kind of a system do we want? Not do we want System A or System B, particularly if System A is described as "state" and System B is described as "market"; that is a false dichotomy, and only muddies the waters. Hence the Excurs that follows, an attempt to deal with how the question is asked, in the context of the urban development issues I know something about.

excurs 2

STATE VS. MARKET:
TREACHEROUS ALTERNATIVES

The historical irony of the *Wende* in the DDR was that, just as the state was being converted from a one-party dictatorial instrument into a democratic participatory one, it was being reduced in its power and stripped of its legitimacy; just as the domination of a political elite was being broken by massive popular protest, the way was opened for the domination of a new economic elite that would equally exclude popular participation in key social decisions. The widespread confusion about the concepts "state" and "market," in which "market" becomes an ideologically loaded synonym for "reform," contributes massively to this irony. Things were being said in the East about the "market" that even conservatives would blush to claim in the West.

The fallacy of the "state/market" dichotomy as a formulation of the alternatives that were before the DDR should be clear ("socialist/capitalist," "public/private" are equally misleading for that purpose; I'll come to them later). In the first place, the "state/market" dichotomy assumes that the two are separable, rather than inherently related to each other; many formulations in fact assume that markets came first and states then intervened in them. In general, however, modern markets are more creatures of the state than the state's predecessors. No market of any size can function without state-enforced property rights, without a legal—that is to say, state-defined—status for contracts, without public regulation of times and places, without currency, etc. No one in the West would contend that a pure "market" could exist in a capitalist society; Paul Samuelson, in the standard elementary textbook on economics used all over the United States, speaks of the pure market as an economists' fiction, and calls the United States a "mixed economy"; how much more would be that be true of West Germany, for instance.

Karl Polanyi makes the point even more strongly. His discussion in *The Great Transformation* is at bottom a convincing documentation of the extent to which the private market, by itself, does not even adequately serve the purposes its own willing participants seek, and has been continuously limited, modified, buttressed, regulated by the state throughout the history of capitalism in order to permit its continued existence; absent such nonmarket actions, Polanyi shows, market systems would have been their own gravediggers.

The second fallacy involved in the "state/market" dichotomy is that, to the extent that "market" and "state" are relevant categories, their role can be seen by examining the relative size of each in the society, and that size can be usefully represented in terms of contribution to GNP, the size of the state budget, or any similar measure—or that reasonable conclusions can be drawn from any such numbers about the nature of the society. But the truth is that the *substance* of what happens, both in the government and the private sector, can be very different even when the respective sectors are of similar size in two countries. The government can play the same proportional role in two economies, but government policies and priorities may nevertheless be very different. By the same token, the market may be used as the mechanism for the same range of decisions in two countries, but the actors and the resources available to them and their access to power may be so different that the mere statement that the market is of comparable size says very little. The relative size or strength of the state or of the market says little; better ways of seeing the important differences might be to look at who—what groups, classes—are involved in making decisions as to the use of resources and their distribution, in what relations of power they stand to each other, to what extent the profit motive fuels their actions, who in reality is able to determine state decisions, and so on.

The third fallacy involved in the "state/market" dichotomy is the assumption that there is a simple and universal content to each of the two concepts. But the definition of the state has been a source of controversy from the beginning of political thought. Marx's definition of the state as the "executive committee of the ruling class" must at the very least be modified by a consideration of the role of bureaucratic structures as independent actors, and whether party hierarchies can appropriately be called "classes" is unclear. However that may be, the *form and method* of governing by the state can vary widely. The DDR was a centralized, hierarchical, party-dominated state. West Germany, as far as its state apparatus goes, is also largely centralized but much less party-dominated; parliamentary democracy is its method of organization. Other variations exist: the United States is much less centralized than either of the German states, and in times of turmoil more direct forms of public action have existed here than are expressed in parliamentary form.

The market is also a concept with a variety of meanings. Basically, the market is simply a place or a forum where exchange takes place, where immediate prices are determined, in large part through bargaining between buyer and seller, where supply, demand, and costs of production play a key role. In this sense the market certainly plays a greater role in West Germany than in East. But one could imagine quite other forms of market: for instance, one where the motivation to make profit, or the drive to accumulate capital, would play only a subordinate or no role (as in the nonprofit or public enterprise sector, for instance), or one where production but not distribution would be determined by market bargaining (as with social housing in Sweden, for instance). To speak as if there is only one kind of market, a private profit-driven market oriented toward the accumulation of capital in individual hands, is to load the ideological dice shamelessly.

A classic example of the confusion in terms and of its political use is the argument made by Konrad Adenauer after the end of World War II. The opposite of the totalitarian fascist state was alleged to be the "right" of private ownership of the means of production, which under this banner was made a fundamental right in the Western zones, even though private ownership of the means of production had also been a characteristic of fascist Germany. "Private ownership" and "state authority" were thus set up by Adenauer as opposites, although the preceding twelve years had just shown how compatible the two in fact could be.

To conclude: "state" vs. "market" as a formulation of the alternatives that were facing the DDR is badly misleading. Not only does it suggest a factually incorrect separation of the two; not only does it conceal the substantive forces operating through the two forms; not only does it blend into one term very different concepts; it also, and here lies its practical danger, excludes alternative approaches from consideration.

In fact, societies could be envisaged in which the economic alternatives, the production and distribution of goods, are determined by:

- A profit- and accumulation-driven *private market*, with various degrees of regulation (for example, automobile production in the West).
- A *social market*, with limited or no profit or accumulation of capital (for example, nonprofit universities in the United States, the postal service in West Germany).
- A *centralized state*, according to the dictates of a political elite (for example, military production in the Soviet Union).
- A *decentralized, democratic state* following directly expressed public priorities (for example, some local government activities in the United States).

Some element of each, but in widely different proportions, is found in most developed countries today. The DDR is overwhelming based on a centralized, nonmarket system. But the alternative is not only a profit-driven private market system; it could also be a "social" market, or a democratic public system, or some optimum combination of the two. The question is not a quantitative one: what percentage should be allocated to each method of decision-making; but a qualitative one: which is the dominant mode, the mode that defines the system. And the alternatives are not confined to the dichotomy "state" or "market." Elements of both are in all alternatives.

The nature and role of a market have direct political concomitants. In terms of power relationships, the political alternatives could be listed as follows:

- Domination by an elite whose position is based on economic power.
- Domination by an elite whose position is based on political power.
- Decision-making without domination based on either economic or political power; i.e., substantive democracy.

Put differently: political rule can be by an economic elite, a political elite, or a majority not dominated by an elite.

Political power can be based on economic power, as it tends to be in capitalist systems, despite the forms of liberal democracy. Political power can be self-perpetuating, as it has been historically in absolutist systems, and as reformers believe it has tended to become in rigid "socialist" societies. Or political power can be generated by popular consent and with popular participation, as both the bourgeois and the socialist revolutions promised.

What does historical experience suggest as to how markets fit into these political alternatives?

A private market tends to produce an *economic* elite. Those who have acquired economic power through the private market have the means to become politically powerful; political equality is limited by the economic inequality produced through the private market. In those countries having the most formally open political systems, there is a constant tension between the concentration of economic wealth and the processes of democratic decision-making; measures such as limits on campaign contributions are typically necessary but insufficient answers, and the advent of mass communications and sophisticated advertising and public relations techniques compound the problem. It is the genius of the market that it permits effective domination by an economic elite through invisible and inevitable-appearing market processes, rather than through the visible exercise of political power, at least under normal conditions. Political opposition to economic power becomes that much more difficult. Quite private-appearing economic market arrangements, as in housing, contribute to the maintenance of political power. The private market both permits the concentration of economic power and permits the economic elite to maintain political control. Historically, the private market has been an essential part of the capitalist system.

The subordination of the certain extreme consequences of a private market is not inconsistent with the continued domination of an economic elite; such subordination may in fact strengthen and legitimate such domination. The term "social market" is in fact often used to describe sectors of an economy removed in whole or in major part from the operations of the private market. The case of land use is a classic example. The Weimar constitution of August 11, 1919, included the following provision:

> The allocation and use of land will be supervised by the state in such fashion as to prevent misuse and to lead toward the goal of providing every German a healthy home and every German family, particularly those with many children, a home and a workplace appropriate to their situation.

More than one hundred years ago, Marx foresaw the logic of such a provision when he commented that the private ownership of land interfered with rather than furthered the interests of industrial capital. Whatever the internal conflicts within a private market *system* (a system in which the private market is dominant, whether it coexists with a social market or not), it remains a system in which those in decisive positions in the private market dominate. The partial existence of a social market (better called a socially regulated market, as in the Weimar Republic, contemporary Sweden, to some extent most contemporary Western European countries, least of all perhaps the United States) within a private market system is very different from a social market *system,* in which the social organization of the market is dominant. In a social market system those holding political power, whether democratically achieved or not, dominate.

But the expansion of the private market can also serve to weaken political domination built on nonmarket power. The expansion of the private market in the fifteenth through eighteenth centuries is an example. The freedom of the towns, representative democracy, civil rights, are all results of the transition from feudalism to capitalism and the expansion of the private market. They each significantly weakened the domination of a political elite (the feudal structure). Private markets, however, at first coexisted quite peacefully with the expansion of central political control through the monarchy. In the transition from feudalism to capitalism, the forms of liberal democracy played a major role, but the extent to which liberal democracy meant full democracy remains contested. It is in this sense that Gorbachev spoke of the socialist revolution as advancing toward the—as yet—unfulfilled promises of the French revolution. However one judges the political aspects of the transition, the role of private markets was to further the substitution of rule by one class for rule by another, rule by an economic elite for rule by a political elite.

The historical experience, therefore, is that private markets tend to support the establishment or maintenance in power of an economic elite, but have under specific historical circumstances accompanied an expansion of democratic forms and broader popular participation. Nonmarket directive systems have been used primarily to maintain, but also at times to weaken, the power of existing elites (as in the French and Russian revolutions); the extent to which nonmarket revolutionary systems inevitably substitute rule by one elite for rule by another has long been the subject of intensive debate.

Thus history does not permit any simple correlation between market and nonmarket, on the one hand, and rule by an economic or political elite on the other. Private markets have served both to strengthen and to weaken elite rule; directive systems have worked both to narrow and to extend, at least in transitional periods, popular voice and control.

Social market systems have too short a history to allow for many conclusions. Some in the Soviet Union, at least, are optimistic about their possibilities. Thus a Soviet economist has written:

> In those countries in which there is socialism and the market has remained in existence, it has been a market of competition, but with a different structure of property rights and a different form of power, to wit, democracy.

Political democracy and social markets support each other, the argument goes. If so, a social market is a necessary but not sufficient condition for a democratic participatory political system. It permits democracy within the sphere of the market, but it does not determine whether the decisions made by and through the state serve the purposes of an elite, for whom the social market becomes a concession made to legitimate political power, or whether those state decisions have been arrived at through nonhierarchical, popular, open, and participatory processes.

The current Soviet discussions seem to recognize both the possibilities and dangers more clearly than do the mainstream discussions in the DDR (perhaps because they are, in the Soviet Union, more theoretical?). Gorbachev's words hint at a possibility that is different from both the existing private market systems and the existing non-market systems, and seems to be leading toward what I have been calling a social market system, placing it in the context of political changes as well:

> In the Soviet Union, we are replacing the administrative-command system with a system based on initiative and economic independence, and we are extending the rights of producer collectives. In short, we are democratizing economic life and restructuring property relations. Many new forms of economic organization are emerging, such as leaseholding, cooperatives, etc. Within the framework of restructuring the whole society, all this creates certain dangers. It is important that processes do not get out of control, so to speak.

How are those dangers to be avoided, those processes controlled?

> ...we want to give socialism a new lease on life by promoting greater democracy and *glasnost*, enabling people to become involved once more in political and economic processes, ending the alienation of the individual from property, government and culture, and making the social process more dynamic.

Whether these words have any practical result of course remains much in doubt. But the options deserve further consideration in other countries also, and briefly, but abortively, seemed to be on the table during the first two phases of the *Wende* in East Germany.

journal

THE SECOND PHASE:
DOWN WITH THE OLD,
THE NEW COMES LATER

**From the Opening of the Wall
to New Years' Eve at Brandenburg**

November 9

To Prague by sleeper for a conference of Architects, Planners, and Designers for Peace. A typical old-fashioned "international peace movement" kind of conference: supposedly a very general topic, peace and the environment, unanimity about everything, everything so general no one can object, mainly Easterners, some Western sympathizers. The DDR had hosted many such conferences in the past, generally useful for the person-to-person contacts and the informal discussions, but strictly party-line in all official aspects. Had such an event been held in the DDR today, the tone would have been open, there would have been controversy, resolutions from the floor, criticisms of speakers, real discussion. But Czechoslovakia was still where the DDR was a month ago (how quickly events have moved!), and we didn't have high expectations. But we were curious, and in particular wanted to see how the DDR representatives would interact with their (erstwhile?) colleagues in Czechoslovakia.

We picked the sessions we went to carefully. At one, on historic preservation, someone from the DDR League of Architects spoke (in Russian!) and showed slides of historic preservation in the DDR, how beautifully the buildings had been restored, how proud the DDR was of its heritage and how much it was doing to preserve it. We had of course just been in Quedlinburg and knew what the backs of the very buildings whose facades were being shown looked like. And we knew how few towns had even that much work done on them. What cynical dishonesty!

We had a couple of names of dissidents from the Campaign for Peace and Democracy in New York, and Jim Morgan of the U.S. Architects, Planners, and Designers for Social Responsibility also had a few. We finally got together with one of those whose names we had, Rita Klimova, in a hotel lobby in downtown Prague. She spoke fluent English, having lived in the United States as a child during the war, and was a close associate of Vaclav Havel's. [She was later appointed ambassador to the United States!] The previous weekend there had been a demonstration, largely of students, at Wenceslaus Square; a number had been arrested, there were rumors of mistreatment. We had seen the stories in the paper, a little note saying there had been an illegal demonstration provoked by troublemakers where thirty-seven or so rowdies had been arrested. Rita was troubled; she said the group around Havel was disturbed by the event, it had not gotten the mass turnout they had hoped for, the group was deciding whether it didn't have to change its tactics, to try some other means to put pressure on the government, one that did not expect masses of people to take to the streets.

[This discussion has since come to symbolize how events can outpace the plans and expectations even of those most closely involved. The following weekend there was a larger turnout, the police violence was so shocking that mass turnouts followed, and within a month the regime had been toppled.]

November 10

At the conference plenary I introduced a resolution from the floor (in itself not an action in keeping with conventionally accepted standards of conduct at such a gathering!) saying politely that the conference considered democracy to be closely linked to aspirations for peace and environmental protection, and calling on all governments to permit the maximum of free assembly and discussion of public issues. In introducing the resolution, I said I felt it particularly important that it be discussed and adopted because of the recent arrests in Wenceslaus Square.

There were violent objections from the hosts of the conference, with the head (or spokesman) of the Czech Association of Architects denouncing the resolution as rude and unwarranted. The chair called a recess and invited me to a closed session of the executive committee, where they tried to talk me out of it. The U.S. representative backed the resolution, as did the Soviet delegate, at least as I understood him, but the Czech was unalterably opposed. He did a little harangue in which he said he had been invited to a conference in Florida several years before, had been disturbed by the treatment of blacks that he had seen there, but that he would never have dreamed of offending his hosts by saying anything about it. I told him it would have been much better if he had, it would have contributed to, not interfered with, greater friendship between the Czechoslovakian people and the people of the United States; but I don't think he understood. In any event, even a compromise formulation was not acceptable to the Czech, and when we went back onto the floor and voted, the resolution lost, but the point was made.

[I got a letter from Jim Morgan several months later saying that the officers of the Czech Association of Architects had all been ousted and the spokesman at the Prague conference in particular was in disgrace. Things do change.]

November 11

The Wall has been opened? It's hard to get news in Prague; we can't get an English-language newspaper anywhere, except the official *News* put out for foreigners. Even *Neues Deutschland* isn't available here; by Czech standards it's subversive. But our friends heard rumors on the radio. When we visit in the evening, we try to get listen to the BBC, but unsuccessfully. We find it hard to believe. *(A photo of the Wall, with the "Death Strip" between the two sides, is below.)*

Bruno Flierl had given me a typescript of some papers put out by

the Research Group on the Theory of Socialism, which he thinks are very good—the most far-reaching, thoughtful, constructive attempt to present a reform model of socialism that he's seen. It's a heterogeneous collection of pieces by people working at the Humboldt, primarily in philosophy, but also in law, social science, perhaps other fields. The ideas had been worked out over the preceding years, that is to say, before any changes were in view, and the group had been protected by Dieter Klein, prorector of the faculty at Humboldt to which they belonged, which had enabled them to have ready some of the few thought-out and detailed pieces on the reform of socialism that could stand the light of day under the new circumstances. Some of the work was quite theoretical, developing what is here fondly called a *Gesellschaftskonzeption*, a "concept of society," something no self-respecting writer should be without, and quite interesting, if very academic. But other pieces dealt with concrete proposals for reform in specific areas: the media and travel regulations were the two I particularly noted.

The travel proposals struck me as particularly interesting because, coming from such a "radical" group, they were quite moderate. They proposed creating a general right to travel, but then suggested a set of administrative regulations, passport and visa requirements, applications and permissions, that seemed to leave far too much discretion in bureaucratic hands—even though there was the presumption of the right to travel, absent strong countervailing reasons. But if this was what the "radicals" were thinking, it was very hard to take seriously the idea that the Wall would simply be opened. It makes the account reported earlier (see November 8) that much easier to believe.

November 19

After a lecture in Prague, sightseeing in Brno, several days in Bratislava attending conferences and lectures, then back by train to Weimar. We had to change in Leipzig. Long lines at the railroad station in Leipzig: lines to buy tickets to go to the West, lines to pick up the fifteen Deutsche marks spending money that each resident was allowed (in exchange for the equivalent Ost mark). It's hard to overestimate the feeling of being locked in, the DDR-claustrophobia, that ordinary people felt under the complex and tight travel restrictions prevailing before November 9; once the door was opened, *everybody* wanted to go through it, just to see for themselves what they had been kept from seeing all these years.

November 24

It's hard to get any work done, so much is happening. To get to my office at school, I have to walk down a long corridor lined with bulletin boards. Some time ago they were neatly apportioned among all the official groups: each class had one, the staff had one, the party organization had one, the trade union had one, the Free German Youth (FDJ) had one; one was for recreational activities, one for culture, one for the governing board of the department. Now they have all been taken over by leaflets, statements, replies to statements, calls for this action, criticisms of that one. Some were typed and signed by several people, some scrawled and signed by one. But almost all were interesting. It takes half an hour just to walk down the hall and look at the material added since the day before.

The ferment is a little incoherent, but there is a sense of excitement, of wanting to change everything, of participation and argument. A new student organization is in formation; the FDJ members argue about whether to criticize or to join; some want to link with other schools, others want to organize their own group first. Curricular reforms are proposed in one memo, other reforms in others, the signers of the first proposal denounced in a third. Revelations about party abuses or administrative stupidities are clipped from the papers and posted, others are set out accusingly in anonymous letters. Everybody is calling meetings, challenging decisions made at meetings, demanding meetings to discuss meetings. Exhilarating, but a little overwhelming too, for us; it's hard to tell the real thing from the talk.

I'm disappointed that more attention isn't being focused on concrete city development and housing issues, the kinds of questions one would expect HAB students and faculty to be particularly interested in and knowledgeable about. I can't help very much on the organizational or directly political work, but I can make a contribution on the substance of planning and housing policies. [Excurs 3, which follows, is part of the result.]

December 5

The Leipzig Monday marches, according to all the media, are turning away from their original direction, becoming strongly nationalist, strongly, even viciously, antisocialist as well as anti-SED, waving West German flags, tearing down DDR ones. I have heard similar stories about the Weimar Tuesday marches and rallies; Ute Schäffer told me she and some friends were going to the rally this evening to show that at least some people disagreed, some people still stood for a reformed socialism rather than a blind going over to the West. I decided to go down and see what it was like.

The march was every bit as nationalistic as the reports from Leipzig suggested. Despite the driving rain, mothers with children in baby carriages, young men in leather jackets, middle-aged citizens, all types, were there. A good many carried the West German flag, there were few DDR flags to be seen. There was no one remotely left among the speakers, nor anyone who said a good word about the DDR. Ute's small group, bravely waving its DDR flags, was so clearly out-numbered that no one paid much attention to it. In Weimar, at least, the pro-West German crowd was clearly the majority.

December 8

There is at least one interview or Round Table discussion on television every evening dealing with events in the West. Not too much new information, but the programs do leave images of people, or of types of people, that merge in one's mind with positions and statements. Two of these seem to have a basis in fact:

The editor of *Die Welt*, a widely read business-oriented newspa-per in West Germany, is on a program with both East and West Germans discussing the future of the DDR. The positions are unre-markable: one of the DDR participants speaks of democratic social-ism, another attacks central planning; the West Germans advocate the market. But the gentleman from *Die Welt* does it with such arrogance, such contempt for those who disagree, such an air of superior knowl-edge and experience, that he symbolizes for us an element in the West German approach that we find very disturbing. In a situation in which millions of people are going through epochal changes in their way of life, in which almost everyone with integrity is questioning, probing, looking for solutions, unwilling to take things for granted or accept answers just because they are authoritatively given, here is a posture from the West that continues what has just been rejected, that treats them as stupid children, is infantilizing in its every tone and gesture. His political approach and his manner is unfortunately typical of many leaders, both in business and in politics, who are increasingly involved in the future of the DDR.

Steffi Spira is on another such program, broadcast from Vienna. She was at the November 4 demonstration, a little old (in her eighties?) lady with great dignity and stage presence, obviously known and respected, whose concluding comment, as the last speaker of the day, was, "So I think the leaders of the SED should do what I am about to do—step down." And she did, to rousing applause. On this program, however, she has another arrogant know-it-all opposite her, quoting statistics and citing economic laws that prove beyond a doubt that socialism is absurd, that free markets produce everything worth having, from consumer goods to social justice—all within a basic framework that says, look, dear lady, your system has just failed, ours is on top of the world, why don't you just go home and tend to your knitting and let us do it right for a change. Steffi is clearly not in a position to deal with the numbers and economic laws, and doesn't try to. Instead, she makes a little speech about her life, her values, how she has fought for them, what justice and equality and democracy mean to her, that people should come before money and might. There is now a real possibility of implementing these values in the DDR, she says, and perhaps to do so better than in the West. The people of the DDR deserve the chance to try. People in the audience at the TV station clap.

Steffi Spira represents a type for us too: the old communist or socialist, politically active before World War II, sometimes but not always a party member (another example is Stefan Heym, who never joined the party; others were in and out or had troubles in), but dedicated to the cause in their bones. Some, indeed, may have become Stalinists, or kept quiet in the face of evident injustice, in the belief that their cause would thereby be advanced. They are people of unquestionable personal integrity; personal gain or personal power is no motivation for them. But they have a different set of experiences than their younger compatriots, almost speak a different language; they are critical supporters of what is happening today, but not its leaders.

There are many in the generation that came of age immediately after the war who have similar values, grew up believing that building socialism would lead to a better way of life, and adhered to those values despite mounting evidence that the effort was going astray. Most had come into conflict with the hierarchy; many stayed in the SED, others left. While, again, many are people of unquestioned integrity, today their credibility is limited.

The real leadership must come from new people, new movements. Some of the people we've seen or heard on TV or read are very impressive—Jens Reich, Friedrich Schorlemmer, Gregor Gysi, Wolfgang Ullman, Ina Merkel—but we don't know them very well. Nor do we know how strong their groups are. New Forum seems the strongest, even if it seems to vary greatly in its composition and goals from place to place. The future of the reform movement within the SED is hard to judge. In any event, it seems to me that the hope for the future lies in this age group.

The problem with watching television these days is that it's so interesting; all the toadying is gone, there's real news—and it's from the DDR, not the West. People used to think that they could only get straight news from the West, that only in the West could people speak their minds freely:

> Honecker is taking a vacation in the summer, and sees a glorious sunrise. "How wonderful to see you," says Honecker to the sun. "I greet you on this glorious day."
>
> "It is an honor to rise for you, Comrade Honecker," says the sun in reply, "and a pleasure to be of service to the leader of such a great land."
>
> The day wears on, sunset arrives, and Honecker says to the sun, "Goodnight, dear sun, thank you for a splendid day."
>
> "Oh kiss my ass, you stupid little man," says the sun.
>
> "What's the matter?" asks Honecker. "This morning you were so polite and friendly!"
>
> "Yes," says the sun, "but now I'm in the West!"

December 10

I would really like to get to Berlin for the balance of our stay. Nothing against Weimar, I say to Frances, who likes it here; it's just that everything is happening in Berlin, or at least visible in Berlin; the scale is bigger, national government decisions take place there, it's where the action is. Of course, much is happening here too, and more in other cities, perhaps even more typically and importantly; but for an outsider Berlin is the place to be. (And besides, I like big cities!)

Frances has said okay, so I've asked for a transfer through all the channels I can think of. No one has any objections, everyone will support it, but no one seems quite sure who makes the decision.

In the meantime, I have plenty to do on the "State and Market" paper for a forthcoming Swedish volume on Eastern European housing, and for a working group of the European Housing Network.

December 14

A sudden idea: with all the work I'm doing, and all the ideas that are being generated around urban issues, city planning, housing development, the protests and the demands and the drafts of proposals, shouldn't we try to put together a book that combines some history and description of things as they are, how they got that way, and what can be done. Obviously I can't put it together by myself, but I've talked to Fred Staufenbiel and he's enthusiastic. The list of contributors is easily put together; the field has attracted, maybe by its nature attracts, idealists, critics, sensitive people, and the DDR is small enough so that they all know each other.

Who we should get as a publisher is a more difficult problem. We want to get the book out quickly, to have some influence on the current situation, presumably before the elections (likely to be in the late spring). That means a West German publisher, under normal circumstances, since no house can work that quickly in the East. But we want it to have an influence in the East, and for that a West publisher is not right. Who would we consider in the East? Dietz Verlag immediately comes to mind; they've published Fred's books in the past, are solid and sympathetic and now reform-minded. But they were (and still are) the official publisher of the SED, in fact belong to the SED. If they do it, our book will be considered SED propaganda. So we have to look around at who else there might be in the DDR. Akademie Verlag, the publisher of the Academy of Sciences, is probably the best, both by way of quality and prestige. Fred will explore.

December 20

Everything seems to be set for the transfer to Berlin, starting January 15. I'm very pleased! But we're a little anxious about the apartment. I've really pressed to get us a phone; I think that's what I miss most here in terms of technology.

December 22 - January 1

In Hamburg over Christmas, where we visited our son and his wife and our grandchild, in their subsidized social housing in St. Pauli. It's quite newly built, three rooms, quite adequate for their needs, run by a nonprofit. The other tenants told the management they wanted someone with a child when the apartment opened up because the yard in back had a sandbox and play equipment and they wanted it used and cared for. Otherwise Harold and Anette would never have gotten it; there are long waiting lists for apartments in Hamburg, as in every other major city in the West. They had actually wanted to be in Tübingen, but searched for several weeks in vain and ended up back in Hamburg, where Anette's mother could at least offer them temporary accommodations. They pay

about 700 marks a month in rent, a hefty chunk of their living expenses, the street is noisy and the neighborhood heavily trafficked; but otherwise quite pleasant.

I spoke at a "Church and City" group meeting the second evening after our arrival. I was interested in going over our formulation of the situation in the West, in terms that would be meaningful in the East as well, and showed some slides of New York City, both its allure and its problems. The Westerners there didn't see New York City as similar to Hamburg; here, they thought, the gross problems were under control, the actual problems more subtle. I tried to take some slides that might at least symbolically represent the situation in the West: a department store with a railroad station tucked in one corner, symbolizing the domination of the private over the public; beggars and peddlers on the streets; sex shops and yuppie boutiques; the prevalence of advertising. Even with all this, the West will still look glamorous in the DDR: new shops, plenty of goods, well-paved streets, bright lights, variety. But the contrast is visible: symbolically, the railroad station is inside the department store in the West, the store inside the railroad station in the East.

New Year's Eve at the Brandenburg Gate *(see photo of the Gate itself on previous page)* illustrates the point. It has been heralded all over Europe as a giant festival; every television station on the continent, it seems, is there to record it, frame it, interpret it, help in its creation, as we can see watching from Hamburg. It is a drunken celebration, people climbing up, not only on the Wall, but on the huge Brandenburg Gate itself, and then on the statue of a chariot and four horses at its top. [The damage to the statue led to its being taken down for difficult and expensive repairs.] The DDR flag that was on the gate is hauled down, pulled back up, back down, replaced with the West German flag. Fireworks are provided by the state; people come from all over the East and West to celebrate. Champagne bottles abound; the only way people tell whether they are embracing people from the East or the West is by the labels on the bottles. But just what are they celebrating? Simply the fact that they can celebrate, together; that the past is over. What do they want? Anything else but what they had, in the East; in the West, maybe just more nights like this. In West as in East, those celebrating most wildly feel neither the responsibility nor the power to make the hard decisions as to the future.

After New Year's, I have enough time free to do some thinking and to work on the housing material I've been gathering. My article has to end with an overall evaluation, including some broad-scale judgments that I probably don't have the statistical evidence to prove but which I'm pretty confident about because of all the talks with people and the reading and looking I've done. It's intended to provide some facts and to stimulate some thinking, at least. An abbreviated version follows.

excurs 3

WHAT'S SOCIALIST ABOUT CITIES AND HOUSING IN THE DDR?

The way people lived in the DDR, and the cities they lived in, are both similar to and different from the way people lived in other, non-"socialist," countries. What difference did socialism make?

Just what "socialism" means is a large question, but fortunately not one that needs be answered here. I include in the term certain aspects of the DDR's economic system: social ownership of nonpersonal property, limited economic inequality, the substitution of planning, social consciousness, and ideology for profit as the driving force of economic activity. Not that these were ever fully developed in the DDR—in only a very limited sense was ownership "social," for instance. The political structure of the DDR, on the other hand, was far from what one would expect to find in a truly socialist society: highly centralized, undemocratic and nonparticipatory, dominated by a hierarchically organized political party, substituting the indoctrination of ideology for voluntary participation as the basis for legitimacy. The disjuncture between the claims of social ownership in the economic sphere and lack of democracy in the political sphere led to consistent tensions within the system and often produced internally contradictory results. Therefore it seems to me important to separate out the economic from the political in order to get at the underlying question.

What difference, then, has socialism made to urban life in the DDR? The question is not an easy one: there are differences between, say, DDR cities and U.S. cities that have to do with "socialist/capitalist" differences, but such differences have both economic and political aspects, which need to be separated if we are to understand causes and effects. Further, there are differences that have to do with national culture, with the overall stage of development and level of prosperity, with cold war alliances, with the different consequences of World War II, and so on. And what about the future? Were the cities of the DDR becoming more and more like those of Western countries, was there evidence of convergence, or were there contrary tendencies, stemming from their different pasts, that would have led cities and housing in the territory of the DDR to differ significantly and permanently from cities and housing in, say, West Germany?

Let me try to answer these questions by comparing cities and housing in the East and the West. Five separate questions need to be answered:

(1) What are the similarities in urban development?

(2) What differences in urban development are unrelated to differences in the economic and political structures of the two countries?

(3) What differences in urban development can be explained by differences in economic structure, along "socialist/capitalist" lines?

(4) What differences in urban development can be explained by differences in political structures?

(5) What can debates about urban and housing policy during the *Wende* and after unification tell us about the success or failure of their various ingredients?

What are the similarities in urban development?

Some striking aspects of urban development in the DDR—the large monolithic high-rise housing developments built on the edges of towns, for instance—are not unique but are simply different from developments in countries like West Germany in quality, scale, and era of construction. For in the West, as in the East, similar overriding historical conditions, largely resulting from wartime destruction, prompted similar responses. A brief review of the evolution of such policies shows both their similarities and the similarity of their causes:

- An early rush to clear inner city areas for new construction, as rapidly as possible, to meet existing shortages and erase the rubble of destruction.
- A period of rapid housing construction to meet immediate needs, with limited standards and low quality.
- An early concentration of investment on rebuilding, expanding, and modernizing industrial capacity, rather than on improving housing conditions above a minimum threshold.
- As capacity increased, a focus on quantitative expansion of the housing supply, expending as few immediate resources as possible, resulting in the construction of large developments on empty land provided by mass clearance or available at the cities' edges.
- The development of an industrialized building capacity to fit into that focus.
- As the pressure of immediate shortages lessened, a shift in focus to improving quality and diversity.
- Similarly, an increasing acknowledgment of the importance of such factors as historical continuity, spatial identity, social amenities, and, somewhat later, ecological considerations.
- A reflection of that shift in increasing attention being paid to reconstruction and/or preservation of the inner city.
- An increasing understanding, the result of pressure from users, however expressed, of the desirability of mixed-use developments and of mixing housing types in residential areas.
- As a result of all of the above, the decreasing desirability of large homogeneous housing developments at the cities' edges.
- A declining concern with the large-scale developments after their completion, leading to increasing conflicts over the need for repairs and improvements arising from

normal aging, abnormal occupancy patterns, and rising standards of living.

These historical patterns can be found in both countries, although they differ in degree and timing. Industrialized construction never dominated building in West Germany as it did in the DDR, the construction of large developments at the edges of cities continued much longer in the DDR than in West Germany, etc. But the underlying patterns listed above, among the most striking features of DDR urban development to outsiders, are not unique to the DDR.

What differences in urban development are unrelated to differences in the economic and political structures of the two countries?

Just as the similarities noted above are not related to their differing forms of economic or political organization, so are some differences in the forms of development. They may arise from *international influences*, beginning with the adoption of Soviet models of planning and construction, tapering off as East German experience and self-confidence grew, then (since November 1989) shifting toward West German influence; or they may arise from *mistakes*, in the sense of choices among alternatives realistically available within the system (a judgment of course open to widely varying positions); or they may arise from *shortages* (which of course may or may not be explained by economic and political differences), shortages either of labor or materials. These were increasing problems in the DDR, caused by other factors but assuming an independent role and leading to an increasingly inescapable dependence on the dominant forms of planning and construction, and limiting the possibilities of implementing even desired alternatives.

Among the aspects of DDR development that might be explained by these nonsystemic factors are:

- The priority given to industrial growth over development of the urban residential environment, a consistent feature of DDR policy through the early 1970s, resulting from pressure from the Soviet Union, and an internal (and subsequently considered mistaken) striving toward autarky—a priority that in turn created severe shortages in the housing sector.

- A subsequent ("corrective") overallocation of resources to quantitative improvement of the housing stock, at the expense of investment in modernization in other branches of the economy, and at the expense of improvements in quality.

- Thereafter, a failure to recognize the need to shift from new construction to rehabilitation, from quantitative to qualitative goals, from uniform to variable construction, resulting in part from the centralized power of the building *Kombinate*, the large, centralized building enterprises, and the exigencies of central planning, but also to some extent unnecessary and inefficient, resulting from, pardon the word, simple stupidity.

- In fact, much of the homogeneous bland uniformity of housing in the DDR can be attributed to unnecessary (as opposed to inherent) rigidities of the central quantitatively oriented planning system.

- Some of the poor choice of locations, lack of facilities, sterility in design likewise come from mistaken planning assumptions, assumptions not unlike those characterizing some Western planning: that social benefits will automatically flow from physically adequate housing, leading to neglect of resident preferences—a neglect in turn not easily corrected because of an undemocratic and unresponsive political system.

- A fixation on the ideological implications of housing policy, in order to differentiate West German from East German policies and to legitimate the social order of an independent East German state.

- A lack of a relationship between rent and housing quality (including equipment, location, age), leading to a significant misallocation of units by household size and the lack of an ability to implement housing choice privately, partly prompted by the inherent hostility to markets characterizing the system as a whole, but far exaggerated and excluding the expression of choices even where a social market could have provided for them (see Excurs 2 above), out of what might again be called stupidity.

In each of these areas there is a mixture of causes at work, but in all of them neither the economic nor the political system dictated the extreme form of the results.

What differences in urban development can be explained by differences in economic structure along "socialist/capitalist" lines?
If I have correctly separated out those aspects of urban life in the DDR not caused by its economic or political characteristics, the remainder should fall into one of these two categories. Those attributable to its form of economic organization, or to its economic theory, might be listed as follows (in each case, differentiating them from those of the West):

- Uniformly low rents, running at 3 to 4 percent of income, with high rents being no more than 30 percent above low rents, resulting in affordable housing for all, but also in significant misallocation of units by household need. (Those overhoused having no financial incentive to limit their housing consumption.)
- The integration of housing at the neighborhood and building levels across income groups, although small privileged groups (functionaries, the *Nomenklatura*) had significantly better housing, in separate buildings but not separate neighborhoods, and older persons tended to have older housing in older neighborhoods.
- Decision-making in the political, not the economic, sphere as to both general principles and detailed implementation of housing policy; hence also only a mediated influence of demand on supply.
- Comprehensiveness of housing policy, including public control over new construction, allocation, rehabilitation, sale, management, financing, demolition.
- A narrow range of new housing, from the best to the

worst, and a narrowing difference in the quality of housing in general, as the older more spacious units deteriorate and new units are of a more uniform quality. Positively viewed, equality in housing; negatively phrased, an oppressive and unnatural homogeneity.

- The allocation of housing (with important exceptions) according to need, with no one lacking adequate shelter, even those at the bottom of the income ladder.
- A strong priority for nonprivate forms of housing ownership, whether state or cooperative, the prohibition of new private rental housing construction, the devalorization of existing private rental housing, and the encouragement of private home ownership only as supplemental to other forms of housing, and then with only very limited rights of disposition.
- An ability to effectuate changes in housing policy rapidly, including construction, once a central decision has been made.
- The minor importance of credit in housing policy, in either direction: credit availability neither significantly promoted, nor did the shortage of credit restrict, housing construction.
- Very restricted private property rights over either land or housing, essentially limited to rights of use.
- Control by the state over the allocation of land for housing, as to extent, location, etc.; thus complete public control of the location of new housing. While controls over land use in West Germany are much stronger than in, say, the United States, the necessity of paying market-determined prices for land that is publicly desired limited land use controls even in West Germany to a far narrower practical range than in the East.
- Deemphasis on commercial uses of downtowns; downtown locations for "uneconomical" housing development.
- Strong emphasis, both in planning and in implementation, on child care, social, cultural, and recreational facil-

ities being integrated into housing developments, this being one of the few cases where, although planning goals are similar in the East and West, implementation was much stronger in the East.

■ Restrictions on the choice of housing, monopolistic housing production firms, and inadequate incentives to labor, all connected with the difficulty of integrating a social market with a socialist economy; restrictions on choice that go across the board, where similar restrictions in the West are based on income, being more severe at the bottom but much less severe toward the top of the income ladder.

What differences in urban development can be explained by differences in political structures?

■ An ability to effectuate rapid change in housing policy.
■ The uniformity of planning and construction standards and architectural forms; neither the expression of preferences allowed by the market nor the experimentation and variation permitted by a decentralized democratic structure were permitted.
■ The neglect of neighborhood issues, rehabilitation, improvement, development of services and facilities, in older neighborhoods, which might have led to feelings of neighborhood or regional autonomy and endangered loyalty to the center.
■ Undemocratic decision-making as to general principles, and no regard for individual preferences as to detailed implementation, of housing policy.
■ The exclusive reliance on industrialized housing production techniques susceptible to central control and planning but resulting in a powerful industrial housing construction lobby.
■ Low productivity in the housing sector, with small wage differentials and monopolistic construction firms.
■ The overreliance on quantitative and easily measurable

goals because they are easily subjected to centralized planning and control. The corresponding neglect of the small-scale and flexible rehabilitation of older areas because it is difficult to implement in a centralized political and economic system.

- A rigid allocation system, under tight central control.
- The use of the housing allocation system to reward political loyalty; while the advantages accruing to the powerful in the West are far greater, both comparatively and absolutely, than they are in the East, in the West distribution is based on economic status and in the East on political status.
- An ambivalence toward history, which is subordinated to ideology.

What can debates about urban and housing policy during the **Wende** *and unification tell us about the success or failure of the various ingredients?*

People's day-to-day lives often have more influence on their political activities than abstract ideology or remote national events. Housing and urban development are day-to-day issues. Community-based citizens' movements drew much of their impetus during the *Wende* from urban problems: bad housing conditions in Leipzig, in the eroding inner city as well as in the large bleak new pre-fab developments on the outskirts, are part of the explanation of why the demonstrations began and gained such strength in that city. *(The photos on the following pages show such developments in East Berlin.)* But in the areas of housing and urban development many realized that the new market-based forces might not provide the solutions they sought either. A Peoples' Building Conference in early January 1990, convened by local members of some of the national citizens' groups and a coalition of neighborhood associations, was still largely devoted to flaying the old *Kombinate*, the abjectly dependent local officials, the spineless city council; few new ideas for action came out of it.

The most immediate effect of the January conference was a halt to further construction of some panelized units, but without any decision about an alternative. At the same time, serious consideration was already being given at the national level to the hard details of possible alternative policies. Even in the unification contracts, drawn up much later in the year, urban and housing issues were left to be debated and decided by the individual states (which could of course delegate to individual communities) or even an ultimate all-German parliament.

Do the controversies about housing and urban development that accompanied the *Wende* and unification suggest what aspects of prior policy were successful, what had failed? Is there any positive correlation between those policies that continued to have support and their

origins in socialist economic policy, or, conversely, a correlation between urban failures and undemocratic political processes? I believe so. A brief outline of what was and what was not controversial supports that conclusion.

Two issues stand out as most controversial: the sale of publicly owned land and rent reform.

The sale of land was one of the earliest visible threats that those in the East faced by the opening up of their country. As soon as the *Wende* began, speculators from the West began to buy up the claims of dispossessed or uninterested Westerners to East German property, claims that up until then had been considered worthless. Cars with West German license plates cruised residential areas photographing houses for potential investors. Since the law prohibited unauthorized sale to noncitizens, the West German real estate association warned its members against using front men to buy East German property; but everyone knew that it was going on. In the city centers, the pressure from Western interests to buy land early was strong. Banks, advertising agencies, law offices, technical experts of all sorts, the tertiary business services sector, all looked for space; most cities developed catalogues of offers, but waited for legal clarification before they actually sold off any property. The possibilities were numerous: the party's planning for inner-city development always outran its resources, so that prime empty spaces, cleared for future developments that never came, remained in the center of many towns. In Leipzig, for example, public firms interested in paying for the eight high-rises planned for the city center were never found; only one was built, and that as social housing (not the planned use for the space). But as economically effective demand grew during the *Wende*, there was renewed interest in the remaining seven sites.

Leipzigers took notice; so did Berliners. On the Baltic shore, there was fear that summer places would no longer be available for Easterners. Foreign firms explicitly demanded the right to own DDR property even before unification; land was con-sidered one of the few things the DDR had to offer to joint ventures from the West. The opposition to these threats focused on the issue of "sale"; the dominant defensive thought was to allow only *Erbpacht*, essentially 99-year leases. That such leases can lead to as much damage as a sale, that the market pressures they can generate will subvert public planning goals just as sales do, was not understood. In "negotiations" with Western buyers, most DDR citizens were babes in the woods.

In the event, the pressures did not mount as much as was anticipated because the infrastructure and environmental qualities necessary to support high land values were often missing. Providing these is, however, simply a matter of time; sources of pollution are being steadily removed, roads improved, services provided. The initial shock of "selling out our land" was not as great as had been anticipated. But the cumulative effect will be every bit as great. Resistance will be locally (or state) focussed, rather than national, but it may yet prove to be very deep and to have lasting effects.

As to rent reform, here the issues are clearer and people can visualize dangers much more readily. When letters from an absentee landlord arrived at one building in Berlin, notifying the tenants that their rents were being reviewed and informing them that some tenants would be asked to leave, a tenants' association was quickly formed. A citywide Tenants' Union followed thereafter, and then a national union. At the first meeting, current single-family owner-occupants threatened with claims of former property-owners from the West, who claimed that their ownership had survived the "illegal" nationalization of many properties in the late 1940s and early 1950s, asked to have their concerns included in the Tenants' Union statement; they were turned down by a divided vote, on the ground that tenants were tenants, owners were owners. As time went on, however, the alliance between the two groups became very close. In both the local and national election campaigns in the spring of 1990 all the parties, from PDS to CDU, promised that current owners would be protected against pre-nationalization claims. But none of the parties made an issue of protecting public ownership of multifamily houses from such claims; that remains a time bomb whose impact may only be less noticeable because it goes off a little bit at a time. But almost all agree that the security of occupancy of the present good-faith residents of both public and privately owned housing must be protected, whatever changes in legal title may ultimately take place.

There had been general agreement, even before the *Wende*, that, regardless of how private absentee owners were handled, some reform of the DDR's rental system in municipally administered housing was necessary. Subsidies in general, including rents, needed restructuring. Bread was so heavily subsidized that it was cheaper than the grain with which it was baked; farmers fed bread rather than grain to their pigs (the stories went) because they saved money that way. Television sets, on the other hand, cost far more than in the West. And rents were about one-third of the cost of maintaining and operating housing. All this was because prices were administratively fixed, according to political goals: everyone should be able to afford bread and housing; television, on the other hand, was considered a luxury.

As integration with the West proceeded, prices were restructured. Prices for children's clothing were raised at the beginning of 1990, with a corresponding increase in the allowance paid parents for children; new price increases were to be accompanied by increases in pensions, disability payments, etc. Although income never rose enough to offset the increase in expenses, at least the theory made some sense. Initially the thought was that, with the same logic, rents could be raised and a housing allowance added to offset the increase. But protests were so strong, as were the arguments of housing professionals that rents were not a simple commodity-subsidy question like bread (rents only remotely affect supply, monopoly affects prices, present flat 1 mark per square meter prices don't reflect values, units are misallocated, ownership pros and cons have to be considered), that rent reform was initially shelved.

The ultimate compromise, as part of the unification package, was that rents would be raised, but slowly, with the details left to the states.

These two issues—rent reform and the sale of publicly owned land—aside, other urban and housing changes were hardly open questions during the *Wende*. Take the preservation of older housing in central cities, for instance. Everyone was for it. When the head of the leading institution for historic preservation in the DDR, Peter Goralczyk, was asked whether it makes any difference *who* lives in the housing to be preserved, he answered flatly, "No," and was not challenged; issues such as gentrification were unknown and their advent was not recognized. By the end of the *Wende*, private landlords, in the view of the DDR ministry of building, were to be encouraged to invest in their buildings by permitting rents that would return a profit on such investment; how that would fit into a new overall rental structure they simply did not know.

Some urban reforms, on the other hand, were undertaken with clear objectives and overwhelming public support. The huge building *Kombinate* were broken up. Decentralization of housing construction to the local level was endorsed by all parties; the hope was that it would help neutralize the power of the building sector as a whole, although similar policies in the United States have not had that result. Training in rehabilitation work was supposed to replace education for mass prefabrication. Private architectural and planning offices sprouted up, and much public work was contracted out to private firms. That trend was heightened by the lay-offs of thousands of governmental workers in these fields. Wages rose in the building trades (but not to West German levels); so construction workers would stay in the field (and in the country); they had been lower than much factory pay, and the work is harder. The West German law regulating private contracts has now been taken over intact, as have the peculiarities of building contracts. The formation of smaller private building firms is being encouraged. Various forms of housing tenure are being taken over from the West. Currently the focus is on smaller scale cooperatives, but condominium ownership of single flats is also on the agenda.

So: Security of residential occupancy was clearly an achievement of the DDR that its residents felt strongly was worth protecting. The same was true for the low rents, even if the uniformity and the extreme subsidies were considered excessive. Public ownership of land was considered of major importance, even if the actual uses made of that ownership were hardly optimal. Centralization of control of urban and housing policy at the national level, and unresponsive public decision-making, were universally disliked. So was the monopolization of building activity in giant *Kombinate,* and the fixation on prefabrication that accompanied it. Neglect of maintenance and rehabilitation, the decay of central-city housing, was universally condemned. Lack of variety, in tenure forms, in architectural styles, in living possibilities, was everywhere considered a problem; if equality and lack of segregation were considered virtues of the old system, uniformity, homogeneity, were considered major vices.

Putting all this together, one may well conclude that the socialist economic base of urban and housing policy in the DDR produced its major successes, although it also created some serious problems; and that its centralized, undemocratic political system, coupled with shortages at least partially beyond the DDR's control, accounted for the major failures in its cities.

journal

THE THIRD PHASE:
THE NEW ARRIVES
(from the West)

**From the Brandenburg Gate
to the National Elections**

January 10

We have moved into our new apartment in Berlin. It's on the fifth
floor of a walk-up, a new prefab concrete panel construction, of
course, built as in-fill on a street very close to the center of the city,
near Rosa Luxemburg Platz. In layout, space, etc., one prefab concrete
panel apartment isn't very different from any other; no surprises for
us in this one. The technological standards are higher than in Weimar:
this apartment has a small fully automatic washing machine, for
instance, and the television is color rather than black and white. Most
important of all, though, there is a telephone! I feel as if I'm back in
touch with civilization.

The apartment is apparently rented on a permanent basis by the
ministry of higher education and then assigned to visitors coming

---

through according to need. We pay 300 marks a month in rent, somewhat higher than normal because it's fully furnished but still very low indeed by U.S. standards—I'd guess, at official exchange rates, one-fifth what we'd pay in New York (at unofficial rates much less than that). The occupants of the other apartments in the building seems to be heterogeneous: some with children, some without, civil servants, a night shift factory worker, a policeman, some elderly. Only three of the twenty-two families seem to have cars.

The apartment is a large three-room unit, two bedrooms, living-dining room, kitchen, bath, hall with storage. It is fully furnished, and

linens and cleaning service are included in the rent. There are even some cocktail-table books on Berlin architecture, a number of albums of classical music (including several Schubert song cycles), candles, several sets of wine glasses...luxury for us!

The person from the ministry for higher education responsible for us explained all the arrangements, is interested in what I'm doing, offers to help set up appointments, has some newspaper clippings of interest on urban development issues, and is generally very helpful. We're very appreciative.

The location is great too. It's around the corner from Rosa-Luxemburg Platz (Place), just on the fringe of downtown. It's history is a miniature of the history of Germany. The square itself (actually a triangle) was originally Bülow Platz, named after Prince Bernhard von Bülow, foreign minister and chancellor under Kaiser William II and a great admirer as well as successor to Bismarck. It was a nineteenth-century working-class area, what was called a slum at the turn of the century; it was called the Scheunenviertel, the Barn Quarter. The first step in its "renewal" was the construction of the Volksbühne *(see photo on previous page)*, or People's Theater, built in 1913 and still in operation—"people's theater" because it was to provide theater accessible to the masses on a democratic basis: all seats, for instance, were to be sold for the same price. By the end of World War I, the Scheunenviertel had a mixed reputation as an amusement center, red light district, and illegal market. It became home to increasing numbers of East European Jews, and the area was also subject to a series of anti-Semitic demonstrations and attacks. In the fight against the Spartacists (the nucleus of the later Communist Party of Germany) in 1919, it was a center of resistance. In 1926 the Communist Party converted an office building there into its headquarters, and two years later it moved its newspaper there.

In the 1920s, the Volksbühne, under Erwin Piscatore, was the center of a rich avantgarde theatrical life. But the area retained its reputation as a slum quarter, and renewal projects abounded. In 1929 a number of apartment buildings and stores were built in the modern style, as well as a movie theater; those buildings still stand, but the full project was not realized. When the Nazis took power they gave it an entirely new orientation: Bülow Platz was renamed Horst Wessel Platz. In the words of their publication:

> Bülowplatz! The center of this neighborhood, known and feared throughout the city, is the Karl Liebknecht House. From here are issued the murderous orders of the Bolshevists. The heart of the Communist Party in Germany. Around this house is a ring of the ugliest darkest tenements, filled with the most evil subhumans from all of Germany.... And today, this plaza bears the name of the hero of the National Socialist freedom fighter Horst Wessel, who died for the victory of his idea in the fight for Berlin.

January 17

Finally a chance for a long talk with Bruno Flierl. We had known that he was highly respected as an architectural historian and theorist, that he had had some difficulty with the authorities, that he had had a mild stroke and had been given early retirement from teaching at Humboldt (partly political, we thought), had as a retiree had permission to travel and thus had contacts with people (like us) in the West, and was extraordinarily knowledgeable about architectural history and about the political as well as physical details of urban development in the DDR. But the real story turned out to be more complicated.

Bruno was born in 1927 in Silesia, then part of Germany, now Poland. At the end of the war his family moved to Berlin, the part that became West Berlin; out of hope and political conviction his father took them to East Berlin after the founding of the DDR. Bruno had studied architecture in the West, but moved East with the family. In 1961 he became editor-in-chief of the official architectural journal in the DDR. It was a period, after the building of the Wall, when there was an expectation of liberalization in the air, and he published unconventional articles: critiques of entries in official competitions, for instance, including details about the losing as well as winning entries, and an account of a meeting between the minister of construction and young architects in which they criticized the bureaucracy that constrained attempts at innovation in architecture. For the latter he was called on the carpet by the ministry; he defended his policies, but agreed to work more closely with the ministry in the future. For a while he was kept on as editor, although his sources of information were cut off, and the pages recounting the critical meeting of architects with the minister were physically removed from printed but undistributed copies of the journal.

That couldn't last; under pressure from the party, he was removed as editor and sent to work in the office of the chief architect of Berlin: good practical work should help impose a little discipline on him, was the idea.

After a while he was asked if he would take a position in a new section for architectural theory being opened at the Building Academy in Berlin, and accepted. Things went smoothly for a while; it was a period where there was some idealism in the air, some optimism about building a new society, and things seemed possible that had not seemed so before. Some lively discussions sponsored by his section were typed up and distributed in the form of duplicated copies, for instance, and even retyped by others for wider circulation; not "gray literature," quite, but neither published nor prohibited.

But that didn't last either. In May 1968 Bruno spoke at a conference on architecture held at the institute. He raised the question of the role of the *Auftraggeber*—the public assignment-giver, the "client"—in making architectural decisions, suggesting that open discussion of alternatives, followed by public decision-making was a more appropriate system than unilateral client-dictated decisions. Implicitly—this is my interpretation—he called into question two different sacred cows: one, the sacredness of "professional" judgments in architecture, and thus the aspiration of architects for a higher status and exemption from lay criticism; the other, the role of the party and its hierarchical, undemocratic, and essentially secretive, if not Borgia-like, way of making "public" decisions. In any event, he was roundly attacked by the party functionaries present, and as roundly defended his position. There was a fuss, and thereafter a long discussion as to whether the minutes of the session should be published, as was customary. The president of the institute, after a fight that lasted a year, prevailed and they were published. But this was now in the context of the Prague Spring and the invasion of Czechoslovakia, and Bruno was called in by the powers-that-be and told that he had better suspend publishing his own writing for a while, maybe two years, which meant that no one else would publish him either. He was somehow not invited to conferences, lectures, etc., for several years. But his job was not taken away; just behave for a while, he was told, and no damage done.

So for the next few years Bruno devoted himself to work on his "habilitation," his postdoctoral dissertation, which is necessary for the highest academic degree in Germany. It was completed in the mid-1970s and scheduled for public presentation and defense, as is customary. It dealt with the forms of urban construction under socialism, with much empirical data, largely sympathetic but also critical. One hour before the scheduled defense, the president of the institute invited him to a meeting at the "suggestion" of its party secretary. The committee in charge of his dissertation and those in the academic hierarchy responsible for the granting of degrees were all present. Nothing wrong with the dissertation, the party secretary said. But the secretary for ideology of the Politburo had just made a speech in which he pointed out that systems theory was a bourgeois attempt to cloak the way things really functioned and thus counterproductive in a socialist society; yet Bruno had referred to systems theory positively in several places in his dissertation. Perhaps he might recast those sections in the light of this discussion; the defense could be postponed to give him that opportunity. No, said Bruno; if there's something wrong with the dissertation, the formal public defense is the place to raise it; he wanted to go forward. His committee members supported his decision (I was surprised when he said that, since even the member closest to him had something of a reputation for avoiding confrontations). But it was put to a vote, the decisive members of the academic hierarchy supported the postponement, and postponed it was.

"So what happened," I asked Bruno, "did you ever get your habilitation?" "Sure," he said; "I made cosmetic changes, handed it in six months later, it was approved without a peep, was published by the institute and well received." The powers that be had made their point, asserted their power, and that was what counted; the substantive question was of no real interest up the line.

Bruno remained at the institute until 1979, then moved over to Humboldt University. In November 1981 (the dates are important, for they relate to major events on the international scene which were of critical importance for decisions all the way down the line, as the Prague events were for the publication of the first conference results) Bruno participated in another conference, and he again discussed the role of the *Auftraggeber*, this time in the context of the scientific-technical revolution, a concept very much in vogue in the higher circles of power. He again called for openness and public discussion, for democratic decision-making, with details as to what that might mean for urban development decisions. His comments were received peacefully enough, and written up with other reports in the minutes of the conference. But someone (whether personal animosity was involved or not Bruno doesn't know for sure, but suspects) sent the minutes to higher-ups in the party, probably with an attached note, and a storm erupted: permission to print was withdrawn, Bruno was expelled from the architects' association, which had asked him to attend the conference in the first place, and trouble began to brew for him at Humboldt. Why all the fuss? Because of the Solidarity movement in Poland over the preceding few years; in December 1981 martial law was declared in Poland, and Solidarity banned. Bruno's statement, according to the party, "read like a Solidarity speech"!

The story ends on a different note. In December 1982 Bruno had a mild stroke; he was considered medically unable to work for one or two years. The doctors then asked him if he would be willing to retire fully, which they recommended; if he would be badly upset by not working, however, they would consider letting him go back at no more than half time. No difficulty with retiring, he said, and he now works just as actively, on full pension, as he did when he was working full time. The medical decisions were independent of all political influence, he believes; assuming he's right, the medical and retirement systems seem quite humane to us.

[Actually, the story hasn't ended yet. Bruno was in the front ranks of those marching on November 4 *(second from the right in the photo)*. He is now very active on architectural and planning issues today, including the currently hot debates about the future of a unified Berlin.]

Bruno's story would support a number of conclusions. I know one shouldn't generalize from limited information, but what else are case studies and personal experiences for? So:

The system of rule that had evolved in the DDR has some similarity with Pavlovian training, aimed at stamping out independence and inculcating respect for authority. If there is a sign of independence, the hand gets slapped, the article banned, the position changed. The purpose is not primarily, or not only, to correct a given "error"; what is "error" at any given moment is almost arbitrary, although in the long run there may be a certain logic behind it. More important than correcting error, however, is to implement a given line; and still more is to train to subordination, to automatic loyalty. Nor is personal conviction required; its outward show is enough, for those not near the center of power. No one has decided the system should work like that; it works that way at the very top, those up there handle those under them that way, and so on down the line, naturally and automatically.

A certain level of civilization nevertheless pervaded the process, at least after the 1950s: compared to Czechoslovakia, certainly compared to the Soviet Union under Stalin or Brezhnev, the penalties for disobedience were moderate. Perhaps the consciousness of the history of fascism had something to do with it. In any event, few were jailed, none ever executed; many were exiled, one way or the other, others effectively silenced. Yet for a writer or thinker concerned with interacting with an audience, with communicating with colleagues, with developing his or her ideas in the normal life of the intellect, even these "moderate" penalties are severe.

Finally, I am personally struck by the difference between the way moral decisions are presented in the DDR and in the West—or rather, that they are in fact presented, directly and in unambiguous form, in the DDR, whereas they lie under the surface for most people in the West, needing a conscious effort to exhume and examine and decide. In Bruno's case, there were at least three such decisions: publish or not, defend or not, speak out or not. For many in the West, similar decisions never come up; we just go our way and the logic of the system makes us conform. Sometimes, indeed, an order comes down and we have to decide in good conscience whether or not to obey; blowing the whistle on a superior is still a difficult decision, for instance. And there are limits to dissent and nonconformity; McCarthyism and its mentality are ever present in the background, and can come down hard on those who defy the standards of acceptable conduct. But we imagine we choose our jobs freely, and then do what is required, or dislike it and look elsewhere. Directly political positions rarely have significant personal consequences; whether we write about a meeting or use systems theory or advocate democracy (or anything else) at a conference of intellectuals doesn't involve a moral decision, is not an act of courage. An overgeneralization, of course. Yet in general I think the Western system maintains its order and its hierarchies much more smoothly and invisibly than do those of Eastern Europe or the Soviet Union. (That's also why finger-pointing in the East is much easier than finger-pointing in the West.)

An East German writer, Manfred Kröber, in an interview in

Sonntag, speaks of "the customary opportunism of everyday life: the strategy of survival" in the DDR. That behavior and its moral danger, it seems to me, exists in the United States as well.

January 22 - 26

In Leipzig for an intensive week of lectures, conferences, discussions. We wanted to go to the Monday evening demonstration, about whose rightward shift so much has been said recently, but Siegfried Lassak, our host, who is professor of law at the Technical University, did not want to go—out of a combination of distaste and apprehension, we deduced. Neither New Forum nor the churches any longer give the demonstrations direction; they have become, from all accounts, a gathering place for the German unification movement and an attraction for the far right from West and East. We asked whether the new political complexion represented a shift on the part of the same people who had started marching in October, or whether it was now different people; different, we were told. Were the leaders of October now out of touch with "the people" because "the people" had changed, or (as some voices are now saying) were they never really in touch with "the people" in the first place? Neither, we figured out from our conversations; "the people" is simply not a homogeneous mass, many ordinary people participated in the demonstrations and marches in October, and many, but others, are participating in them now.

The result, however, is a lack of leadership, of direction, for the opposition to the old SED. The influence of the political parties from the West is strong, and most people assume that unification, and a shift from a centralized to a market economy, is inevitable. (But see Excurs 2 on how misleading such an undifferentiated formulation of the alternatives is.) The city planners I talked to had on their desks many requests to buy city-owned land in Leipzig, but didn't know what to do with them; they were simply cataloguing them. No citizens' organization has arisen to present a program and take the initiative to get it supported and implemented. Even the housing conference in Leipzig earlier in the month was more of a negative, stop-the-demolitions, stop-the-environmental-damage, stop-the-prefab-construction conference than one to set guidelines for the future. No organization to take the next steps has arisen.

In my lectures I spoke at length about property rights and the legal structures of planning in the West, including my own experiences as a lawyer in the United States, and there was great interest. But they were more interested in finding out what others were likely to do in the future than in figuring out what they wanted to do in the new circumstances.

And the classic pattern in the United States by which businesses play cities off against each other, to the net benefit of the businesses, seems to be on the way here too. To the question, why doesn't the city simply tell prospective buyers of its land that the land won't be sold, only leased (and only with certain conditions), the planners answer that if we don't sell to them, Dresden will and we'll lose the business. The answer ought to be the same as that one that we recognize, but don't use, in the United States: regional, state, or if necessary national control over specified land use decisions. But that runs counter to the line of thinking that's prevalent here now.

January 29

Thomas S. picked us up to drive us to Ilmenau, about one and a half hours from Weimar, for a talk to a New Forum group. He's just been elected, as a reformer, to the county executive committee of the SED-PDS, from which many in the old leadership have been removed, but there aren't enough younger people like him available to take an active leadership role. He's debating whether to form an independent socialist party or to stay in the SED-PDS.

Ilmenau is a small town in the foothills of the Thuringian Woods, a beautiful setting in a small river valley, defaced by a large factory complex and some standard prefab panel buildings up on a hill. We were invited to speak to the local New Forum group, and were to stay overnight with a lovely elderly couple that had lived there for many years, Andreas and Liesle Schuler. When they told us that they had emigrated to England during the Hitler period, we realized they were Jewish. Most people think that there are no Jews in the DDR (there are certainly very few in West Germany), but either there are more

Jews than is generally known, or we are somehow attracted to Jewish people, or the arm of coincidence is long?

The meeting of New Forum is held in the community room of the Catholic church, in a Protestant town; we are driven there by a Jewish man who used to teach Marxism-Leninism. The meeting is very much in tune with my topic, citizen participation in planning, and the discussion is very pragmatic, dealing with housing finance, rehabilitation costs, decision-making structures; big political questions don't come up, and I'm told people are there from all across the political spectrum, from CDU to PDS to radical left idealists. Almost all belong to New Forum. Rolf Henrich, a lawyer who got into trouble with the authorities for a book called *Der vormundschaftliche Staat* (*The Guardian State*) and who was one of the founders of New Forum, was quoted in an interview with Kurt Mazur on October 26, 1989, as saying: "I can say this plainly and without hesitation to you, I don't know anyone in the 'Forum' who questions socialism." You certainly couldn't have said it without any hesitation in Ilmenau; but it wasn't a matter of immediate concern there either.

Judging from the jokes, central planning à la DDR isn't in very good repute here:

> A lion in a DDR zoo complains to the zookeeper that he's being discriminated against: "All I ever get to eat is bananas and every now and then an apple, but the lion in the next cage gets meat all the time."
>
> "But there's a good reason for that," says the warden. "The lion next to you is in a cage planned for a lion, but you're in a cage planned for a monkey."

February 1

Honecker was taken from a hospital bed by the police and locked up the Rummelsburg Prison, according to the newspapers, the same prison I was in on the night of October 7! Poor Honecker! Neither of us should have had to be there. He was released the next day, for medical reasons, and given refuge in a house outside Berlin provided by a minister who then got death threats for making it available.

Indeed, not so much anger as sardonic tolerance characterized Honecker's reputation. The jokes about him seem endless:

> Someone in the Politburo tells Honecker that in his county there's no more coal to be had.
> "And what do the people do?" asks Honecker.
> "They freeze," he is told.
> "Wonderful how our people know how to make do in any emergency," Honecker replies admiringly.

However, the low opinion was universal:

> Two men, one from the Stasi, are standing in a bar talking.
> "What do you think of Honecker?" the man from the Stasi asks the other man.
> "The same as you do," comes the careful answer.
> "I'm sorry, then I'm going to have to arrest you for calumny against the state," says the man from the Stasi.

February 2

On January 28, Modrow proposed a "Government of National Unity," fearing that otherwise the DDR would be "ungovernable." Certainly the criticism of the old regime is becoming virulent, occasionally violent attacks on buildings, destruction of offices, intimidation of speakers, etc.; and the economic situation is worsening, the exodus across the border continuing. The citizens' movements agree; they will name eight "ministers without portfolio" in the new government. The SPD also agrees, but apparently on the separately negotiated condition that the national election will be moved forward to March 18, with local elections held on May 6, the original date for the national election. The citizens' movements have simply been outmaneuvered politically; the polls all show that the SPD is strong, it has support from the West, the Round Table's vote to prohibit Western speakers in the DDR election campaign, although passed, was immediately greeted by a statement from the SPD that it would not abide by it (and of course it has no legal effect), so the SPD will be much better able to use the shorter time to the election than the citizens' movements. The Modrow regime had recommended, in its first proposal for new election laws, that no party be permitted to receive support of any kind from outside the country. But the Round Table had rejected this because most of the participants saw it as an advantage for the SED alone, because it had the best electoral apparatus within the country. So now the new parties, which led the struggle for democracy, will be overwhelmed by the established parties from *"druben"* (over there in the West). Electoral politics, Western style; dirty, by "moral" standards, but conventional, by the standards of everyday politics. *(The photo below shows Ingrid Koppe of New Forum at a meeting of the national Round Table.)*

Modrow has come out for German unity! Up until now, the PDS has sided with the groups opposed to the unification, looking for some third alternative between the old socialism and the old capitalism; has it now thrown in the towel? More likely, Modrow is still taking the position of "national responsibility," and as such

feels it necessary to be on the same wavelength as the majority, which means for unification, whether he likes it or not. So he advances his own plan, which calls for a united Germany that would be neutral, neither in NATO nor in the Warsaw Pact. Little chance of success! The PDS comes out with a wishy-washy statement that does not disagree with Modrow, but emphasizes that the "values of the DDR" must be brought into any united Germany. Actually, in December he changed the party's name to SED-PDS, and then in mid-January dropped the SED, so it's now only PDS. Hard to tell what this will accomplish.

And just what are the "values of the DDR"?

February 5

Herr Fiedler came to see us on business this morning: he is the young man from the ministry of education who is responsible for us, and deals with any administrative problems that we may have. We end up discussing his situation: the ministry has been newly reconstituted from three separate ministries. (Margot Honecker was the head of one of them before the *Wende*.) The three ministries had a total of 8,000 civil service employees; now the consolidated ministry will have only 2,000. Fiedler doesn't seem to be worried for himself but says that the mood in his workplace is very unsettled. Every day there are rumors about another reorganization; no one knows what things will look like tomorrow. We talk about taking private Russian lessons from his wife, who teaches Russian in a Berlin secondary school. Fiedler says that his wife could come to our place, but we would rather go to theirs because we like to see how other people live. He says that they live in Eichwalde, a little community on the outskirts of Berlin, in a small two-story house over a shoemaker on the ground floor. As he describes it, a beautiful town where many artists and higher officials live. Last week people came and photographed every house in the town. The speculators are everywhere! They are really a slimy lot who produce nothing themselves, are interested in nothing but money, and make their profit from the work of others and from the society. This is a type that has until now been unknown in the DDR. Will people here be able to defend themselves against such types?

The same question came up that afternoon in a lecture by Klaus Brakke from Oldenburg in West Germany. The lecture was at the Institute of City Development and Architecture, of the Building Academy. He related, in the course of his lecture, a remark by Haussmann, the minister of economics in Bonn, that the acquisition of land is not critical for Western investment in the East. Brakke sees this as a concession; Haussmann is more concerned with the interests of big capital than with small speculation or investors in land. Brakke concludes that this weakness opens the possibility of using long-term leases instead of selling land. I look at it somewhat differently: most companies want to pay as little as possible for land; for them, just as for private households, landowners, landlords, and speculators are parasites who take the profits of others without producing anything themselves. And Haussmann also understands that the same essentials can be obtained from a long-term lease as from a purchase. Further, land leased from the city may well be cheaper than land bought from a private owner. The city of Leipzig, as we heard last week, is practically ready to let anyone have land who is willing to build there. Much better to lease from Leipzig than to buy from a greedy speculator. Haussmann is not weak, only savvy. And one must be just as careful with a lease as with a purchase if one wants to protect the interests of the city. Do the officials of the city of Leipzig know how to deal with such questions? The general consensus of those at Brakke's lecture: No.

The discussion had little to do with what he said; the questions were all about how one thing or another is accomplished in the West. It was clear that the participants had long since given up the concept of the DDR as an independent country. The issue was only how best to achieve union.

At noon we had a lunch date with Peter Claussen from the American embassy. Last September, he and his wife had invited us to an elegant lunch at the Grand Hotel. This time we couldn't get near it or any other restaurant in the area; all were full, "Wessies," West Germans, naturally. The prices have been raised and are high for the "Ossies," the East (Ost) Germans, but still a real bargain for the Wessies. So we lined up at a cart outside of one of the restaurants for *Buletten*, DDR meatballs served with a slice of bread and curry sauce on the side. Not bad, and only 1.35 marks ($.80 at the official rate). They could have charged three times as much, and people would still have lined up for them; no market economics at work here yet. On the other hand, the food wasn't great either. As one story went:

> A man buys a sausage at a stand, bites into it, and complains, "These rolls are hard as a rock. They must be at least three days old! Can't you give me a sausage on a roll you got today?"
>
> "No," says the man running the stand. "If you want one of today's rolls, you'll have to come back in three days."

As we sat on the edge of the raised flower beds eating, Claussen told us about the increasing number of visitors to the embassy and its library. Before the *Wende*, when a visitor left the embassy, he or she would be followed and stopped by a policeman or a Stasi officer and asked to show his or her *Ausweis*, "We're looking for someone who fits your description." Then the policeman would read aloud the information in the *Ausweis*, to be recorded by a concealed microphone, and the *Ausweis* would be returned. Later the visitor would be called in by a superior at work (or by a professor, if a student) and, in a friendly way, counseled that going to the American embassy was not the way to advance one's career. Thus, only people already marginalized were likely to go more than once. All this came to an end in November, and now the embassy could hardly keep up with requests for information and visas to visit the United States.

On the late news the reporter discussed the plenum of the Central Committee of the Communist Party of the Soviet Union, and in the course of his report he cited an old DDR song: "The party, the party, It is always right. The party gave us everything, air and sun and light. The party didn't stint; where it was, was life. What we are, we are through it; it has made us rife." (This is my pretty faithful translation!) Can it really be that people sang such a thing?

February 6 - 8

"5th Sociology Congress of the DDR" announces the banner over the podium. A new sociological society, with a different, more participatory style, is about to be founded here; it will run the next big meeting. It has been four years since the preceding congress. This will be the last sociology congress of the DDR, is the joke circulating among the participants. Why? Because next time it will be a meeting of the sociological society of the DDR? No, because next year there will be no DDR.

At the entrance, members of the student council for sociology at Humboldt and Karl Marx universities give out leaflets that criticize the old sociologists who had been subordinate to the central committee of the SED. The students don't want the "new" sociologists to be subordinate to the market. They don't want sociology to be an institution that facilitates efficient production and consumption. "The shift in function leads to exaggerated service to new masters. Again, sociology is the prop of usurpers." Why "usurpers" I don't know, but the formulation "new masters" is telling. The new masters will not be as visible as the central committee was; they will be hidden behind the "market" almost as if the "market" was an entity, instead of just a field on which opposing forces compete.

The congress proceeds exactly like the meeting of any social organizations in the DDR since the *Wende*. (One still says *Wende*, although it is clear that it's more a breakup than a turn.) In the past, the congress was convened by the "Scientific Council for Sociology." No one knew exactly how it was constituted, but that didn't matter: it was the instrument of the SED for the control of sociology in the DDR. All the old leaders sat on it. Now no one wants it anymore, even if it were to be reformed. In fact, the "Scientific Council" has now effectively disappeared. On the second evening of the congress, the sociologists are supposed to elect an executive committee for the new sociological society. Peter Voigt, one of that middle generation who belonged neither to the Old Guard nor to the Young Turks, is professor of sociology at Wilhelm Pieck University in Rostock. Six years ago he wrote an article for the Rostock newspaper, *Ostsee Zeitung*, about social policy questions, in which he reasonably enough stated that social policy had not begun with the Eleventh Party Congress of the SED. Someone in the West saw the article and cited it in a West newspaper and it was picked up in a TV broadcast. The SED leadership heard about it and informed Honecker, who stated: "That man is a class enemy." Voigt was suddenly in danger of losing his tenured position, his right to travel out of the country was revoked, and even his young daughter was harassed in school because her father was such a terrible person. Today, for the rank and file, Voigt not only has credentials and experience but also bears the scars of independent thinking, and were he to run (he refused) he could easily have been elected president of the society.

The national election campaign: a poll of voters in Leipzig asks which party they would choose if the election were held today, and the result is 54 percent SPD, 12 percent SED, 11 percent CDU; astonishingly favorable prognosis for the SPD, explained by most commentators as being the result of social democratic traditions dating back to the 1920s and 1930s; the potential of similar Communist traditions has been vitiated by the actions of the SED over the last forty years.

February 8

Democracy Now, New Forum, and the Initiative for Freedom and Human Rights have joined together to form Bündnis 90. They see themselves as citizen activists who are fielding candidates in this election but who don't want to be a political party. Seems strange to me. The Greens and the United Left, a coalition of tiny left groupings, have stayed out of the Bündnis 90 coalition; they want to be normal political parties. The Leipzig and Frankfurt/Oder organizations of New Forum now refuse to support Bündnis 90 because its politics is too "left."

Last night Frances suddenly developed pain in her knee and could hardly walk. We decided to call a doctor; but how? The telephone book has five full pages of different medical facilities: clinics, polyclinics, medical practices, hospitals, emergency services, nurses stations, local health centers, and neighborhood medical offices. If they all exist, the health services must be terrific and/or very bureaucratic. I call the nearest "medical practice" and ask if they make house calls. For what reason, I am asked. I say that we live on the fifth floor and my wife can hardly get from one room to another. The nurse says that we should call the emergency service. I demur, but then call, explain, say that it's not urgent. No matter, we'll be glad to come. When? Within two hours, depending on what other calls we get. I'm astonished, and even more so when, in about an hour, a young doctor with an emergency service shoulder patch and a substantial bag arrives and climbs the four flights of stairs to our apartment. She examines Frances carefully and thoroughly, writes out three prescriptions, and explains their purpose and how to use them. She answers our questions clearly and competently before leaving. Never a question of who we are, where we're from, are we covered, will we pay.

I take the prescriptions to the pharmacy up the street. The pharmacist gets the three medications out of different drawers. As she hands them to me, I am not sure if I have to pay or at least show my passport and identify myself, but she has already turned away to do something else. Hardly a bureaucratic procedure!

The DDR health services are supposed to be in a deep crisis caused by general shortages and by the number of doctors and nurses who are leaving the country. In some areas this may well be true, but in our situation, the course of the treatment could hardly be better. We had a medical problem, a doctor came to treat it; no question of who we were. The medicines we needed were handed to us without charge. No one mentioned money; health is a universal concern, and it is taken for granted that no one should make a profit out of it. And the system functions without a hitch, at least in our case. It is the matter-of-factness of it that so impresses us. Of course, a society provides for the basic needs of its members, isn't that the purpose of a society? Isn't this a model for how real socialism should function?

February 24

Deirdre Berger, from PBS, the Public Broadcasting System in the United States, called, wants to do a TV film on the decay of the DDR cities, and wants some help. I said okay, but tried to explain to her that not all the cities were decaying, that there's a good bit that has been accomplished, much that is worthy of preservation, that social relations are also important and worth looking at. Not only decay is of interest. Did she understand? We'll see.

February 25

taz, the feisty independent tabloid-sized West German newspaper (it started as an alternative paper after the student movement of the late 1960's, made it financially, and now has editions published in, at least, Frankfurt/Main, Hamburg, Berlin, a good paper with left if sometimes blindly anti-PDS politics) celebrated the opening of its East Berlin office this evening. They were very proud to have been the first Western paper to comply with all the requirements and properly put out a legitimate edition in the East, using primarily DDR people, etc. Their good faith compliance may all have been in vain; the Western papers are already selling like hotcakes here, regardless of whether they've complied with regulations or not, and the more sensational the headlines, the more they sell. It's tough for an honest little paper to compete with the yellow Western press. But *taz* is so much more informative than the standard DDR papers that its almost mandatory reading for anyone wanting to understand what's actually happening. And we have known Georgia Tarnow, a key editor there, for many years. So we went to the celebration.

Gysi came by too; although he's been roundly criticized by *taz*, they share many values and perspectives, and he likes to talk to those who think differently, judging from his actions. And he's got a lot of charisma; he draws crowds wherever he speaks, East or West, and has more charm and certainly more humor than any other major political leader around. We talked with him a little, in between everyone else who wanted to get to him. I mentioned the neglect, in the PDS platform endorsement of decentralization, of any recognition of the dangers of competition among cities, and described the pressure for economic development on the local level as being a significant danger to good planning and urban life, giving the luxury hotel construction in Weimar as an example. He took it very seriously, said he'd think it over; I had the impression he really might. An unusual person, in whom one could have confidence as an individual.

As far as being a spokesman for the PDS, Gysi doesn't do quite as well. He was very defensive on TV recently—of course, he was very much under attack!—but he didn't aggressively put forward his party's platform, refused to predict how many votes they'd get, was overly formal and polite, let the interviewer determine the flow of the discussion. Modesty is certainly a new role for a leader of the PDS, but people expect an attitude of leadership too. Bärbel Bohley, one of the founders of New Forum, gave an interesting interview to the papers today: she does not want to run for office, does not want "to participate in the exercise of power." She is one of the most consistent, as well as courageous, of all the early dissidents; and she was represented by Gysi when there was a fear that she wouldn't be readmitted to the old DDR after a brief trip abroad. Her position reflects recognition of perhaps the central political problem of our times: power corrupts, but without power nothing positive can get done.

February 27

The TV film on DDR cities with Deirdre Berger. We went out on the street to meet her crew and decide where to go, and I told them they could see the range of both good and bad simply from the corner where we were standing. We went down, they filmed and I pointed: on one corner, the playground for the new kindergarten and grade school, built because the standards for the new construction behind us (including the building where we lived) required it; across the street older large houses (four and five story walkups, built to solid middle-class standards) in the process of rehabilitation, but slowly; opposite them, equally old buildings on the commercial street, Alte Schonhauser Allee, built originally to lower standards, un-rehabilitated, dirty, sad-looking; behind them on Mulackstrasse similar buildings being torn down, but one that had been squatter occupied is hung with banners proclaiming, "This building is worth saving; don't let them tear down our neighborhood." That controversy had started long before the *Wende*; now, of course, there was greater recognition of the issues all around. So we filmed there.

Then we went to Sophienstrasse, near the center of town and near the Wall, one of the showpieces of DDR urban renewal, done in part to compete with West Berlin for the 750th anniversary of the founding of the city (two years ago). Typical touristy restoration, with old street lamps and wrought-iron merchants' signs, but up to European standards. A guy came out from an inner courtyard and said, "In back it's still all shit, go look for yourselves." We did, and the rehab really was only for the spaces accessible or visible from the street.

Then to Potsdam, where again there has been some of the best historic restoration, but where there are also many local controversies now. One section of the old city, where Huguenot tradespeople had been settled, was lovingly rehabilitated, and even some small, almost yuppie shops installed. But again, large sections untouched and badly needing repair. The citizens' movement in Potsdam, called ARGUS, led by a very able woman named Saskia Hünike, who showed us around, had already had experience with West German firms offering public-private partnerships: their best offer had come from a Berlin developer who wanted to restore all the facades, but build a hotel behind them, privatize the park and make it into a golf-course for guests, etc. They turned him down cold.

Deirdre comes from St. Louis, is now living in Cologne with a German man. Her parents can't understand how she could do that; they brought her up as a good Jewish girl, in the Jewish tradition; how could she live with a German? Both Jews and Germans have trouble working through the meaning of the Nazi period in their personal lives.

Deirdre told us about interviewing ex-Stasi as they were picking up their unemployment checks from their office. Those she spoke with were entirely "unrepentant"; they simply did not understand why this was happening to them. I told her of my conversation with the Stasi who drove me home on October 7; his reaction to, "Why are you doing this work?" was, "For my country; wouldn't you do the same for yours?" I think he meant it just as sincerely and naively as Oliver North when he defended his lying to the U.S. Congress. Patriotism is as much an opium as religion, and when combined with self-interest, it's impenetrable.

Meeting with the nascent Tenants' Union in the evening. Bernd Hunger proposed the formation of three working groups: on legal issues, rents, and ownership issues. The decision is made to combine legal and ownership issues, and to postpone dealing with rents until later. So the danger that what are really political problems will be handled as legal problems, become technical issues for technicians, as so often happens in the United States. I proposed a Round Table on housing, a slightly corporatist idea, but what the hell, politically it would have great potential for publicity and organizing. But no action was taken on it. Bernd still believes that if we write a solid persuasive position paper of three pages or so, we'll have accomplished something—the myth of the benevolent state rears its head again. Unfortunately it doesn't work that way in any democracy I know. Oddly enough, it might even be more likely to have worked in a centralized system like the DDR, if one got to the right person (and if there were a "right person" there!).

Figuring out how to make a political difference, now that the system is presumably democratic, isn't so easy. They want to put together a set of demands for all political parties, and present them at a mass meeting in a few days. I suggest that they should also formulate a set of questions to put to the party spokespeople, so that they can either get some commitments or at least see exactly where each stands: What's your position on raising rents? On continuing social ownership? etc. It was a brand-new idea for them, although I suppose it would be routine for us.

February 28

Now it's official: the reform groups that have been sponsoring the Leipzig demos every Monday have withdrawn their sponsorship. It's been clear for several months that the demos have been drawing more and more right wingers, the original participants have more and more withdrawn; now the divorce is final, the sponsors disown the demonstrators. Monica Maron, a writer expelled from the DDR several years ago and now among the more virulent critics—not only of the old regime but of anyone who ever had anything to do with it—takes the position that the idea of "reforming socialism" and the talk of "democratic socialism" is all a cover by the party for its efforts to regain power, or sheer stupidity by people taken in by the party. She also thinks that all the intellectuals in the DDR (all except her and those like her who chose to or were forced to leave) colluded with the SED to get personal privileges for themselves. She would make the turn of events in Leipzig out to be the alienation of the intellectuals from the working class; the workers never wanted a "reformed socialism," she would argue, that was just the intellectuals' self-delusion. To us the turn of events in Leipzig sounds more like the taking over of street demonstrations by other groups than those there at the beginning. The 100,000 in October, who marked to speeches calling for reform within the system, must have included a few workers too, one would think!

March 2

Visit to Akademie Verlag with Fred Staufenbiel, to discuss our book on housing and urban development in the DDR. An outdated building, with odd additions, long passages, of course still a guard/porter at the entrance, and a manually controlled gate to let cars in (or keep them out). A pleasant conversation with our editor, a glass of schnapps to celebrate the completion of our proposal and its acceptance (do they do that in the West too? a pleasant custom). Now we have to get the book together! The idea of separate editions for West and East, or separate distribution channels, which we had played with, is now totally outdated; Akademie will distribute both places. We might, looking backward, have published West and sold East too, but it leaves a better taste in the mouth to publish East if one wants to address East problems.

In *Neues Deutschland* today, some quotes from West German officials on their intentions: border troops from the West should replace DDR troops at the Oder/Niesse line with Poland, because one can't "leave the control of the German-Polish border to DDR border patrols, which are so hated by the Poles because of their chicanery. That goes for DDR customs officials as well." Further: "There isn't the least desire, in the West German foreign ministry, to take over DDR diplomats...they are not 100 percent, but 150 percent, former SED members." They are only interested in "a few of the DDR's embassy buildings." The arrogance is unbelievable. The comment on SED membership is undoubtedly correct, but it hardly means they are all incompetent; nor does it even say much about their personal ideological positions. High officials in the United States embassies regularly change with changing administrations, but the civil servants under them don't, whether they're registered Democrats or Republicans. Professional foreign service people are likely to be just as nonpolitical, to be required to keep their personal beliefs to themselves just as much, in the East as in the West or the United States.

The anticommunism of West German ruling class is understandable enough. The populist red-baiting, the resurgence of the far right in East Germany, is harder to understand. Fred Staufenbiel told me this morning that he was having supper in Weimar a few days ago and several others at the table (one shares tables here without hesitation, a Germany-wide custom, very unlike the United States) made anti-foreign-worker cracks. He demurred, said after all they produced for the country too, why treat them differently. The response: "You must be one of those red pigs too!" What brings that on? Blair Ruble writes, in his report on his visit to Leningrad, of the rise of Russian nationalism, often in ugly forms; he says he thinks it would lessen if economic conditions improved. In other words, nationalism and racism as an expression of frustration? Of course, to some extent. But shouldn't forty years of socialism here, or eighty in the USSR, have given some understanding of what nationalism and racism are?

I was at the new private copy shop around the corner from us this afternoon. A long line; I didn't have the patience and left. All of a sudden, out of nowhere, comes a copy shop, and suddenly the demand, previously nonexistent or invisible, is overwhelming. That's an example of how a market *should* work: a new good or service is offered, by someone willing to take the risk that it's wanted, and people take it up: the better mouse-trap argument for capitalism. No one would dispute that such a new service is desirable, no one gets hurt or put out of business by it, things get done better or faster. Not like the multiplication of virtually identical products, the stimulation of socially useless activities or desires. And the money, even here, is available to pay for them. And for items that are not so clearly desirable: imported cucumbers cost 11 marks, compared to huge local cabbages for less than 1 mark, and yet people wait in line to buy the cucumbers.

A little story that illustrates the extent to which the East German election is a matter of West German politics: late at night on the way home today, a conversation between two slightly drunken men on the East Berlin subway: "Well, how does the election look to you?" "Oh, great, finally we can get our Willy!" "Willy? Willy who?" "Why, Willy Brandt [the popular former West German chancellor], you jackass." "He's not running in *our* election; what about Boehme [the chair of the East German SPD, who *was* running]?" "Boehme? Who's Boehme? It's Willy we want!"

The latest poll shows Modrow increasing his credibility rating to 87 percent. This despite his acceptance of the top spot on the PDS ticket. Triumph of personality over policy. And more people undecided than last week: the parties sound too alike. Triumph of centrism and tell-them-what-you-think-they-want-to-hear over honest politics. Getting more and more like a U.S. election campaign every day!

March 3

A story in the paper yesterday of a tenants association in the south summarized the questions they were putting to candidates in the election; today the first mass demonstration of the budding national Tenants' Association began with questions in the same way. They did it just right: first, with representatives of all the parties there, announce the questions; then have a couple of tenant speakers let them know what answers you want to hear; then invite the parties to answer. Classic interest group politics, American style. And the questions were to the point: How do you propose to convert state ownership into public or social ownership in housing and land? Do you oppose the sale of publicly owned housing to private landlords? Do you endorse security of tenure, protection against evictions? Affordable rents? Special consideration for the socially weak? (With a surprisingly strong attack on housing allowances, as being an inadequate answer.) How will you work with tenants? In discussions on unification, will you insist on a whole new constitution, not just the adoption of the existing West German one?

The speeches, on the whole, were good. The tenants' best formulation: "If we're not protected, we'll end up being the last displaced persons of World War II." The politicians weren't as good. The LPDP speaker, the first, spoke for far too long and promised the sky: the value of all publicly owned property in the DDR is 100 billion marks, subtract 25 percent for streets etc. that have to stay state-owned, figure some goes to trusts or utilities, some goes back to the original owners, that still leaves 25 billion marks that should be divided up among all you voters. A ridiculous proposal. Of course people clap anyway, but I doubt if anyone took it seriously. But the speaker also said, put your views on a postcard, send it to the Volkskammer, it will make an impression. The pattern of traditional representative democracy takes hold fast.

No party dared challenge unification; only Antje Vollmer, from the West German Greens—speaking as an individual so as to honor the Round Table demand that outside parties not electioneer in the DDR!—spoke of the usefulness of preserving two German states. Another speaker described the issues being discussed in the committee considering a new constitution for the DDR. It sounded very good: no eviction unless another unit is available for the family being evicted, a right to housing, and property rights subordinated to that right to housing. Zimmerman, from the ministry for construction and housing, endorsed all of the positions of the Tenants' Association. A nice thing to do, but foolish; he's promising more than he can deliver, the ministry isn't going to take a position against city sales of city-owned land, etc. The PDS speaker was weak: you could feel the uncertainty as to how to receive her (after a cold beginning, she was clapped three or four times in the course of a short talk). But she called for tenant ownership, presumably individual, of units, and the importance of protecting the socially weak. The first is treacherous, and would mean tripled costs for most tenants; the latter is precisely the wrong way to get support from people who don't consider themselves "socially weak."

The election slogans are getting sillier by the day. The DSU's is "Freedom Not Socialism," a mixing of categories if ever there was one. The CDU's is, alternately, "Freedom Is Performance" or "Performance Is Freedom"("Freiheit ist Leistung," "Leistung ist Freiheit"). Apart from the fact that both are blatantly untrue, do they think people *want* to perform, that requiring performance will attract votes? And what does, "Don't Worry, Take Gysi" mean?

March 4

The call was for the "occupation" of the Palace of the Republic, by the same groups that had mounted the mass demonstration at Alexanderplatz on November 4, 1989, the demonstration that in retrospect was the high-point of the revolutionary euphoria accompanying the overthrow of the SED. *(The photo on the next page shows the demonstration of November 4 marching past the Palace.)* They call themselves the "Initiative November 4—die Kulturschaffende." There's no exact English translation: the culture-makers would be the literal rendition, cultural workers closer to the sense. But the term lacks the connotation of culture industry that it would have in the United States; "producers of culture," in a society in which production is honest, respectable work and cultural workers are honored, not lowered, by identification with factory workers, might be better. It still smacks a little of the attempt to fit artists into crude Marxist categories: production workers, with what they produce being culture.

But, language aside, the whole system of handling culture, from reliable financial support for poets, musicians, writers, artists, to the links with national pride, to its central place in inner city planning (in theory), is in fact one of the most notable accomplishments of real existing socialism. When Christa Wolf (I think) says that its culture is one of the things the DDR brings to unification with the West, the DDR

 doesn't come with no assets to the marriage, she means it as a real value, just like a factory or an autobahn or a technology.

The purpose of the "occupation" was to prevent any surrender of space in the Palace of the Republic for commercial or representational (symbolizing power) purposes. As a demonstration of mass support, it was a flop; a proposed march to the palace from the Lustgarten, the "pleasure garden" across the street, never took place because the weather was too cold; everyone just went into the palace when they got there. Innumerable television crews and radio reporters and journalists stopped anyone they could get hold of to get a story; the media not only report news, they make it when there's none to report. The doors were open; a family fair was also taking place, with sales of blouses, demonstrations of haircutting, children's songs, etc. Everything was totally peaceful. Many good performances, an ear-splitting rock group, a Jewish musical group (the Klezmatiks), later meetings we didn't stay for. If this arch-Stalinist modern building can be converted into a real people's place of culture, then the argument about physical form determining use is forever settled!

Supper at a basement restaurant in the Nicolai Viertel, the show-place of DDR downtown renewal. Two days ago there was a ruling that Westerners were to pay in Deutsch marks in restaurants, to prevent Wessies from coming over, getting bargain repasts and crowding out the Ossies; but there was general skepticism as to whether it could be enforced. We weren't even asked if we were West or East, nor was anyone else. Regulation of the market can only go so far; if the system creates private motivations that contradict public regulations too widely, regulations won't take hold.

March 5

For my collection of political slogans: "PDS: One Germany, 1:1." Short and to the point, and a good point. The big issue in the agreement that there should be a single currency in both parts of Germany, and that it should be the West German mark, is: at what rate should it be exchanged with the East mark? The official rate is 1:1, and that's obviously the most favorable to DDR residents. The rate used in commercial dealings is at least twice that, the black market rate 7 to 10 times that. So 1:1 should find favor with DDR voters. The PDS obviously has professional help in their campaign. Someone should tell them to stop plastering the subway entrances, etc., with dozens of copies of the same posters; that doesn't impress anyone, and alienates some.

Stories of PDS or any kind of opposition people getting beaten up in Leipzig yesterday; in Erfurt, Bernd's ex-wife was beaten up carrying a banner with a few others at the Kohl talk: "One Germany? Think of Buchenwald too!"

Learn something new everyday department: we had trouble with our TV, not getting Channel 3 (a West station, ARD), the repair man came, said something was wrong with the antenna. Today spoke to the wife of the couple responsible for the building: no, everything's fine here, we're all on the same antenna. But wait a minute: you're in a ministry apartment, aren't you? Very likely your set was adjusted not to receive some channels. Oh come on, I don't believe that! Yes, it was the practice!

Mitterrand wants to guarantee Poland's border with Germany

because Kohl is making such an ass of himself hedging on the question. Does Mitterand remember how World War II started? A frightening thought. Allianz für Deutschland announces its election program at a press conference in Bonn. How stupid can you get?

March 7

Meeting with Schultze and Manfred Richter, at the office for long-range planning. It's on Stroktowerstrasse, off Leninallee, because the head of planning department was an obstinate character, the mayor of Berlin wanted to get him out of the way; when they built this building for the building *Kombinate* for whom a location with good access to roads out of Berlin was important, the mayor sent long-range planning out there too. In the backyard of Berlin, so to speak: symbolic.

The election procedure is outlined in the newspapers. Seems very fair—fairer than ours. Votes are tallied by voting district. It takes roughly the same number of votes to win a seat in each district. Each party gets seats in proportion to its votes. Any unused votes (e.g., if a party gets 40,000 votes and 33,000 are needed to elect, then there are 7,000 "unused" votes, or if a small party gets under the 33,000 votes, then all its votes are "unused") are cumulated nationally and given to the party; it then picks which of its candidates is to receive the unused votes. The West German system differs in that it has a minimum percentage of all votes (5 percent) needed nationally for any party to be represented in the Bundestag; that was deliberately rejected here, because small parties/movements were to be given a chance too. Also, some votes can be permitted for persons, not just parties (a "mixed," rather than a "relational," system). They propose to do that for the local elections here, in May.

March 8

International Women's Day. A march from Alexanderplatz to Rosa Luxemburg Platz, around the corner from us, and speeches there. Good ones, too. On the one hand, the burdens on women in the DDR are the same as everywhere: the double duty of paid outside work and unpaid home work, cooking, raising children, keeping house. But *every* speaker—although there is not a true cross-section, no CDU women, actually no political party women at all, but DFD and UFV (the Independent Women's Federation), both clearly left— spoke of the accomplishments of the DDR and what had to be fought to be preserved in the coming unification: the certainty of a job, of a home, of support for children, day care, education, support for single parents. Equality hasn't been achieved between the sexes in East Germany, but the basic social net has in fact been successfully built; the floor of support is relatively high. In the past that support has been taken for granted; now its absence is experienced as fear, rather than as knowledge, but it is a well-grounded fear.

The most interesting formulation: we don't want a consumption and performance (*Konsum und Leistung*) society. That's classic Herbert Marcuse, and it makes direct sense here, as to both terms. The DDR really is not a consumption society. Its economy is not driven by ever increasing consumption and its people are not motivated by the desire (elsewhere in part manufactured) to consume ever more and more. Neither are its people driven by the need to perform, to produce in a personal and hierarchically, market-determined sense. That is good, in a humanistic sense, but it has unfortunate by-products; the standard of living and of services is correspondingly lower. Nor have people had the freedom to develop their own personalities and potentials as they wished; so the lesser external pressure to produce has not been offset by a greater joy and creativity in freely chosen production. If all the investment in privileges and the even greater investment in the preservation of power had only been invested in the support of individual development, culture, personal expression!

After a talk on public housing at a West Berlin tenants' union conference, during the lunch break, interviewed by a correspondent for *Berlin am Abend*, a popular afternoon newspaper in East Berlin. Also by someone from TV; it turns out from West German cable television, a channel that does real estate marketing! Their card says: "Real estate is now also on television." Ah well! And Hank Bell tells me, by telephone from New York, that the *New York Times* has a full-page ad from a Munich firm soliciting investment (minimum $25,000) in East Germany. Real estate speculators are on the front lines of the private market's invasion of the East. What the reporter for the East Berlin paper tells me, confirms the impression: she says a pending deal between the KWV (Kommunale Wohnungsverwaltung, "municipal housing administration") for Berlin-Prenzlauer Berg and a real estate firm in West Berlin, Data-Domizil, provides for the firm to administer all (!) of the KWV units here—up to 100,000 units! The KWV corresponds to U.S. housing authorities in several ways: it's appointed by the local government but is legally autonomous, and it's thus nonprofit, relatively bureaucratic, limited in its means, and essentially gets its job done; it differs from the U.S. model in that it has nothing to do with construction, and in that it administers far more housing, being the dominant force in almost any housing "market" in the DDR. The pending deal is confidential, but someone made the tenants' union a copy; she'll bring it tomorrow, the tenants' union is planning a press conference to expose it.

March 9

Excitement about the Data-Domizil offer. The reporter from *Berlin am Abend* wrote up the interview with me, stressing the point I had made that in a private housing market a substantial number of people, as high as 25 to 33 percent of the population, were dependant on some form of governmental assistance to get decent housing, and many were forced to live below accepted standards if they didn't get it. Last evening I went through the draft contract between Data-Domizil and the KWV that had been smuggled out, and I gave her my analysis: a horrendous deal, giving Data-Domizil all kinds of options, not only to manage at a profit without any commitment to maintenance or repairs, but also options to buy up those properties they wanted and/or return to KWV management those properties they didn't want or were having trouble with. A pretty onesided deal, with little protection for the tenants. The tenants' union held a press conference at 1:00 o'clock in front of a local KWV office; not well attended, but the housing administration (local and national) will hear of it, and I assume it will have an impact.

Dinner with Valerie Karn, from Birmingham, England, among others. My interpretation of coffee-break socialism came up. She says at her institute the boss insists on a coffee-break, too, one that every-one must attend—so he can see who is there and who isn't. The participants dislike it, would rather not go. A symbolic reaffirmation of my thesis: in the West the coffee-break is to serve the purposes of work; in the East it represents the subordination of work to human space.

March 10

Eberhard Mühlich comes to visit, from Frankfurt/Main, and we talk about the election campaign.

The slogan, "Leistung ist Freiheit," is all over the place on CDU election posters. *Leistung* is a tough word to translate: it means work, accomplishment, production; in Freud, the *Leistungs-Prinzip* is trans-lated as the "performance principle," as opposed to the pleasure principle. I guess the CDU wants to say that, in a desirable society, like that of the West, high productivity creates freedom for the whole society. They alternate it with the slogan, "Freiheit ist Leistung," which I suppose is intended to suggest that once the DDR is "free" it will produce more, and the standard of living will rise. Weird; isn't the implication that freedom means more work, that work and free-dom are the same thing, a turn-off? Don't people also want freedom *from* work? Is that all freedom will bring, more work? No pleasure?

Worse: the inscription on the gate of Dachau was: "Arbeit macht Frei"—"Work Makes One Free." Bruno, whom I had asked about this, held that the CDU was probably ignorant of history, but that the underlying "innocent" similarity in the slogans is no accident. Bruno said the Nazis used the Dachau inscription before Dachau; Eberhardt says it goes back in another meaning to Hegel.

Frances and I both spoke at a gathering sponsored by the Liga, the Society for Friendship Among Peoples, at the residential facility of the GeWi Akademie—"the Academy for the Social Sciences at the Central Committee of the Socialist Unity Party" (sic!). A beautifully restored older building, with an inner courtyard, a complete kitchen, both fancy and high-quality guest rooms for graduate students and guests of the GeWi; the typical privileges of the ruling class, here, not extreme, but nice. The Liga advertised an intensive two-day course for those interested in learning about the United States. They expected twenty-five responses, got eighty, and were very happy, considering it was 200 marks a head. They see the need to establish some measure of self-sufficiency; the good part of the market economy? Friendship among peoples has to pay its own way!

We were to talk about everyday life in the United States, tips for travel, and did so: Americans eat their big meal in the evening, not at noon, bring some pieces of the Wall along for gifts, people are friendly but often in a hurry, you will be exotic, many people won't know difference between East and West Germany. At the end, Fran had had enough of small talk, made a little speech about their right to be proud of their peaceful revolution, urging them to look critically at what they encounter and not shy away from defending their country or criticizing ours. An important point, I think. Remember the Czech architect telling us we shouldn't criticize their handling of demonstrations, he didn't criticize our handling of Negroes in Florida when he was there?

March 11

At a breakfast rally for the PDS in the KWV on our street, the first real sign of anti-semitism we've encountered. From a surprising source: Professor Luft (husband of the finance minister). In his talk, a pretty straightforward party line speech, he made the following argument: "We don't have to get into bed with West Germany, investors from other countries are interested too. Proof: the letter from twenty-four U.S. senators calling for support for reform movements in Eastern Europe was signed by Jewish senators. That means the big U.S. banks are interested." I went up to him afterward and protested: the facts were wrong, Jews did not run the big U.S. banks, the senate vote had nothing to do with Jews or bankers—and the whole line of argument smacked of stereotypes from *Mein Kampf*. He protested that he was not saying that the fact that Jewish bankers were interested was a bad thing; it was a good thing. In other words, he didn't understand the assumptions he was making. I got a little hot, made my point again, then saw that he was turning off; but a bystander intervened and said it was a misunderstanding, a question of words and perhaps of failed sensibility, and I used this to turn moderate and say that he must not realize how his argument came across to others. He took the out, and said yes, he understood that he could be misinterpreted, he would not use that argument again, he appreciated being told.

These people have not had any contact with Jews, have treated the problem of anti-semitism as over and done with, and never thought twice about what it meant, where it came from, how it was expressed. I think Luft would react with horror to the oppression of Jews if he saw it directly; but his thinking fertilizes the ground from which such oppression can come.

March 19

The election results are in:

Alliance for Germany   48.15%

Christian Democratic Union (CDU)   40.91%

German Social Union (DSU)   6.32%

Democratic Opening   .92%

Social Democratic Party (SPD)   21.84%

Party of Democratic Socialism   16.33%

Coalition of Free Democrats (Liberals)   5.28%

Bündnis 90 (New Forum, Democracy Now,
Initiative for Peace and Human Rights)   2.9%

Democratic Farmers' Party (DBD)   2.19%

Greens & Independent Women's Federation (UFV)   1.96%

(The fourteen other parties on the ballot got less than 1 percent of the vote each.)

The first general reaction is, "It's all over." The formulations vary, from "the last free election in the DDR" to "the end of the last chance socialism had" to "now all that remains of the DDR is a footnote in the history books." The folk-saying Andrée quoted was: "Better an unhappy ending than an endless unhappiness." In one way it's true. The election represents a clear triumph of the image of Western private market capitalism over all that forty years' experience had taught East Germans that socialism means. It also shows the power of money and manipulation: the West German publicity and public relations efforts paid off handsomely. The CDU got across the message that a vote for the conservatives was the best way of getting the most help from the West the fastest. The message was powerful even when it was indirect, as in the constant featuring of Helmut Kohl as a speaker at East German rallies. But it was also direct: what else does a placard, "Vote CDU: Friends Help Friends" mean? That simple message got the CDU 41 percent of the vote. The conservative DSU got itself 7 percent of the vote by making a similar connection with the CSU in Bavaria.

For the SPD, West German help was crucial. While the SPD has a long tradition in Germany, in the DDR it had merged into the SED almost forty years earlier and was only reestablished in October 1989, just before the *Wende*. Thus it was Willy Brandt and Helmut Schmidt, old friends from the West German SPD, who campaigned actively in the DDR, plus truckloads of posters, newspapers, flyers, balloons—and personnel—that helped the SPD get its disappointing 22 percent.

The influence of the West German parties can be directly measured. The CDU presented speakers at 74 rallies, the SPD at 60, the FDP at 48, the CSU at 20, and the Greens at 3—proportions close to those of the election results. But more important than speakers was the influence of money spent by the Western parties.

Curiously, West German party money is virtually West German state money; under an old provision designed to avoid one-party domination, all parties represented in the national legislature are entitled to establish nonprofit foundations to pursue party interests, which are then funded by the government. In a special appropriation, the CDU (through its foundation) received 4.5 million marks, the CSU 1.5 million, the FDP 1.5 million, and the SDP 1.5 million. The Greens have in the past opposed such state support on principle, and although they have now essentially reversed their position, they didn't have a foundation at the time of the election and thus got no money and had less to offer the DDR Greens.

The PDS had given almost unbelievable sums (over 3 billion marks) from its treasury back to the state in the process of its reform,

but had clearly kept enough to run a smooth and technically impressive campaign. Only the citizens' movements and tiny parties lacked
financial support (the Greens gave their help, what there was of it, to
both of the citizens' alliances: Bündnis 90 and the alliance of Greens
and the Independent Women's Federation), but made up in the
quality and dedication of volunteers what they lacked in resources.

The regular political party opposition—a perhaps surprising but
accurate designation for the PDS, and meaning those opposing rapid
annexation—did relatively well, while the nonparty opposition, the
citizens' movements, did relatively badly. Seventeen percent for the
PDS, the former SED, was not a bad showing, given the ferocity and
virtual unanimity of the attacks on the old SED over the previous four
months. It is hard-core support, from people who are clear in their
allegiances: it is the only party for which the polls predicted the results
accurately, because PDS supporters knew from the outset how they
would vote. The citizens' groups, which had led the October revolution, had lost their leading role by December. The precipitous opening
of the Wall introduced an entirely new element into the popular revolt
against the centralized state: in addition to the quest for a better state,
a freer society, now the allure of prosperity and plenty which the open
border revealed on the other side. Nationalism seemed the easiest way
to get it, and nationalism, getting more and more rabid, took over the
street demonstrations from the principled citizens' movements. The
movements' own ambivalence about their role, and their initial ambivalence about whether they should participate in the elections at all
or remain grass-roots movements acting as a check on the political
parties, was felt by many voters, including their own supporters.

The arrangements for reporting the results of the election were
symbolic of the whole set of forces that had determined those results.
The returns were broadcast as they came in. (The wits had it that after
the broadcast had run half an hour, a telegram arrived from the
Politburo: "Stop the transmission immediately, report to the central
office within two hours to receive the final figures for the election
results.") ZDF, West German television, covered at the Palace of the
Republic; DDR television played off them. Round Tables in East
Berlin and Bonn were given equal time to comment on the elections.
The whole Palace of the Republic was cordoned off for TV cameras,

for panel shows and interviews, entry only by permission, while the PDS headquarters and the Haus der Demokratie, headquarters of the citizens' movements, limited entry only as they got crowded. The PDS headquarters, in the central committee building of the old SED, itself previously the seat of the national bank under Hitler, was painted, bannered, everything possible to cover over the Reichsbank/SED aura. The symbol of the SED—the shaking hands—had been taken down long ago; in any case, they mean something quite different in the United States.

The practical results are clear. The Liberals will join with the CDU, as they have in the West; that will provide a stable ruling coalition with 53 percent of the seats, 214 out of 400. If the SDP enters into a "grand coalition" with the CDU [as it did], the coalition will represent 75 percent of the votes, and have 301 seats, or well over the two-thirds necessary to amend the constitution and make all procedural decisions. The control by the pro-unification forces seems absolute.

excurs 4

THE POLITICS OF THE *WENDE* AND AFTER

The March elections represented the end of the *Wende* in the DDR and the beginning of the forced march to unification of East Germany with—into—West Germany. But did they represent the utter collapse of socialism? Did they leave any organized political forces behind on the German landscape?

Let me separate the issue into two sets of questions: (1) How could the transfer of power represented by the *Wende* take place so peacefully? Who lost power, who gained it? Was there a historical alternative to the direction the *Wende* took, and could the result have been different? (2) What were the forces involved in the unification process? Who stood to benefit by it, who to lose? What were they, and why were they so weak?

Explaining the *Wende*

As late as the summer of 1989, the political system of the DDR seemed immutable, impermeable to change:

"Do you think the present Politburo will ever be replaced?" one DDR citizen asks another.

"Only two possibilities exist," is the answer, "a natural way, and a supernatural way. The natural way would be that an angel would come down from heaven, and take the members by the hand, and lead them each personally to their eternal reward."

"And what would be the supernatural way?"

"That they would retire or resign."

The story represents the real intellectual puzzle of the *Wende*: how could such a change come about so peacefully and with so little resistance? Within a period of two months (i.e., by the end of the second phase of the *Wende*), the complete and essentially irreversible destruction of a set of power relations had been accomplished. The power of the forty-year-old entrenched SED bureaucracy was shattered, despite its absolute control over the media, the educational system, and all voluntary organizations, despite its truce with the church, its well-ordered internal distribution of power, and above all its apparatus of over 100,000 full-time employees in a mighty state security apparatus, censoring mail, eavesdropping on telephones, keeping detailed files on all residents, calling on millions of willing or unwilling volunteers for information on their neighbors and co-workers, infiltrating every potentially disruptive grouping, with proportionately one of the largest armies in Europe. Was this the first peaceful revolution in modern history?

Was it a revolution in the first place? Without entering the debate over definition, the first phase of the *Wende* involved the destruction of a power structure without the establishment of a viable alternative. This created a partial vacuum into which the ruling forces in a neighboring state quickly stepped, establishing their own domination. Thereafter, economic structures and relationships were also completely overturned. "Counterrevolution" is hardly an intuitively appropriate term for the reversal of a change that took place forty-five years ago (and of course raises the question as to whether those changes were themselves a revolution), but in terms of class relations it seems accurate: those class relations that existed prior to 1933 (and in many ways continued through fascism) were reestablished after the *Wende*, those that were established after the war are now being destroyed. Crudely, the *Wende* might be considered an abortive or potential revolution, unification as counterrevolution, as far as the DDR was concerned.

How could such dramatic changes come about so peacefully? In a nutshell: because the party and state apparatus did not represent a solid ruling class and the first phases of the *Wende* did not represent a shift in major class relations; thus there was no violent or last-ditch resistance. When the real shift in class power came with the end of the *Wende* and the implementation of unification, the dominant forces in West Germany substituted their own power for that which had hitherto dominated the DDR; West German power was so overwhelming that there was no possibility of resistance.

The real ruling powers at the beginning of the *Wende* were surprisingly weak and unable to defend a top-heavy structure from a real challenge. The top of the party hierarchy consisted of a very narrow circle of people; once their position was weakened, once they had embarked on the road of concessions and then themselves withdrew from power, the apparatus they had headed was unable to fend for itself, to stand in the way of sweeping changes. Certainly the contrast with the party apparatus in the Soviet Union is striking; there, it seems, it is a major independent force, capable of sabotaging reform not only from without but even from its own leadership and top ranks.

According to this analysis, not the ouster of Honecker but the resignation of Krenz was the turning point in the *Wende*, brought about as much by the latter's weakness as by the power of the opposition. Certainly the opening of the Wall on November 9 was perceived by many at the time as a panic reaction, quite unexpected by the opposition and going well beyond what they had thought attainable, or even desirable, at the time. But Honecker to Krenz to Modrow (even to De Maizière) were only changes in formal political power, in the superstructure, under which the real economic relationships remained quite stable. The big change is represented by the currency union, the privatization of state firms and/or their buy-up or takeover by private firms from the West. The destruction of the political apparatus in the first two phases of the *Wende* was relatively easy because that apparatus did not have the anchoring in economic relations which, for instance, the Soviet party with its vastly greater privileges and entrenched personal power had; but that destruction left a vacuum, in which the democratic opposition was strong enough to prevent the reform leadership of the party from exercising control but not strong enough itself to take over, thus opening the door to the invasion from the West.

This explanation suggests that the party in the DDR was not in the traditional sense a ruling class, and that its power, though strong and visible, was not rooted in any deep economic structures. Certainly if no ruling class gives up its power without a struggle, the SED in the DDR was a pretty pathetic ruling class. The power and privileges of its members melted away like snow in spring: those individuals who kept any of the benefits of their earlier status did so more because they disowned their former allegiances than because they affirmed them. The reference to the "leading role of the party" was removed from the constitution with the consent of the party; Wandlitz, the private residential enclave of the ruling elite, with its (relatively modest) mansions, security fence (à la California private communities), shopping facilities with foreign goods, separate lane for travel to offices in downtown Berlin, was converted into a rehabilitation center within the medical system. Krenz even let television crews in to show the public the privileges being surrendered. The hunting lodges of a few of the top SED leaders were converted to recreational use for public organizations. Thousands of members of the security police were laid off. Full-time positions for workers representing the party in factories were eliminated. Hundreds of party officials at national, regional, and local levels were forced out of their jobs and lost their privileges. And all without significant national resistance.

I am thus prepared to venture a conclusion, but a limited and cautious one, on the question of the class structure of the DDR and what happened to it in the *Wende*. At least since Milovan Djilas, and in other forms already much earlier, the societies of the Soviet Union and the real existing socialist countries had been characterized as ruled by a new bureaucratic class, of which the party and state apparatus were the decisive components. The experience of the *Wende* does not support that conclusion for the DDR. The political rule of the SED effectively ended with the resignations of Honecker, then Krenz.

Economically, ownership was never taken away from one class and given to another in the *Wende*; it was gradually and voluntarily surrendered by some individuals. The administrative apparatus remained substantially in place. The old Politburo once ruled indeed; but once it was gone, there was a vacuum of power. No class, in the traditional sense, attempted to maintain its rule in its own interest, and no new class took over rule in the *Wende*.

The situation in the Soviet Union seems to be very different, and hence the limited nature of the conclusion I want to draw here. In the Soviet Union a dramatic change at the very top seems to be largely unable to produce change in the party or state apparatus, which seem to have built up power, based on self-interest, quite independent of a few people in the top leadership. The pattern is the exact opposite of that in the DDR. Romania seems similar to the Soviet Union in the durability of its apparatus; the opposition in Bulgaria claims the party there is also clinging to power.

The explanation offered here suggests a two-level picture of "socialism" in the DDR: on one level, a real and major difference in economic structure and economic relations from Western capitalism, largely consistent with traditional concepts of socialist ownership; and, on the other level, a political structure and set of relations not consistent with traditional socialist concepts, top heavy and vulnerable. The political structure was overthrown, or collapsed, in the first two phases of the *Wende*, the economic structure that might have provided a basis for a new form of political decision-making could not survive because of pressures from outside the system. That suggests that the weakness of the political structure is related to its inconsistency with the economic relations over which it presided, that a strong and progressive socialist economy requires a democratic and bottom-up organization both of production and government; democracy being absent, the political being in discord with the economic, the whole structure becomes self-contradictory, stagnates, becomes vulnerable. What replaces it then depends on the context. In East Germany, the presence of the West was decisive; the brief opening for a "third way" perceived in the first two phases of the *Wende* closed quickly. In the other East European countries, neither a third way nor integration into the developed capitalist world seem plausible in the immediate future; a dependent third-world-like status seems at least an interim possibility in several.

Was it then only the Stalinist political structure of the DDR that accounted for its collapse; could it economically have held up in competition with the West German economy had it been better, more democratically, run? What, in other words, does the DDR experience teach us about the economic potential of socialism?

The historical evidence is inconclusive. That East Germany lagged well behind West Germany in its per capita GNP is hardly debatable; while the figures suggest a gap of only about 20 percent, no one believes them, and everyday experience showed a startling difference in the standard of living, from cars to housing to clothes to food to gadgets. That demonstrates beyond doubt which has the superior system, argued the conservatives in West Germany and indeed in the United States. But the comparison is fundamentally flawed. In the first place, more than half of the industrial base in the Soviet zone was destroyed in the war, while the corresponding figure in the Western zones was under 20 percent. While the Western zones (after their unification, West Germany) received a large part of U.S. Marshall Plan aid, the DDR was paying reparations, in money and materials and whole factories to the USSR. U.S. capital collaborated with the existing German industrial and financial leadership, much of it heavily involved with fascism, to rebuild the West German economy to the mutual profit of both; in the East, anti-fascist feelings and fear of German strength led to the elimination and exile of almost all those who had played any leadership role in the past, and to a deliberate Soviet policy of suppressing German growth. An initially backward Soviet Union, tremendously weakened by losses from the war, led by a repressive and unbalanced regime using military might as a substitute for the economic power it did not have, was no match for the United States in the support it could give its allies in Europe. Much of the difference between the two German states, after forty years of such history, can therefore be explained without any reference to socialism or capitalism.

But not all. There are sound reasons for skepticism about what the results of competition between the two systems could have been expected to be, even if they had started even. West Germany, Sweden, and the United States produce as efficiently as they do in part because of an international division of labor: the capitalist standard of living includes Haiti as well as Switzerland, Ethiopia as well as England, the underpaid and repressed of Korea as well as the overpaid of Wall Street. A socialist country, presumably, precludes exploitation of such international divisions. At home as well: would a truly socialist country compete with West Germany in the use of material incentives to stimulate faster, less autonomous, labor, subject to the threat of discharge and degradation? Would it use the promise of personal wealth to encourage sixty-hour work weeks and workaholism to drive workers to ever greater activity? Is the shifting of the cost of environmental degradation from industry to the public, contributing to the production of endless commodities, a shift to which socialism would contribute?

Of course a socialist country would be expected to have some advantages in the competition. The abolition of the waste of advertising, of manipulations of ownership, of the maintenance of power, of the production of unneeded goods—all these should be an advantage. The unleashing of the forces of personal creativity should find its reflection in material production as well. But the DDR never got that far. In the real world, betting on East Germany's success in face-to-face competition with the West, even given a different political structure in the East, would have been betting against the odds.

The Performance Principle was much discussed in East Germany in the months leading up to unification. Its absence under socialism was presented by Westerners as a fatal flaw of socialism; the reform socialists in the DDR joined in calling for its implementation. On the face of it, the call for a return to the Performance Principle by the advocates of a democratic socialism would startle anyone who had lived through 1968 or read the literature on those events. Yet that call for performance is hardly a rejection of that literature, certainly not literally, since the work of the Frankfurt School, indeed of most recent Western Marxists, was largely unknown and unavailable in the DDR. But, beyond this, the criticism of the Performance Principle has been a historical one; its linkage to the systems of class domination is hardly contradicted by any experience of history to date. The assumption of a society of plenty, in which utopian aspirations are realizable and thus no longer utopian, underlies the call to aim beyond performance to freedom. The society that would make that possible did not exist in the DDR.

Indeed, the dilemma is hardly a new one. In connection with events in Brazil, but perhaps equally applicable to Eastern Europe, the editors of *Monthly Review* quote Engels, writing in 1851 of Thomas Münzer:

> The worst that can befall the leader of an extreme party is to be forced to take over the government at a time when the movement is not yet ripe for the domination of the class he represents and for the measures the domination of this class requires.

Herbert Marcuse quotes Lenin as writing, in 1918:

> In reality, state capitalism would be a step forward for us... If we would have it in Russia, then the transition to full socialism would be easy and certain.

Must a prematurely socialistically organized society then return to capitalism before it can achieve mature socialism? Or would a less fully developed socialism have to intensify the application of the Performance Principle to production, rather than ameliorate it, in order to progress to its abolition? The question is academic today, since even in the Soviet Union implementation of a close relationship between performance and pay is taken as necessary by all sides in the debate. Yet speculation as to the answer is relevant to an understanding of the economic stagnation in the DDR.

By providing personal security regardless of performance, a change in the set of motivations that drive individual actions may have been produced in the DDR, undermining a pillar of the Western system of accumulation and discipline. It briefly looked as if political freedom might provide an opening for motivations that would fill the gap. The flowering of expression, of activity, of social involvement, that erupted in the first phases of the *Wende* was unbelievable. External events certainly helped precipitate it; Czechoslovakia went the way of East Germany in part because East Germany already had gone that way, and the Hungarian border opening led into the crisis in the DDR. But what erupted once that opening appeared cannot be explained by external events; it reflects what was there, and clearly was there through all forty years. Might it have been possible that that political energy would have been transferred to economic activity, had West Germany not interfered? No one can safely say; I would not have written the possibility off. Or, theoretically, if the Performance Principle is put in place, not from above to support accumulation and domination, and then internalized, but rather from below, as a democratic choice, externally agreed upon and controlled, perhaps the result would have been different. Marx, at any rate, saw the need for performance as a component of socialism in a transition to communism; perhaps it needs to be more fully implemented before it can be abolished.

After the *Wende*

To the second question, then: whatever there was of socialism in the DDR, will it leave any organized political forces behind? If so, can they be expected to retain any influence after unification?

The first place one might look for the effects of forty years of DDR socialism would be in the traditional working class. Their pay was substantially less than that of their Western counterparts, and their hours somewhat longer, but their working conditions were in many ways good (e.g., lack of pressure, speed-up), and they had full job security and good benefits. Good health care could not override serious environmental hazards, but it was nevertheless a very important benefit. Apart from their pay, East German workers had many advantages their Western counterparts did not enjoy.

But working-class interests in job-related conditions never found independent political expression. The one major attempt to express them, in the resistance to centrally imposed increased work norms, led to the bloody suppression of the June 1953 uprising (although thereafter norms were in fact brought back down). Over the past forty years the trade unions were thoroughly integrated into the party apparatus. After October, they were completely discredited; their former head, Harry Tisch, with his hunting lodge patrolled by the police, in the middle of a nature preserve, is currently under indictment. Although the old party-led trade union federation was cleansed during the *Wende*, it never regained any credibility under the new circumstances. And individual workers are not likely to be very militant in the future either: for most workers who have jobs, the prospect of higher pay scales at DDR rates approaching those in the West makes a little bit of capitalist exploitation tolerable, at least in the short run. As the realities of life under capitalism slowly become clear, however, the opposition will mount and then some of the socialist background in the experience of DDR workers may again be brought into play.

The strong union movement in the West might have been expected to be energized and perhaps radicalized by a perception of the directions opened up by DDR rhetoric, if not DDR practices, for workers. And the Western unions' own interest in avoiding rate-cutting competition was heavily at stake. But some of the East demands were disconcerting to the Western unions; a new trade union law, for instance, passed by the Modrow government just before the election, guaranteed workers rights in the management of companies, prohibited lock-outs, and was stronger than anything in the West. Ideologically, the West German unions were simply unwilling to buy it. They have made their own peace with West German employers, and as long as prosperity continues, they will stick with it rather than embark on new and uncharted waters. They are also still unwilling to work with leaders from the former DDR, with their taint of a formerly Stalinist union movement.

The second of the forces created by the DDR that may survive the *Wende* are the dissidents, left intellectuals, artists, church leaders, active women. They were in the leadership of the opposition to the Stalinist SED, and the spokespeople of the opposition in the first phase of the *Wende*. They were both within and without the old SED, in fact both within and without the old DDR, since many had been forced to leave the country because of their views. They founded New Forum and the other oppositional groups represented at the Round Table before the March elections. The intellectual opposition included such old dissidents as Stefan Heym, principled socialists who identify the legacy of the DDR with the striving for a humane socialism, and such younger dissidents as Bärbel Bohley, who came to her beliefs very individually and totally outside of, and in conflict with, the party. Within the PDS, what is left of it, the reformers are dominant, and some young people have been attracted to the party as a way of participating in organized political action. Similarly among students: a few small independent groups with left leanings were created, and are again mobilizing around current issues. The Greens in the East, sympathetic to the left in many ways, have learned some of the critiques of the West from their Western colleagues, but they have thus far deliberately kept ecological issues central to their activities; efforts to define such issues broadly and form left alliances have met with opposition within Green ranks.

The former-DDR intellectual opposition is, however, internally divided and seems to have concerns that diverge from those of the majority of the people—or of the voters, at least, judging from the results of the elections. A sometimes bitter and generally fruitless discussion has taken place about whether the intellectuals have

"At least say something about the weather."

either misunderstood or betrayed the workers, whether they were ever actually in accord, whether it is the intellectuals with their ideals of political freedom or the workers with their pursuit of a higher material standard of living that are the real motors of reform. That raises the whole question of whether it was political or economic motivations that led to the *Wende* in the first place, and how the two were related.

Political dissatisfaction with restrictions on freedom of expression, of travel, in the arts, in government decision-making, had been continuous in the DDR. Economic dissatisfaction had waxed and waned; over most of the DDR's history, there had been economic growth, conditions were consistently better than in the majority of other East bloc states to which DDR residents could travel, economic security was provided and could be relied on. In the 1970s, growth in many areas was in fact ahead of that in West Germany, although in absolute terms the standard of living lagged well behind (official statistics that suggest a narrowing gap are hard to interpret, and in recent years increasingly inaccurate). But by the mid-1980s stagnation was evident, and the contrast with West Germany increasingly glaring. Both the exodus over the Hungarian border in the summer and the later out-migration over the open border to West Germany were caused by the economic lure of the West; the chafing under political constraints may have played some role in the early days, but none after November. And the exodus to the West continued well after unification, as unemployment in the former-DDR mounted.

Despite this, the leadership of the reform movement, both outside and inside the old SED, was moved by purely political goals—purely, in the sense that the demands for economic reforms were not demands to improve their own economic position, not demands of a class or a group for improved material conditions for themselves, even though the demands included economic reforms for the benefit of all. The nationalist revival in the second phase already began a turn to more material concerns: nationalism was equated with unification with a more prosperous West Germany, and the prosperity was at least as important an attraction as the common nationality. Ironically, the third phase, while it was played out in a political election campaign, involved almost exclusively economic issues. The conservative victory was a victory for economic assimilation to West Germany. Political democracy was by then hardly an issue.

But political democracy, certainly parliamentary democracy, is not identical with freedom, which is the better term for the initial concerns of the reform movement. The big question is the relation of the demands for a better material life, and for political, intellectual, and economic freedom. The unspoken assumption is that they all go together, that each will support the others. But the tension among some of them is clear. A return to the Performance Principle is demanded of the people of the DDR after unification, with material incentives for better work, reduced laziness and waste, and increased productivity, thus raising the standard of living. But most people also expect independent trade unions, as well as reduced working hours, increased vacations, benefits at least as good as what they had in the

East or could get in the West. Under most conditions the two de-mands—for greater production and greater benefits—go badly to-gether. As Gorbachev has seen, even the minimal demands of organized workers for decent conditions can interfere with maintain-ing current production in mines and factories. In an economic system in which job security is one of its real claims to success, the threat of unemployment and reduced income that is the underside of the Performance Principle is already beginning to encounter resistance. The West, capitalism, is hardly perfect here; "free" trade unions have not succeeded in producing a share of the wealth for workers propor-tionately as favorable as it was in the East. Nor is the Performance Principle, understood as reward in accordance with work performed, rampant in the West, unless stock brokers, lawyers, and bankers are to be considered thousands of times more productive than factory workers, teachers, and cooks.

These issues tend to be defined in the current debate as "social" issues, in contradistinction to political and economic issues, but they are perhaps the point where economics and politics meet. And here is also where workers and progressive intellectuals may agree. In this way it is possible that two of the organized survivals of life in the DDR—working-class organizations and oppositional intellectuals—may strengthen each others' influence in a campaign to achieve social justice, combining material prosperity with real freedom. But that is a long-term perspective.

Another reason to expect a left opposition in the DDR might be that socialism had indigenous roots in Germany (as in the USSR), a native tradition to draw on, local leaders to rely on after the defeat of fascism. No doubt true to some extent, but the overwhelming majority of prewar Communists were murdered in fascist concentration camps, the Moscow hand in the imposition of the East German regime in 1949 was ungloved, the pompous pedagogic insistence on the legacy of Marx, Engels, Luxemburg, and Liebknecht has as likely led to their irrelevance as to their hallowing.

The third political force (after workers and intellectuals with dissident political ideals) that may survive unification lies in urban residents and agricultural cooperative members, whose living condi-tions—housing in particular—have been thrown into crisis by unification. Uncertainty over property rights, and specifically uncertainty of their ability to remain where they are, is one of the main fears confronting DDR residents today. The community-based citizens' movements that provided much of the initial basis for the October changes, to the extent they have survived, are beginning to realize that these new market-based forces may not provide the solutions they still seek. New neighborhood groups will undoubtedly spring up, as they have in the West; but in the DDR they will have memories of a system in which real estate developers were not to be feared, in which rights of use were proclaimed as natural and rights to speculate unheard of. Again, this force of neighborhood concern is more a potential than actually organized, but its emergence (or re-emergence) is a strong likelihood.

To conclude: While the dominant forces in the early phases of the *Wende* succeeded in overthrowing an authoritarian political structure, their focus was more on reforming than on rejecting the economic and social aspects of socialism as it existed in the DDR. The overpowering presence of the West in the East after the March elections resulted in a complete formal rejection of the East's economic system. But, ironically enough, that may lead to the revival of some of the earlier socialist concerns in the DDR: workers, seeing a worsening rather than an improvement of their conditions under capitalism; intellectuals, no longer split about the approach to a vanished party apparatus and still seeking a freedom that they find is curtailed in the West as well; and residents and neighborhood groups finding housing conditions and city life subject to new and hitherto unknown threats—all these may find in the forty years' history of the DDR some aspects worth preserving in their new situation.

part 2

UNIFICATION—MISSING MARKS?

Introduction: The Three Phases of Unification

To put the process of unification in perspective, let me first provide a brief overview of the major events before telling the story as we personally saw it from our vantage point in East Berlin.

March 19, 1990, was the effective end of an independent DDR. The CDU having won the election, the question became not whether but how full absorption of the East into the West would take place. As events were to prove, unification took place in three phases: the first involved preparing the political groundwork for virtually unconditional annexation—begun even before March 19, reinforced beyond cavil by the strong CDU showing and unquestioned CDU-SPD dominance in the local elections of May 8, 1990; the second phase prepared the economic groundwork for complete unification, and culminated in the currency union of July 1, 1990; the third phase was the formal and legal establishment of that economic domination through the imposition of West German law (according to the terms of the contract between the two German states of October 2, 1990). The upshot was the consummation of political unification, achieved in the all-German elections of December 2, 1990.

None of the winners of the DDR's March national election had any doubt as to why they won. Without the existence of the CDU in the West, the CDU in the East would have been just another "bloc party," a willing participant in the "Democratic Bloc" of political parties that governed the DDR, a willing accessory to SED rule for forty years, surrendering any potential independence in return for a few seats in the Volkskammer, a few mayoralty slots, a nice building and a newspaper and a hotel and a few other perks. Because of its affiliation with the West CDU, however, the East CDU had unlimited money, nationally known speakers, a polished political organiza-tion—and above all a claim to leadership in the East on the basis of existing power in the West. The implicit campaign theme was, "We've got it; if you want it, vote for us." The "it" was not so much lofty principle, freedom or equality or democracy, but, quite simply, Deutsche marks. There was no question that the CDU did have them, both as a political party and as the ruling party of a wealthy state. And there was no doubt that many DDR citizens wanted marks, feeling themselves unjustly deprived, and voted for the CDU to get them. And their rationale: if the DDR system had been a failure, let us go to the diametric opposite pole for a cure, was not without logic.

Much the same was true for the SPD. Without the SPD in the West, the SPD in the DDR would only have been a handful of dedicated malcontents, without a clear program, with few leaders (and none without some shadows over their pasts), and above all without the resources or skills to run a serious election campaign. Here, however, there was something more of an indigenous tradition to fall back on: before the war, Leipzig, Dresden, the industrial cities of southeastern Germany had been bulwarks of the SPD. But the strength of that tradition was much exaggerated in the original optimistic forecasts of SPD victory. Not only was the old tradition already at least fifty years behind the times; it was also tarnished with its association with the left, with socialism, with allusions to class and to welfare and to equality, exactly the rhetoric that most DDR voters had grown to distrust intensely over the recent decades.

What hurt the SPD in the East the most, however, was probably the weakness of its West German counterpart, which seemed to be more carping and back-biting and playing politics than offering a real alternative to unification on the CDU's terms.

The miserable showing of the groups that had initiated the *Wende* also had something to do with their relationship to the West: very simply, they had none. They received no money, no personnel, no publicity, no political counseling, nothing but constant verbal kudos. And they had no links to influence in the West that they could promise those who voted for them. The Greens got a little, but just a little, help from the Greens in the West; but because they had originally taken a principled position against Western interference in Eastern affairs, the West German Greens held back. And in any event, they were not that rich, were internally divided, and they could in no way represent power in the West: only principle.

So the March election, symbolically in the defeat of groups like New Forum that had been the champions of the *Wende* and politically in the victory of the pro-unification parties whose orientation was not to reform in the DDR but to join it with the West, signified the end of the *Wende* and the beginning of the march toward unification. The SPD entered into a grand coalition with the CDU, thus achieving the two-thirds majority in the Volkskammer needed to amend the DDR constitution and eliminate all possible legal obstacles to unification. A few of the more old-fashioned principled SPD leaders at first held back from such a coalition, but the charge that they were holding themselves back from the common work of unification became too much for them, and they joined. With hindsight, this might have been a mistake; had Western SPD politics established clearer policies or leadership, the Eastern SPD might have carved out a separate and attractive identity for itself. As it was, not many saw any particular reason to vote for it over the CDU.

The national elections produced a government that was able to "negotiate" the terms of unification—"negotiate" in quotes, because while they were legally and politically authorized to do so, they were hardly inclined to be tough bargainers, owing their positions as they did to Western help. Kohl and Bonn called the tune; De Maizière and his cabinet danced to it, occasionally grumbling, a very few times arguing, but never fighting.

So from mid-March to May there was a series of visits from Western officials to the East and vice versa, providing information and working out details of the merger of the two systems, department by department, agency by agency, industry by industry, institution by institution. West Germany was alas busy gaining the necessary international approval for the process; at international meetings, the DDR representatives tagged along, said yes to whatever West Germany proposed.

Various interest groups in the DDR tried to lobby for their own protection: enterprises, universities, academies, cities, the elderly, tenants, women, sportspeople, and others. They had a little influence in a few areas, but not much. Kohl knew the politically sensitive areas: pension payments to the retired, abortion, rents, for instance, and compromises were worked out on those, sometimes simply by deferring decisions or relegating them to lower levels of government. The process involved more West Germany deciding what it wanted to do than it did negotiating conflicting Eastern and Western interests.

New Forum, the citizens' movements, the Greens, the women's organization, protested loudly, eloquently, logically, at many of the decisions made by the CDU-SPD government, but to no avail. The PDS likewise objected, voting with the smaller parties perhaps more often than the latter liked, but between all of them they had less than a third of the votes and were thus effectively powerless.

The local elections, which took place in May and which some observers (including this one) had expected might reveal second thoughts about unification, as its concrete meaning became more evident, revealed no such thing. It simply confirmed the results of March; the PDS lost a little, the CDU gained a little, the SPD obtained a plurality in a few cities, East Berlin most notably, but the general trend toward subordination to the West German pattern and parties was maintained.

Thus the period after the March 1989 elections, after the end of the *Wende* represented the consolidation of West German rule in the East. The issue was no longer *whether* it would take place, but only how and when. The Article 23 issue was symbolic of the narrow range of remaining political alternatives. Article 23 of the Basic Law of the Federal Republic of Germany provides that the Basic Law may be applied to other German territories if they join Western Germany. That is the route Kohl and the conservatives in the DDR advocated. It therefore was, legally and symbolically, the West taking over the East, not two independent states negotiating a merger; it was not even the people of the two states voting to establish a single state, as the SPD advocated. The PDS took the position that a new constitution should be adopted by a popular vote after an agreement on the conditions of unification had been negotiated between the two states.

Thus, the opposition in general conceded the inevitability of union; only a few splinter groups on the left took a flat position against. A slower timetable, protection for existing East German rights, a "socially responsible" process, a new constitution and legislation combining the best of both systems, rather than a takeover of the West German model—this was the opposition platform. But it did not get far. The appeal to DDR loyalty, the evocation of a DDR "nationalism," fell on deaf ears. West German wealth and power were too strong, too attractive, the DDR past too tarnished.

The march to full unity thus went forward with scarcely a hitch. A first contract between the leaders of the two CDU governments of East and West Germany was signed in July. What is notable is that the issues being negotiated were economic: crudely, how capitalist principles of doing business—and, even more crudely, how Western capitalists—could operate in the DDR. Political issues were postponed until later, in fact until the signing of the Unification Agreement on October 3. The hope was that even before then West German capital could get in the door and begin to work. It was a hope not to be fulfilled, but that realization only came later.

The main debate in the late spring was about the ways in which the Deutsche mark would be introduced as the currency of East Germany. Economically, that was a *sine qua non* of unification; without it, West Germans investing in the East could not get their money out. The popular demand for a 1:1 exchange was only in part met (only the PDS and a few smaller parties had made it an official part of their platforms): up to 4,000 East marks per person could be exchanged for their equivalent in West marks; beyond that the rate was 2:1. Given that the black market rate had been hovering around 8:1, that didn't seem to be such a bad deal; but because East German businesses could only exchange at 2:1 and had to pay wages from then on at 1:1, the strain on businesses was substantial.

The events that followed the currency exchange, which went into effect July 1, were almost anticlimactic. The economic barriers to West German business penetration of the East were overcome with the currency union. That ended the second phase of unification and opened the financial door to unlimited economic penetration by West German firms into the economic system of the DDR.

In the third phase of unification, the remaining legal barriers to that penetration were addressed (although not all were resolved): in particular the two thorniest, the privatization of the firms through which the DDR's state economy was organized and the sale of publicly owned land in the DDR to private parties. For the former, a trusteeship was established in the DDR, given rights of "ownership" in all DDR-owned businesses, and mandated to sell them off. For the latter, the sale of real property, the claims of various private owners antedating the conversion to public ownership had to be dealt with, a process not yet complete, and the municipalities which came into control of previously nationally "owned" land often did not wish, or were not able, to sell off their holdings as quickly as a few West German investors wanted. Neither the sale of publicly owned enterprises nor the restoration of all property rights issued were to be resolved even until the date this is being written.

The other legal barriers were much simpler to deal with: East German law simply had to be made to correspond to that in the West. That was done in the second formal contract of unification, signed in October, which effectively annexed the East to the West under Article

23, and applied West German law to the territory of the former DDR, lock, stock, and barrel.

The rest consisted of complete political consolidation of the two states, and ran from the Contract of Unification of October to the all-German elections on December 2, 1990. After those elections there was a single administration and legislative body for the (former) two countries. The weaknesses of the opposition on both sides were manifested in the dismal showing in the December elections of the SPD, whose only criticism of Kohl's policies was that they were going too fast. Internationally, with what looked like a 7 billion mark pay-off to the Soviet Union, in any event in no position to object, and with multiple promises of good behavior toward its western allies and the United States, all the rights of the victors in the war against Hitler were abrogated; pundits raised questions as to who, when all was said and done, had actually won that war.

During this entire period, most people in the DDR, from conservatives to liberals to opposition, saw the serious problems visible in daily life as transitional, as being difficulties created by the complexities of unification and the time necessarily involved in achieving its fruits. With hindsight, now that more time has gone by and West German investment in the DDR has not reached anywhere near the levels that had been predicted, now that the costs of unification have been admitted to be grossly underestimated, now that the level of predicted unemployment in the DDR runs in the millions and indications of its reduction are nowhere in sight, now that the costs of environmental clean-up have been realistically assessed, the question may be asked whether political interests did not run way ahead of underlying economic interests. If the process of unification had slowed down after the currency union, if the DDR economy had in fact been allowed to coexist with investment opportunities desired (in what we now see as quite limited quantities) by the West in the East, the people of both territories might have been much better off. But that is speculative, and only time will tell how disastrous the situation in the DDR will become. The process of unification, which provides the backdrop for the following pages, gave evidence enough of problems in the future.

journal

THE FIRST PHASE:
THE WEST TAKES OVER

From the National to the Local Elections

March 20

Back to routine, the research on city development I'm theoretically here to do. A visit to Michael Breuer, state secretary (the top of the "civil service" administration in a ministry) at the ministry of building and housing. He had risen to be chief architect of Rostock under the old regime; whether he was a party member or not I don't know, but he was independent, fought for his city, dealt unbureaucratically with his own staff, and was widely respected among professionals West as well as East. He quickly came into prominence in the *Wende* as someone who combined high professional competence with reformist ideas. He will decide shortly whether to leave the ministry or not. If Elmer Pieroth is appointed minister of finance, a West Berliner, a businessman accused of shady dealings (a firm he was heavily involved in financially, doctored the wine it sold, he disclaimed knowledge), a convinced conservative and wheeler-dealer, but the person the CDU has suggested for the position—

Breuer will leave; it would symbolize the intention of the new ruling party to dismantle the entire housing and community planning structure that Breuer is committed to improving, not destroying.

De Maizière has been summoned to Bonn tomorrow; the announcement of when he's going—these West Germans have no shame at all—is made by the party head of the West CDU, Ruhe, casually at a street interview as he is leaving an "inspection visit" to Berlin. Asked whether the SDP will join a grand coalition government, he replies, in effect: They'd better. Poor De Maizière: yesterday evening he was on a TV discussion show with Henry Kissinger (by remote), Genscher, and others, and had to struggle to get in a word edgewise.

March 21

Fran's shopping survey, of all the supermarkets on the trolley line between the medical clinic she attends and Rosa Luxemburg Platz, showed substantial differences in the variety available. A result of social segregation, differential services for different neighborhoods, as we're used to in the United States? No; we're told by Wolfgang that it depends on the skill, tenacity, and willingness to tip the delivery men or the manager of the store. Hardly consistent with socialist theory but in part reassuring. The *Nomenklatura*, with the exception of the very top, live in privileged housing, but throughout the city; the buildings are segregated but the neighborhoods not, so the shopping is not.

Three hundred skinheads, after a football game yesterday, attacked a squatter-occupied house in Schönhauser Allee, threw stones, etc. Squatting is almost an institution in West Berlin, and has produced some decent housing by squatters doing self-help, as well as very progressive housing and rehabilitation policies in parts of the city, particularly Kreuzberg. The squatters in East Berlin have gotten help from friends in the West, and are by and large sincere, committed young people, often with anarchist political leanings, with unconventional life-styles but hardly criminal or irresponsible. But they violate some conventional mores, and the far right finds them a handy target to attack. The police declare themselves "over-taxed" and provide no protection for the occupants.

March 23

Anita Bach reports that there is deep uncertainty at the HAB in Weimar about prospective cuts in personnel. In earlier stages of the revolution, those teaching in sections of Marxism-Leninism—essentially what we would call the social sciences—felt threatened, with some reason; those sections were by and large dissolved, although in fact most were simply rechristened social science or something similar, and I do not think many people have been fired. That may of course be different soon. But Anita says the problem is not directly political. The student-faculty ratio is half that in West Germany, she says, not only in Weimar, but in the DDR generally. Why? Two reasons: professors here spend more time on their teaching, advising students (from what I hear of the care with which they work with doctoral students, I am very impressed—or perhaps ashamed of how little we generally do in the United States!), etc. The faculty are expected to be at their posts during the working week; not like the United States, or West Germany, where most professors consider themselves largely independent entrepreneurs and spend a minimum of time in their offices. That's the first reason for the high faculty-student ratio in the DDR. The second reason is the cumbersome and bloated administrative apparatus, the procedures to be followed, sign-offs required for any little thing, etc. That's something that shouldn't have existed to begin with, of course, and that even a purely democratic, non-Western-oriented revolution would (should) deal with.

March 24

Interview by Steffi Knopp of the *Wochenpost*. She's very interested in some comment about my father; she's gotten the one book of his she could out of the library here, but says he's little known, that neither the Frankfurt School nor the events of 1968 nor the Western student movement or new left are part of consciousness here. I told her I had seen the library cards stamped "Only for special access" in my father's books at the main library in Leipzig.

March 25

A talk this morning by Adel Karasholi, a Syrian-German poet, about the situation of foreigners in the DDR. "Syrian-German": only an American would use such a term. There are not hyphenated Germans in either Germany, East or West. There may be Germans from Poland, or from Hungary, or from Russia; and there may be Bavarian Germans, or Saxon Germans, or Germans from Thuringia. But they are Germans; that is an ethnic identity, based on ancestry, not place of birth. The law in West Germany entitling all "Germans" to admission and citizenship, in any of the prewar territory of Germany, is the legal reflection; it is based on parentage. Such a concept is inconceivable in the United States. Individual citizenship is based on the legal citizenship of the parents, and has nothing to do with ethnic origin. Even the long abandoned "melting pot" approach made "American" a matter of culture and values, not of ethnic origin.

The setting of the talk was also remarkable for us: the ornate Apollo room of the state opera house. Such spaces as these are what are needed to make a downtown function well as more than a commercial and business center.

The physical space reflects something of the ideological importance attached to such events as this talk; although this one was very sparsely attended, and then by a largely older and well-dressed crowd, the official importance of *Kunst und Kultur*, "art and culture", is very much greater than in the United States. When East Germans talk about what they bring to a united Germany, "culture" is always high on the list, and I think it is not only the normal DDR share of authors, playwrights, etc., that is meant, but also the public value placed on culture as a contribution per se.

The content of the talk was more consciousness-raising than analytic or programmatic. What we remembered were the first-hand anecdotes: Karasholi's being refused service in a plush hotel in downtown Berlin because he was not a hotel guest, when three Dutch visitors who walked in right after him were served immediately and without question; they were not "foreigners." The saleswoman who insisted on answering questions in pidgin German, although he asked questions fluently and speaks with almost no accent. The "Ausländer Raus" ("foreigners out") written in the snow on his car on Christmas morning. The teacher who called a blond, blue-eyed Syrian youngster with a long Arabic name, *schwarzer*, "blackie."

He deliberately stayed away from politics. He spoke clearly of the increasing scale of such actions, the depth and prevalence of prejudice, and near panic in many communities in the last few months as it has spread—newly locked front doors, organized community watches, advice not to go out alone in the evening—but without purporting to explain. I commented briefly in the discussion about the likely connection to a chauvinistic arrogance particularly strong in West Germany, at least with people like Kohl, whose whole bearing is domineering, but it was the last comment made, so no response.

The role of the police also brought interesting comment. The moderator, from the ministry of culture, commented afterward innocently that he hoped that the full force of the law would be used to avoid hostile incidents, and that the police would control things like the recent Leipzig demos better to stop the attacks on foreigners that were taking place on their fringes. The person who had introduced the speaker took exception, protesting that this opened the door to Stasi-like control tactics. The speaker apologized immediately. It reminded me of the "the state is incompatible with democracy" hypothesis at the Moscow conference, and I later spoke of the importance of legislation, and of its enforcement, both in restraining hostile action and as a means of education. The somewhat myopic but understandable anti-state stance of many, after forty years of Stalinism, is deeply ingrained.

March 26

An appointment in the afternoon with someone from the city planning office who had met me at a talk in West Berlin, where I had said that West Germans could learn something from the East. There were six people present when I arrived, and I was astonished at their questions: essentially they wanted an outside opinion of what they were doing—what was good, what bad, what we call a brain-storming session. They asked, for instance, whether, in the light of all the criticisms they have recently heard of the anonymous large industrially constructed estates, I thought their whole building policy under the 1973 building program was wrong. And they really wanted to know! I said, no, what was wrong was that it was *all* that was done, that had it been part of a policy in which there was also rehabilitation, small-scale construction, etc., it would have been fine—and that some of the criticism of what was bad about prefab construction was more a criticism of shortages of materials and appliances than of their planning work.

The discussion was wide-ranging and very open. They asked about ownership; I advocated continued public (municipal) ownership, but with resident participation in management decisions, decentralized administration, democratic public discussion and control over plans and changes. They asked about co-ops; when I said I saw co-ops without resale restrictions as identical with privatization, they were surprised but quickly convinced. They have simply never seen private co-ops in action. We agreed that a *Sperrklausel*, a prohibition against resale with profit, was desirable; I explained how they worked in New York City. They asked about *Wohngeld*, "housing allowances"; I said fine *if* most of the market was in the public domain, but not if the bulk of the market was private, in which case *Wohngeld* would only increase the profits of private landlords. We talked of speculation, private vs. public building companies, taxes, rent control, etc. For me, a fascinating discussion.

At the end, they said, essentially to each other, that they needed to find some method of discussing and recommending policy among themselves (I had commented that I had discussed similar subjects with others in other departments and ministries, who knew nothing of them), that there was a policy vacuum that was dangerous. One of the many defects of a hierarchical administrative structure is that information goes up (and perhaps down) the line of command, but not across it.

Watched Marcel Ophuls' Barbie film last night. Fascinating, technically and substantively. The film exposes, quietly but all the more effectively, the rationalizations people used afterward to justify their Nazi or collaborationist activities: everyone did it, we were gentler than others would have been, let bygones be bygones, I did it for my country. In the DDR these issues have never been faced; the Nazis were someone else, the DDR was always anti-Nazi and Communist, it has nothing in its own past to examine or understand.

March 27

Went to a conference of the Society for Social Policy, at the Academy of Sciences. The report dealt with social services, including kindergartens, child care, recreational facilities.

I had not realized how large a part of such services were organized through enterprises, by employers for/with their employees. We had noticed in the Soviet Union that the cafeterias also sold groceries, that employers held yoga classes, etc., but thought of those as either compensation for a lack of "normal" provisioning or as marginal. But the system is well developed here, and eminently logical: child care at work, health care, including polyclinics, at large factories, vacation homes provided by employers, and on and on. It reflects the centrality of the workplace in everyday life, and a direct connection between work and leisure, or work and the rest of life, that makes psychological as well as logistical sense. If enterprises are organized solely for profit, this is all wasted money for them.

March 28

Skilled workers, plumbers, electricians, are postponing as much contract work as they can because they figure the Deutsche mark will be introduced soon and they'll get paid more; until then they're working slack as much as they can. The housing administration sends an electrician to look at a modernization job; he comes, looks, and is about to leave; he's asked by the tenant what happens next, he shrugs and says it's not in his hands, tries to leave again; is pressed, says they'll probably come back to lay out the work. Two weeks later he reappears, makes eight chalk marks on the wall in five minutes for where the outlets should go, leaves again. That was a month ago; no action since then.

> A man comes to order a Trabant [*see photo next page*], for the delivery of which, he is told, there is a ten-year wait.
> All right, he says, but just when will it come?
> In 1988, he is told.
> What month?
> April, probably.
> What day?
> Well, if it's that important to you, we'll put it down for April 15.
> In the morning or afternoon?
> For goodness sake, why do you have to know so precisely?
> Because the plumber promised to come in the morning!

That was an old story. The situation now has other causes.

Employers are now refusing to hire mothers with small children at home, or pregnant women; they are laying off foreign workers before "Germans"; they are closing, or planning to close, health facilities, day-care centers, etc., that they have previously subsidized. They are doing all this because they are preparing to be "competitive," to compete with firms that have no social obligations and are bound by less demanding laws. The laws of the DDR have not changed; no big fight to repeal them was mounted; employers just ignore them, and get away with it, because they "have to." Who makes them? No single person, no party or institution; the force is internalized, and all the more difficult to fight.

The discussion came up at supper last night, with Erika Planitza, the sister of a friend of ours in New York, a pediatrician living on Leipziger Strasse, her son-in-law, a philosophy graduate, and several other friends. They were all deeply depressed; no one knew what was going to happen, but it looked bad, as if the CDU victory had swept away all they had struggled and hoped for over the years. For us, the tone of the discussion was discordant: it was passive, others were doing bad things, others should do good things, no one was taking charge, the future was so uncertain. It's unfair of us, as outsiders, to criticize this fear of uncertainty; we live in a prosperous society, we have no personal fears of falling through our own safety net. It's not so much the fear of uncertainty, however, but the passive reaction to it, that bothers us. We formulated it last night (with them) as a lack of experience at competing, an immaturity (*entmündigung*) perpetrated by a system in which choices only needed to be made, only could be made, within a very narrow range, and competitiveness was never called for.

But on reflection I don't think that's the right formulation—or substance. It's not that the DDR has been a planned society with too much security, or that the desire to plan and be secure are bad values; planning and security are good things, and don't contradict self-reli-

ance or initiative. It's that the DDR (as a country? as a ruling party? as a ruling hierarchy?) has not had a purpose, a vision, a goal, other than preserving its own rule, i.e., stability, with no boat-rocking. There's been no struggle to improve things, build a new and different life, help third world countries, try out more democratic forms, experiment with life styles, forms of economic organization, even technical solutions. People have forgotten how to struggle, how to fight, even how to figure out what to fight for. That's what's missing: not competitiveness, but a fighting spirit.

We learn little things about the DDR everyday. Erika is going to take six months off, at 70 percent of her pay, to take care of her daughter's six-month-old baby so the daughter can study. That's provided for in the law! It seems a really civilized idea.

Meeting at the Cultural Workers' Club. This was a panel discussion on "The Future of Berlin: From Confrontation to Cooperation." The place was mobbed; the room was not the expected one, too full, too hot, tables weren't removed, etc. There was an entry fee, according to the plan and the tickets and the announcements, but no one remembered to have someone there to collect it—so they didn't. Market thinking doesn't come easily, fortunately!

One theme was East/West; plans are still being made in the West without consultation with the East, the new competition for Potsdamer Platz, a central area right at the border between East and West Berlin, was done exclusively in the West, etc. Agitation about that, but I think outdated. A man who works for city planning in East Berlin reported on the thinking of the unofficial regional committee for Berlin. He spoke of planning for a greater Berlin, on the assumption that Berlin will be the capital of a reunited Germany. He described its advantages at the center of the axis from Moscow to Paris and from Stockholm to Italy. My blood curdled at the prospect of a new Germany dominating Europe that he conjured up. Fortunately, Bruno Flierl said approximately what I felt as soon as the man had finished; the response was that he was only reporting the thinking of the committee. The basic conflict, as I said in the discussion, is between the use of the city to meet the needs of its residents, and the use of the city to meet the needs of international business and ambitious politics. But people continue to focus on Potsdamer Platz. It's the standard tactic: divide up the big question into a set of little ones, let them win some of the little ones and lose the big one.

Argument about the Wall; I think it should be treated in separate pieces, according to where it is, in the middle of the city, Brandenburger Tor to Potsdamer Platz, it should be salted and left barren, like Carthage; a combined remembrance of Fascism and the Cold War. Excurs 5 below gives more of the argument.

March 29

To Rostock by train to give a talk at the Wilhelm Pieck University. They're already beginning to describe it as "Rostock University"; will there now be a political test for the dead namesakes of schools, streets, airports, parks? Ah, well; one has to admit they overdid it a little. We love Rosa Luxemburg, but every city doesn't have to have a Rosa Luxemburg Strasse!

The congress hall, or convention center, near the railroad station in Rostock is a *Schwarzbau*, Peter Voigt told us. What's a *Schwartzbau*, we asked? The direct translation is "black construction." in the sense of "black market. Why? because it was built although it's not in the plan. At first I thought of the boat in the Moscow reservoir, but that's "black" in a different sense, much more akin to self-help, privately done, off the record. A congress center is a huge thing, very visible and designed to be prominent; nothing "off the record" about it. The analogy is much more to the mural in the train station in Dessau that we had first seen August 29. The SED leadership in Rostock simply decided it ought to be done, and they bludgeoned everyone into doing it even though it meant unceremoniously violating—"amending"— the plan.

The afternoon lecture went well; slides of New York, questions and answers.

The evening discussion was quite different. It was supposed to be about student life in the United States, but picking up on Fran's earlier refusal to be drawn into trivia, even if it was explicitly asked, I talked about the organization of higher education in the United States, the peculiarities of a private system, the students' worries about jobs, the lack of room for curiosity, the impact of military research and the dependence on contracts, the presumptions about the "naturalness" of the private market, the current debates about ideology. General surprise; they had thought that America was a "free," nonideological country. But they liked the ability to postpone decisions as to careers until much later in school.

March 30

A new book has just come out with extracts from some of the estimated eighteen kilometers of papers put under seal in the Stasi archives, but it sells out as soon as it arrives anywhere, and we've only been able to see excerpts in the newspapers. The book is classic *Bück-waren*, "stoop goods." Stoop goods are a minor but symbolic characteristic of the DDR way of life. They are the goods in short supply, like the Stasi book, which, when they arrive in a store are put under the counter by the shopkeeper for his or her special customers; the shopkeeper has to stoop to get them out. The shortages that lead to such practices are (at least historically) characteristic of East European socialist countries. The adaptation to such shortages by reserving and stooping, rather than selling on the black market, is characteristic of the DDR: a nonmercenary evasion of the centralized system, which hardly deserves to be called corruption, but certainly "irregular" from the point of view of the state. Not the market, but personal relations, soften the impact of central controls.

Trabant joke, new version:

> Walter drives a new Trabant; he doesn't have the money to buy a used car, he says.

You used to have to wait ten years for a new car, since demand didn't affect supply. Now, with used cars coming in from the West to meet an almost insatiable demand, you can get a new and heavily subsidized Trabant right away; in fact, they're afraid they won't be able to sell what they have produced and are cutting back on production.

April 1

In Hamburg with the Voigts from Rostock. Reflection on how odd it is that we, Americans from 3,000 miles away, are showing a West German city to the Voigts, who live 150 miles away but have never been there.

Reflections also on consumptionism: Heidi Voigt, principled, committed to the ideals of the DDR, but little traveled, fascinated by the range of consumer goods available, buying herself a little colorful vest she couldn't get in Rostock, loving the window shopping, but also repelled by the same consumerism, preferring life back home.

April 2

Arrived in Budapest. A great deal of uncertainty about the future here too, but a very different feeling from the DDR. Here it's simply uncertainty about the future, but it's a quantitative change, not a qualitative one, that's expected. There's always been a significant private sector in the economy. In housing, for example, an active private market, with private construction, etc., always existed side by side with the public sector.

In the DDR, the feeling is quite different. Something entirely new is coming, is anticipated with some uncertainty, feared in many places. Things are not under the country's own control. It is more as if there is going to be an invasion, an occupation by a foreign power, peaceful perhaps, friendly even, but definitely foreign, and definitely taking decision-making away from the locals. The Hungarians don't feel this: Hungary is and will remain their country, and they will be making their own decisions, right or wrong.

April 3

Discussion at the institute of town planning in Budapest, previously ministry-supported but now working under contract for towns, regions, the ministry, even private parties. Before it had five hundred professional members; now it has three hundred: each is required to produce ten times his or her annual salary each year in contracts, to cover overhead, etc. When capitalism comes, it comes with a vengeance!

I gave a talk dealing with gentrification and my expectations for Budapest. Agreement on the analysis and the trends, but the surprising question raised: were there enough yuppies in Hungary to make a difference? The argument: Hungary was still essentially early industrial in its economy, yuppies are a product of a postindustrial society, therefore they will not arrive on the scene for some time. I argued that internationalization of the economy would produce a yuppie class not based on their role in national production, but in distribution and in internationally based services, tourism, commerce, etc. But the point is interesting in its relation to the DDR: I think, for some time to come, the yuppies, and the gentrification, will be West German-led, not DDR people "making it," and will lead to tensions all the more severe because they will be West/East tensions as well as class and residential tensions.

April 4

The market is supposed to correlate supply and demand; in a planned economy, the plan does. Thus when they don't correlate, planning is blamed. An empty office building stands in the middle of Budapest; the ministry of construction's plan was not integrated with the plans of those ministries that might provide the occupants. The same in Leipzig when the university tower was built, and essentially the same with the high-rises around Alexanderplatz; the occupants had to be searched for, and the buildings were not ideally designed for their ultimate users. But is it planning per se that is to blame? Or merely poor planning? The general perception doesn't separate the two:

> A lion escapes from the zoo, is not found for fourteen days, then is suddenly brought back to his cage. A fellow lion asks her, "How did you get along for so long without being noticed? What did you live on? How were you caught?"
>
> "Oh, it was easy for a while," the escapee replied. "I got into the Central Planning Commission building and each day I ate one of the commission members, and nobody ever noticed. But then by mistake I ate the cleaning lady, and they hunted me down and put me back in here."

Certainly a market doesn't solve the problem; look at the office tower in Frankfurt that has been empty for many years, the 16 percent vacancy rate in New York City's new office buildings, etc.

The latest scandal in Hungary is perhaps a foretaste of what may happen in the DDR. The Socialist Party, the reformed old Communist Party, has just sold four major regional newspapers to Springer Verlag, the most reactionary and vicious of the big West German media giants. The party first formed a private corporation to which it transferred the papers, and it then sold them to Springer; no one knows where the proceeds of the sale will go. The old Stalinists are the first to get into the private market game, partly because they hold the power and control the assets, partly because they have few scruples about going with the tide for their own benefit.

The worry about not enough gentrifiers seems serious enough here; I visited the upscale supermarket that replaced the old market hall next to Klauzel Ter, the center of planned and initially subsidized (the money has run out) gentrification. But the demand wasn't there and they had to reconvert half the space into a down-scale farmers' market. Which is worse, too little or too much gentrification? Many Hungarians envy the DDR; the ex-socialist Germans, they say, at least have someone who wants to buy their country; Hungary is up for sale but no one wants to buy. That's of course exaggerated, but reflects a real difference in the two situations.

April 9

A central defense of the DDR's housing policy has been that it fosters a "socialist way of life"; Fred Staufenbiel's several studies of cities in the DDR all start with several sets of quotes from authoritative sources—e.g., the Central Committee of the SED or Honecker—as to what a "socialist way of life" is supposed to be. Authority or not, the content of the definitions of the "socialist way of life" never made much sense; they included being kind to the elderly, having a rich cultural life, being healthy, raising children in a supportive environment—what nonsocialists would disagree? The word that's used these days by those concerned with the positive values in the DDR is "solidarity," as in "a society of solidarity."

What brings all this to mind is a side comment by one of the Czech participants at the Budapest meeting. He had just visited West Berlin for the first time, at a conference that was attended by some 400 people, maybe 300 West, 100 East Germans. He and one or two other Eastern Europeans had been told in advance not to worry about accommodations, they would be put up privately. And indeed at the end of the first day of the conference the chairperson asked for volunteers to put up Eastern visitors overnight. Six people raised their hands, and the Czech found a suitable host. In *East* Berlin! It turned out that every one of those volunteering was from the DDR.

April 11

A phone call from a person I didn't know, a Michael Plötschke, asking if I wanted to meet with Professor Steinitz, the head of the PDS commission on the economy, at 3:00 p.m. today; Thomas Simon, of the Liga, the Society for Friendship Among Peoples, had suggested it. Certainly I did.

The meeting was in the building that had been the seat of the Central Committee of the SED. The monstrous hulk in the center of the government quarter of the city, behind the new ministry of foreign affairs, walking distance to the Palace of the Republic, having been built in 1936 by the National Socialists as the headquarters of the national bank, we noted how appropriate it was that the seat of real power was in the same building before and after the war, although formal power both times was elsewhere!

Half of the building had already been given over to other uses, the Jewish Cultural Association, for instance, which we had visited a month ago, but the PDS had used the big hall for their election returns affair and in the last few weeks the building had been livened up with banners, pictures, signs, posters, so that it looked almost human. The CDU and the SPD wanted the building for their representatives in the Chamber of Deputies, who had never before needed an office, and for the various party representatives' offices, again a new need. The PDS had said yes, since they agreed that the building belonged to the state, but please wait until they had a chance to move to another party building. Agreed; but then a problem of title to that building turned up, and the move was delayed. Finally, the week before the Chamber of Deputies was to meet, the PDS was given three days' notice to move. They left, reluctantly taking down all the indicia of their change of tone from the walls, the paintings on the front, etc. They still had a few offices on the fourth floor, and a little desk in the lobby: a sorry comedown.

The social relations within the old SED must have been incongruous, and some of them survive: an odd mix of Communist comradeship, German order, and hierarchical power. I was met in the lobby by Plötschke, a pleasant young man, and taken up to Steinitz's office. How things worked in the old days was clear from the setting: an anteroom, then a secretarial room, and then a huge office, a desk with a huge conference table, with places for thirty or forty people (could it have survived from Schacht's times at the bank?), a view of tulip beds out the huge windows—all together as representative of domination in its way as any feudal palace.

Coffee was served by a very polite and friendly secretary from china cups. Steinitz was still at a meeting of the parliamentary caucus of the PDS, so we went in with a Rolf Kühnert, a member of the executive committee of the party, and talked while we waited. The social relationships were odd: Michael and Rolf used the familiar form of address to each other, as comrades, although they had never met before, and Steinitz did also when he walked in, but when Kühnert had to leave he asked Steinitz if we might be "permitted" to remain, a formal request that apparently came naturally to him but seemed to me very out of place within a comradely organization—but very in place in the room and the building and the old SED.

The substance of the discussion was not striking. I told of some of the pitfalls of the free market in housing as we had encountered them in the United States—homelessness, staggering rents, segregation, congestion—and spoke of some of the difficulties of implementing government decentralization, with its resulting intercity rivalries. He described the programmatic proposals of the PDS; quite sophisticated, including commitments to decentralize communal decision-making but include equalization provisions on the distribution of tax revenues to help cities in difficulty. The program is described in a pamphlet that is part of a series called *Discussionsangebote,* or "Offers for Discussion," an effort to have positions discussed democratically within the party before they are adopted. But they of course have encountered the obvious problems of democracy; were they to wait to take positions until a full internal democratic discussion had taken place, they would lose all political momentum. So they fudged it; their program gets discussed in parallel with its public presentation as the official party position. Certainly a very competent program, from a party that might have built a democratic and social government; but it won't have that chance anymore. Had it reformed itself on its own initiative, something might still have been possible; once it lost the initiative in November/December (to Kohl, not to the opposition), its future powerlessness was assured.

The mood was one of matter-of-fact pessimism tinged with sadness, but not with nostalgia. Michael Plötschke had started studying physics and wanted to become an atomic scientist, but, after a year, he said, it was clear they didn't need more atomic scientists (or perhaps he wasn't a top one), and he decided to pursue another interest, foreign affairs. The place you did that, in SED Germany, was the College for Government and Public Law, where he studied for five years, then served in the DDR embassy in Washington. Then he moved over to the international relations division of the PDS; he didn't know his way around the building yet. Now he's uncertain about his future; he'd like to go back into the foreign service, he really liked the United States, but he doesn't know whether there will be a new *Berufsverbot*—the West German legislation prohibiting Communists from working in the civil service, applying to him, or not. A decent and effective person; I think he would serve any civilized government well. But that's not the criterion likely to be used.

The pessimism and sadness ran not only to the exclusion anticipated from the new government; it also related to the attitude of the other left and oppositional parties. Weiss's withdrawal from the Easter march had just been announced; they felt it typical of the undeserved and purposeless hostility of many of their natural allies against the PDS. They understood the causes; as Kühnert said, in describing an article on the elections by someone from New Forum, when they spoke of Kohl benefiting from the results of forty years of Honecker and his like, they were right. But when Gysi went over to the headquarters of the citizens' movements on election night to express solidarity with New Forum and the other pioneers of the October revolution, he came back completely shattered; the opposition was embittered and blamed the PDS for its defeat. It's a depth of bitterness and hostility that's hard to understand; I want to make a concerted effort to find some people who take this view to see if I can get a handle on it.

On the way home I stopped by to pick up a pair of pants that I had left so that the pockets could be replaced. They were left at an *Annahme*, a "pick-up place," where everything from laundry to shoes to umbrellas go for repairs; they are sent on to the appropriate repair facility, then returned. The pants were back, with a little note: "These pockets can't be fixed. Please return them with material for new pockets. Please undo the sewing that was done to try to fix them." If I were to do a *Berufsverbot* for anyone, it would be for the person who wrote that! And they expect to be able to compete???

April 12

To the doctor's again, because our grandson broke the bottle with the pills for Fran's knees; splinters of glass mixed with the pills and all had to be thrown away. This time we went to the local medical practice, the second floor of an older apartment house, perhaps six rooms, two doctors, two nurses; no appointments possible, but we were in within five minutes. A pleasant young woman doctor, friendly and businesslike, took our blood pressure although she could just have prescribed, and we chatted a bit. She talks to Fran, examines her, gives her a new prescription. My pulse is slow; she'll send me for an EKG, do blood tests only if the EKG gives cause for concern. All is free; the decision has nothing to do with money or cost. Not an economical approach, she admits, but it provides good health care. She says she could theoretically get us a bill so we could reimburse from our insurance, but the rates would still be very low and the paperwork wouldn't be worth it.

All her West German colleagues are telling her that fee-for-service is the only way to go, but she doesn't like the idea: a lot more bookkeeping, a commercial instead of a personal relationship with patients. But it's coming, she's sure. And it will improve some things: some of her colleagues will work harder when there's something directly in it for them, some of her patients won't come, particularly the elderly ones, just to talk, when there's nothing really wrong. Of course, the talking does good too, and it lets the doctor get to know the patient.

Some change is noticeable already: younger people are less likely to come in to get written up as sick, not because they will have to pay but because they're afraid it will hurt them at work, and unemployment is now a real threat.

So capitalism in the medical care system will correct some abuses, but at the same time will take the heart out of a set of noncommercial relations that were at their best really human and desirable.

Thomas Simon (his wife is a doctor) later gave me some gross measures of what the doctor at the medical practice had told us: a 30 percent reduction in patient visits, because people are afraid to take time off from work. If a child is just a little sick, the mother will take it to kindergarten anyway, not take the day or week off because she is afraid she may lose her job. Doctors in Prenslauer Berg, a mixed community with many singles, young people, alternative types, poor people, see an average of seventy a day, often having trouble finding time for lunch; in middle-class or single-family home areas, they may see twenty. But doctors in middle-class areas are now worried that they will not be able to make the fee-for-service arrangement pay. Many doctors have left for the West, but there are no long waits for appointments (our experience was typical) because fewer patients are coming in, many doctors are working harder, and some of the medical bureaucrats are treating patients again, as a result of political changes.

April 13

We went on a visit to the Staufenbiels. They live in a double apartment on the tenth floor of a new (late 1960s) highrise on Hans-Loch-Strasse. The rooms are generous to begin with, but they were able to get a double apartment because of the number of people in their household when they moved in: six at the time. Now they have only three, but still the same apartment. That's the famous misallocation problem. It's almost system-independent. The problem, large families in small units, small households in large units, is considered one of the most serious current problems in social housing in West Germany. It's the same problem many older people have in the United States, living in single family houses that are much too big for them, hard to take care of, and expensive; but they've lived there all their lives and don't want to leave. Here the problem is less for the individuals, because rents are so low, and maintenance is essentially public; but the misallocation, socially viewed, is the same. The only real answer is to provide a more attractive alternative to the empty nesters, and that requires a surplus of housing of a standard, and at a price, that no society has yet been able to afford, or at least to produce under its existing housing system. Raising the price is no answer, although it's a practical one: it's using penalties rather than better options to resolve the problem.

The new cabinet is announced. Only two things remarkable to our eyes: 13 out of 24 have Ph.D.'s (estimates are that 80 percent of the PDS candidates have advanced degrees), and only 3 are women, and then only in secondary or stereotypical "women's fields": Family and Women, Youth and Sports, and Commerce and Tourism. Both are European cultural phenomena rather than just DDR. Professional competence has always held a higher political value here than in the United States, partly from a belief in rationality and the usefulness of technical knowledge to solve issues we would consider overwhelmingly political, i.e., interest or value conflicts, partly because higher education is considered an accompaniment of status. The frontier mentality, anyone can get rich on their native intelligence and/or hard work, all doors are open, is a typically American attitude; the rest of the world knows better. Three out of 24 slots for women is not disproportionate to United States experience; we would expect a little more criticism, or at least commentary.

[Later information: 25 percent of the CDU representatives in the Volkskammer have doctoral degrees, 33 percent of the PDS's. None of the Liberals are women; 24 percent of the SPD, 15 percent of the CDU, 42 percent of the PDS, and three out of eight of the Green/Independent Women's coalition are. In the last case, of course, it was the election law and the stubbornness of the Greens that prevented the expected minimum of 50 percent women from being reached; in the joint lists that the Greens/Independent Women put together in each district, a Green was always in the No. 1 spot, an Independent Woman in the No. 2. Since they nowhere got enough votes to get two spots in any one district, they ended up with all Greens in the Volkskammer, three of whom happened to be women. The Greens then refused to give up any of their seats to their coalition allies—which in turn led to the dissolution of the coalition.

[In the United States, by contrast, 22 of 436 representatives are women—5 percent—and 1 of 100 Senators. Ph D.'s, on the other hand, can't be calculated; the official statistics, characteristically, only give occupation in phrases like "agriculture," so one can't tell whether a person is a tenant farmer or a multimillionaire absentee landowner.]

Bruno Flierl and Lili Leder came over for supper, carrying a bouquet of flowers for each of "our three women" (Fran, our daughter Irene, and our daughter's child, Tabitha). Bruno has just, to his surprise, gotten a four-week reservation at one of the Cultural Workers' Club summer homes on the Baltic coast. Everyone had assumed the Western invasion would have meant no vacancies anywhere. It's not quite clear whether these units were simply bound by contracts signed before the *Wende* or whether the Western demand hasn't been as great as anticipated, or whether many people simply prefer the old arrangement. It was in any event a real benefit of life in the DDR: vacation places were socially distributed, not subject to market competition, purchase, and sale to the highest bidder.

April 16

To Ina Merkel's with the whole family for an evening's talk. She lives with Thomas Flierl and they have two children, 13 and 7. She has been a spokeswoman for the UFV (the Independent Women's Federation) very outspoken and sharp, a guest on many talk shows, interviews, etc. In her early thirties, she is clearly a member of the intelligentsia. The apartment an old building, 1890s perhaps, in sad disrepair on the outside but still showing that it was once middle-class housing, with curved staircases, multi-room apartments, decent-sized rooms. It is well fixed up, bookcases, hi-fi, computer on the desk in the living room (no separate work-room/study available). The children, by American standards, were extraordinarily well behaved, greeted each of us at the door, came in to shake hands with everyone when they went to bed; nice, but (and?) German.

The conversation turned very quickly, as I had hoped, to the question of the relationship between the PDS and other groups. I asked why the resistance to working with the PDS in a common opposition. Her answers were clearly deeply felt. I list them, but they were all part of a single discussion:

- The PDS had never undertaken self-criticism; it simply assumed it was a new party, gave lip-service to "responsibility for the past," but never more. (An analogy, perhaps, to the failure to come to terms with the Nazi past? A complicated question. Who has the responsibility? The individuals who were in the SED before, certainly, as individuals. The party, to the extent it considers itself the continuation, or at least heir, of the old.)
- The PDS is opportunistic: on the question of abortion, at the national Round Table, it was PDS women who insisted on removing the most explicit definition of women's rights, although they had agreed in principle on the entire statement. It sends its representatives to church when it thinks that will look good politically.
- It's not democratic; decisions like the one to go to church should have been discussed, the UFV goes to great lengths to try to have grass roots democracy, the PDS acts like a party used to direction from the top.
- Old personnel are still in many party offices, particularly locally.
- In its dealings it uses power. It still sends the UFV bills for rent for its offices, although Gysi promised they would be rent free. They haven't paid yet, and won't, but don't like getting the bills and having to keep protesting.
- They screwed up the one chance that existed for a durable DDR legacy, through Modrow's inaction and weakness, and then capitulation to the German Unification hysteria. Modrow also held back for an unconscionably long time in recognizing the Round Table as an element of government, and in dissolving the Stasi. Nor did the PDS ever criticize the Modrow regime.
- They were more concerned with their party's position than with what happened in the country. On election night, they were elated with the results because they did better than expected; the UFV, on the other hand, were depressed because of the conservative victory more than because of their own loss.

The criticisms are very understandable, although some issues are more complicated (the role of the Round Table, for instance); but the main reaction we had was that she had an abstract expectation of what the PDS should/could do that was not realistic, that much of what she was criticizing was inevitable (that the party should try to maintain its income, that it should "play politics," that it should emphasize the new over laying out the old). Running through the discussion was the image of the large, rich, powerful PDS playing hardball in the big leagues, in comparison with the young, poor, struggling, idealistic UFV, consigned to playing softball in the countryside. The image isn't wrong; the question is simply, how should the two relate to each other? Clearly the initiative should have come from the PDS; but signals could also have been given that it would be well received.

April 17

A dark day, with storm clouds. Outside our window is a construction storage facility: piles of sand and cinderblocks, storage sheds, toilets. Two streetlights on tall poles make it usable early in the morning or at twilight. Those lights have been on, day and night, since we moved in. No one has the incentive to turn them off? Or knows how? On a dark day, they're a conspicuous symbol of something!

A taxi to a meeting in West Berlin. East taxis don't like to cross the border; they charge by distance, and if they have to wait at the crossing they lose money. Why not charge for waiting? Their meters aren't set that way. Why not a flat charge for crossing? It's not regulated that way. Why not informally? That's not sanctioned. Tell that story to someone in Poland!

Supper with Andrée Fischer, from Dietz Verlag, who wants to publish our diary. It remains "owned" by the PDS. In Western terms, the ownership relationship is weird; Dietz is not a separate corporation whose stock is owned by the PDS, there is no legal entity recognizable as Dietz; it is simply "part of" the PDS. They are now trying to establish their independence, which involves, since they operate at a loss, bringing in some profit-making books, in a new entity they want to form, one that will publish belles-lettres. Which is where we fit in, presumably. Fran is concerned that they will be tempted to take whatever we give them, regardless of quality, assuming that they can sell it on the basis of the name and the subject. Is it co-optation of us? No and yes—no since we can say what we want, including criticism of the PDS; yes since many more people will see our names on the publication list than will ever read a line of what we have written, and will take our appearance as a form of endorsement. Fran sees this as a form of unconscious exploitation by Dietz—and of course she is right. We need to deal with it in two ways (presuming we go forward with publication with Dietz, to which I think we are in good conscience committed since they suggested the idea): our own concern for quality in what we are writing, including editing, omitting trivia, careful judgments; and perhaps an explicit discussion of the issue in a foreword of some sort.

Andrée's background is interesting: Jewish, born in exile in France, early childhood in Mexico, to the DDR in 1947, a committed socialist and an SED member, she has struggled with the SED bureaucracy and attempted to defend the integrity of Dietz over many years, and feels a strong loyalty to it now. She is noticeably without bearings under the new circumstances; the eternal world is changing unpredictably, her internal values are shaken, the locus of discussion (and of fighting, for that matter) has been removed, she feels she can only wait and see what others will do, and in the meantime try in little ways (like helping to found the subsidiary) to prepare. She has even considered picking up on her Jewish identity, and went once or twice to the Jewish Cultural Association, but she didn't pursue it further. Left-PDS relations are an inevitable topic of conversation. She is shocked at the bitterness people like Konrad Weiss feel toward the PDS. She tells the story of waiting on line after the war and hearing a woman near her express sympathy with poor Göring, who now was having such a bad time of it. No one expresses such sympathy for the deposed SED leaders, as the elderly and sick Honecker found out when he tried to move to a normal small community and people lined the streets banging on the car he was in, telling him to keep out.

The generation gap may also make a difference. We have lived through the beginning of the Cold War, with its McCarthyism. Out of that experience comes an instinctive distrust of those who dwell on the evils of Communism, at the expense of united action against the right. Many criticisms of Communist parties and their actions were justified; but the question is rather one of priorities and the differentiation between internal disagreements and class enemies. As Andrée argued, the SPD was probably guilty of as virulent anti-Communist, and anti-working-class, actions in the period after World War I as any right-wing party, including military oppression. She told the story, apparently well-documented but unknown to us, of the joint Communist-Social Democratic governments in Saxony and Thuringia after World War I, in reaction to which the German SDP expelled every SDP party member who had participated. Yet the SPD remained a party of the working class, and thus should be treated differently from a right-wing party.

Who the members are is therefore not decisive; the CDU probably has overwhelmingly working-class members in the DDR too. The question is how the party sees itself. Those now in their thirties, the Ina Merkels and Konrad Weisses, did not go through these historical experiences; their overwhelming experience was oppression by the PDS. That there is no chance of that role continuing, not so much because the PDS is reformed but because it has been denied any access to state power, is a realization that will only come with time. In that sense, it was easier in the United States; in the civil rights and anti-Vietnam movements, anti-communism might have lurked in some corners, but was seldom an issue; few in the movements were asked where they came from, only where they were going.

April 18

By coincidence the draft of the contract for unification is printed in *Neues Deutschland* on the same day as the text of the new constitution for the DDR proposed by the last Round Table. The contrast is striking. In the Contract it is not only proposed that any reference to socialism be taken out of any law in the DDR, but also that the principle of "the priority of private business activity" be established: the private comes first, the public should "interfere as little as possible. The only constraints on private business activity are that it be undertaken in "good conscience, with faith and honesty." As for social consequences: the economically weak should be protected from "inappropriate disadvantage." Appropriate disadvantages, of course, are all right.

The draft constitution, on the other hand, continues a long-standing DDR (actually, socialist) tradition of distinguishing between personal and business ownership. Rights of personal ownership and use are guaranteed against state interference, in a manner parallel to that of the Contract, but for business uses, the public welfare comes first. Ecological considerations must be respected, cities and the state are authorized to engage in business activities, private monopolies are forbidden, the use of land and water is to be limited in the interests of future generations, every worker in any enterprise has the right to participate in decisions affecting it. The draft constitution may be the most progressive document of its kind around in the world today (more on it in Excurs 6). Its chance of passage is minimal.

For lunch, we happened to be at Alexanderplatz and went to a place that features *Palatschinken*, thin pancakes with any of an assortment of fillings. Watching the man behind the counter was an experience. There were apparently only two people working there, in a place that seated perhaps thirty at tables and twenty at the counter. The man behind the counter did the *Palatschincken*. He had two grills and they were going constantly. He would pour with one hand, reach with the other hand to spread the batter evenly with a wooden tool placed exactly where he could get it without looking, turn and take an order or accept payment or serve an order, bend back to flip over one end of the *Palatschinken* that was on the grill, check what filing was to be in it, pour it in, reach over to an exactly placed spatula and pick up the other edge of the *Palatschinken*, pick up a plate with his other hand without looking, slide it under the *Palatschinken*, with three more expert flips of the *Palatschinken* fold it over the filling without letting a drop spill, and put the plate on the counter behind him; and all this with a constant fluidity that involved not a wasted motion. The whole performance was a pleasure to watch.

The eating place belonged to the state concern, and I am sure he did not get paid extra for the skill or speed with which he worked; but he was obviously proud of what he did, and was pleased when we commented. We were obviously not the first people to appreciate his art. I don't know if socialist economic relations foster such a relationship to work or not, but at least they don't prevent it.

In the evening a meeting of the Tenants' Union. I went to see if they would get back to the ownership question. But when I got there I was asked if I would represent the union at a meeting of an informal neighborhood Citizens' Committee, in Prenzlauer Berg; all the others wanted to stay for some important discussion. I said yes, and went. My own role was small, just to describe the background of the Tenants' Union which I did; but I was very interested to see what the difference would be between such a meeting and what I was accustomed to at home. By and large, very little. Everyday concerns: tree planting, dog shit, traffic, rents. The Parks Department offered a list of plants available to put in front of houses; old-timers rambled a little about garbage pick-up on their street; a younger man pushed for the group to organize itself more formally and be accredited as a Citizens' Committee; it had apparently begun as an outgrowth of the former state sponsored Residential Area Committee, but no one wanted to keep that identity. The main difference from a similar gathering in a middle-class neighborhood in the United States was probably that they expected more of their government in the DDR; but the tone of the meeting, and the citizen-to-government relationship, were otherwise very similar indeed. Surprising!

April 19

To Thomas Simon's house to see the TV film that Deirdre Berger was working on when I spent February 27 with her in Berlin and Potsdam. I thought the commentary was much oversimplified, but the visuals were good, and how much can you get across in fifteen minutes? The group included, at our request, two SPD members, plus Michael Plötschke, whom I liked very much. One of the SPD guests was Elke Judersleben, a candidate for the Berlin city council, who came from the same election district as Plötschke; the other was Peter Kunstlich, a former teacher who quit in frustration at what he calls the nonsense he was supposed to teach his students. Elke joined the SPD because she read the party program and liked it; she acknowledges that she might as well have joined New Forum, and she doesn't understand the SPD's objection to working with the PDS, whose program she also likes. Peter was cynical about the SPD, as well as about all the other parties; he believes the opposition should work together and is disappointed that it isn't doing so. Asked by Elke why he wasn't speaking out in support of joint actions (her position), he said that he had decided not to say anything if it wasn't going to have any effect. He didn't realize, I think, what he was saying: that it was exactly what many good SED people over the past forty years had used as their excuse for going along. "Die Schere im Kopf," "scissors in the head," as the saying has it about self-censorship.

April 24

Spoke this evening at a meeting convened by the senator for city development and the environment of West Berlin, Michael Schreyer. In West Berlin the senators each head administratively a department of the city government, and collectively act as the legislative body for the city, somewhat akin to the commission form of municipal government in the United States. Schreyer is quite left, a member of the Alternative List, and concerned to deal with a juggernaut that seems to be mounting around Daimler-Benz' proposal for a highrise at Potsdamer Platz. The meeting was in connection with the opening of an exhibition on the forthcoming competition for the area. Potsdamer Platz had been the transportation center of Berlin, one of the most crowded and used of all the central squares of the city. In the division of Berlin, it was split between the two sides, and the Wall was then built across one edge; the East Berlin side was then named Leipziger Platz. The exhibition was mounted at the Esplanade Hotel, one of the only two surviving buildings at the site. [Someone later said that if a competition for a plan for a united Berlin had been brought up nine months earlier, it would have been considered a contribution to the Cold War; no one imagined such plans would have any relevance for at least twenty-five more years.]

The sensitivity to the issues of the fascist past displayed in the exhibition was substantial, but selective. At one point in the notes for the exhibition, there was reference to the importance of the past in the planning of Potsdamer Platz, with a specific note that the relationship to the Prince-Albertstrasse area (where the Gestapo jail and interrogation quarters were), and Hitler's Bunker, should be included in that past. But in the pictures in the exhibition itself, one tableau depicts the square's history in the chronological unit 1900-1945, with no portrayal of the Nazi plans for Berlin—which would of course, had they been shown, have raised some interesting questions about their similarity to certain present proposals; particularly the representation of power that Hitler's planning and Daimler-Benz's proposed highrise both had, if in different ways.

The procedure for the competition is, to my mind (and that of many others), completely backward: first a competition for the physical development of a central crossroad, then a discussion of goals and ideals for all Berlin (the discussion I was invited to), and sometime later decisions about regional issues, whether Berlin will be the capital city, if so what offices will move there from Bonn, etc. To make matters much worse, Daimler-Benz has expressed an interest in 160,000 square meters of office space on Potsdamer Platz, including a highrise component, and the senate is offering them a reduced price for the land (which it largely owns) and instructing the competitors to include the Daimler proposal in their plans.

The discussion was highly intelligent and sophisticated. Some complained about the likely social segregation, the West becoming the "good address," the East the "bad." The lack of citizen participation in drawing up the program for the competition was raised; so were regional issues, traffic problems, cultural needs. A large audience, with a lively give and take discussion; better than a similar discussion would have been in New York City, I think.

I spoke in favor of the concept of a modest Berlin, as contrasted with a mighty Berlin. For the first time that I can recall in Germany I identified myself as a Jewish emigrant. My utopia for Berlin (the title of the meeting) was a modest, resident-oriented, user-controlled, historically conscious, ecologically sensitive, speculation-free Berlin. Much applause.

A slightly edited version appears as Excurs 5.

April 25

Little things: in the U-Bahn stations, and not just at Alexanderplatz and not just since the *Wende*, there is artwork: painting or posters or photographs, some avant garde, often very political, changing quite frequently, obviously done with love and without political or aesthetic inhibitions. In New York City, and in most Western countries, there are huge advertisements instead.

Our host in Dresden was Heinz Schwartzbach, who has the chair in city development at the Technical University of Dresden. He lives in a one-family house at the end of a dead-end street south of the city, very close to the gigantic university campus. He bought the house several years ago; it was in sad shape then, and the city was glad to sell (he, of course, has only user's rights to the land, but now wants to get legal title). He did—contracted out—a lot of modernization: put in new floors, built out the attic, added a separate unheated little house on the side, glassed in a sunporch, probably re-did the electrical and plumbing systems. How was he able to get it done, get the materials, the labor? Well, each application was separate, and each counted toward the city's rehabilitation quota in the official plan; he figures he must have accounted for at least four dwelling units rehabilitated in the official statistics since each application counted as one unit rehabilitated—so he contributed his bit to the fulfillment of the plan!

In conversations in Dresden, I pursued the question of why New Forum and the other citizens' groups in the city that had been so prominent in the first phases of the *Wende* dropped down so far in the vote and in public visibility. There are at the moment fifty-four official citizen's committees in Dresden; to be official one simply has to register and then becomes entitled to access to information, etc. Of the fifty-four, about twenty are subject-oriented: ecology, birds, bicycles, etc.; the others are territorial, what we would call neighborhood groups. I would expect there to be close cooperation with New Forum, a substantial base for votes, etc., but that has not developed. Why not? The citizen's committees "don't trust the New Forum people—they're all intellectuals, are pushing their own ideological goals." Some unfortunate confirmation of the intellectual/working class cleavage. We'll have to explore further.

Heinz told a story about hanging curtains in the windows of empty houses when the city council or party leadership came to visit, as a form of Potemkin Village show. I commented on the analogy when I showed the slides of the "occupied-look decals" in New York in my talk the next day. Odd how such similar and irrational practices crop up in such different systems: tsarism, real existing socialism, real existing capitalism.

April 26

In the morning, with an hour free, I walked down to Pragerstrasse, one of the most overblown pedestrian malls I have ever seen, ugly, monotonous, three identical prefabricated concrete hotels, a slab apartment house across the way, one-story commercial buildings plunked in the middle, four housing towers across the top. Yet apparently functioning fairly well, which just goes to show that people, not buildings, make a city center. A terrible case of gigantomania, but also harking back to the desire for places for parades and large public assemblies, called for by the SED in its planning schemes, and justified as bringing the people together, defending the principles of socialism. Actually it seems to me exactly parallel to Hitlerian mass psychological bids for support. But ineffective for the SED; remember the old lady's reactions to the troubles of the old Göring and the old Honecker? I think the support of the majority of Germans for Hitler outran the support they felt for any recent SED leader.

In the particular amalgam between Germany and fascism that produced Hitler, the uneasiness about German nationalism is for me almost greater than that about fascism—at least while in Germany, and while not immediately confronted with a fascist threat. A speaker on the radio today used the phrase "Nazi-Germany." It bothered me; the implication, as he used the phrase, is that there was, from 1933 to 1945, a Nazi and a non-Nazi Germany. The truth is there was a phenomenal identification of Germany with Nazism during this period; one didn't modify the other, the two identified with each other.

Certainly there was another Germany, but it was in the camps, dead, in flight or emigrated.

The Nazi past comes up all the time. Should the Frauenkirche, the Church of Our Lady, in Dresden, be rebuilt? It is an overwhelming ruin, much different in its impact from the Gedächtniskirche, the Memorial Church, in the center of West Berlin. The Gedächtniskirche is artistically, in a way ostentatiously, preserved, saying: we don't need to have this ruin here but we of our own free will decided to leave it; after all, look around you, here's the real Berlin, we wouldn't have to put up with this ruin if it didn't serve our purposes. The Frauenkirche is different. It shows both the splendor of what was destroyed, and the extent of the destruction (the Gedächtniskirche doesn't; it more resembles a deliberately created monument than a church destroyed in a bitter fight to the end). I would perhaps prevent more pieces of the Frauenkirche from falling down (a large chunk of the front facade recently fell in), but I would leave the trees growing in the middle, the pain of having a ruin where a tourist attraction should be, the symbol not only of the extent of devastation but also a monument to how ineradicable the legacy of the events that produced it is. Indeed, it was Anglo-American planes that dropped the bombs that burned it, as the civic literature tirelessly repeats, and perhaps—or almost certainly—it was a barbarous extension of the war to bomb a civilian population; but the bombing was much more the product of Nazi than of Anglo-American inhumanity. And of Nazism that was German, and of which Dresden was a committed part. I would leave the church stand as is, and permanently ring off the area around it. Time does not heal all wounds, nor exonerate all perpetrators.

The Jewish synagogue in Dresden, burned down on Krystalnacht, was not rebuilt. There is now only a small monument to where it was, a stone menorah with an inscription. On the site itself is a transformer for the city's electric power system. To hell with trivial sentimentality; there are no Jews in Dresden now, let bygones be bygones, rebuild the Frauenkirche, why even keep the silly stone menorah standing?

At the entrance to the wide Pragerstrasse and the commercial center of Dresden there is now standing (in both senses) an assembly of *Ausländer*, "foreigners"—that is to say, Poles, people from Arabian countries, Turks. The term foreigners doesn't include Americans,

French, British, in everyday use; there's a clear racial/economic underlay in *Ausländer*. Pragerstrasse is not like Via Utca in Budapest, where the whole street in the heart of downtown is lined with peddlers, mainly from the countryside, selling things they themselves have produced. Here it's selling things bought cheaply elsewhere, T-shirts, soap, toiletries, all those goods where the cost of distribution is a large part of the price and thus where the spread in cost between manufacture and sale to customer is large enough for small private entrepreneurs to squeeze out a profit, à la Haiti. One sees the same thing sporadically in East Berlin, at street fairs, etc., and continuously in West Berlin, at what's been known as the "Polish market," but it's a relatively new phenomenon in the DDR. I find it unsettling, a symbol of international disparities; but those disparities exist whether they're so visible or not, and the street markets reduce rather than exacerbate them. Yet what a lot of the world's effort goes into distributing what's already been produced, instead of into producing things!

April 27

Getting (or not getting) visas is a beautiful example of the differences between U.S. and DDR ways of life. Fran went with her sister Barbara and her niece Rebekah to get their visas renewed (they had come in on a one-day visa), and thereafter to get them registered with the police. They were asked for 55 marks each. Rebekah's attitude was immediate: to hell with it, we won't pay, we'll fight with them at the border when we go out; what are they going to do to us, at worst we'll have to pay then, at best we'll be home free. The professional analogy in law: competent lawyers don't tell their clients to do what the law says, but to examine the consequences of doing or not doing it, and then decide. The DDR reaction is quite different, based in part on centuries-old European traditions, particularly strong via Prussia, and in part on forty years of Stalinism, both of which make obedience to the state a virtue in itself.

A particularly painful example: "Gib dem Lehrer seine Ruhe," "Give the teacher his peace," said to a school child who has just been asked to say or do something in school that he/she considers nonsense or wrong, and is told by the parents to comply anyway. That I don't think would happen with us.

There are other contrasts between West and East:

> A DDR construction worker crosses to the West and gets a construction job. After a few days, he complains to his foreman that his wheelbarrow squeaks. His foreman asks, how does it sound? Whe-e-e-e-e-e, Whe-e-e-e-e-e, Whe-e-e-e-e-e, he replies. The foreman fires him.
>
> Puzzled, he looks for another job, and gets one. Again he gets a squeaky wheelbarrow, is asked how it sounds, replies Whe-e-e-e-e-e, Whe-e-e-e-e-e, Whe-e-e-e-e-e, and again he's fired. He turns to a fellow worker from the West who had overheard the incident and asks, can't you even complain about anything around here? Sure, says the man, but around here, when a wheelbarrow pushed by one of us squeaks, it's supposed to go Whee Whee Whee Whee Whee Whee Whee!

That night we are invited by Thomas Simon to a social get-to-gether at the Liga. It is part of their effort to be self-supporting by offering two-and-a-half day intensive "introduction to the United States courses," 200 marks (about $125) per person for nonmembers, half that for members, barely covering costs but generating contacts and members. They can't use the Academy of Sciences residential facility anymore, as they had when we went on a previous occasion, because there are too many better paying demands for it.They asked me to speak for twenty minutes; I said okay but with family, and it will be in English; it should be fun for Barbara and Rebekah.

On the way out to the session, we passed a factory that makes concrete panels, which was working around the clock. How come, given all the objections to prefabricated buildings? They have to finish what's started, close gaps left by withdrawal of firms from other parts of DDR, which had, weirdly, always come not only with their own workers but with their own panels. You certainly can't blame that kind of thing on central planning; it seems to me more the opposite, poor or missing planning. In a market economy, the consumers punish firms that are stupid; in a planned economy, voters should punish stupidity, but in this system weren't able to. A defect of Stalinism, not socialism.

On the way back to Berlin, Thomas asked if we wanted to go to Torgau, on the Elbe, on Sunday, where every year the anniversary of the first meeting of Soviet and American troops at the end of the war against Hitler is celebrated. We said sure!

April 28

A social evening at Manfred Zache's. The subject got onto sports, and the DDR's pride in its achievements, Olympic medals, and so forth. Well, he says, for kids that are topnotch, they go all out: they have to practice five days a week, have special instruction, later special schools, and are treated as privileged people. But for ordinary kids, the system just isn't interested; either you're a star or not worth attention.

The jokes don't stop. People still don't trust *Neues Deutschland*, which has removed the statement, "Organ of the Central Committee of the SED" from its masthead but is still owned by the PDS:

> Honecker and Kohl agree to have a race, to see whose system produces the better runner. Kohl wins. The headlines in *Neues Deutschland* read: "A great victory for socialism! Honecker wins a glorious second place! Kohl comes in next to last!"

April 29

The trip to Torgau was delayed by a farmers' demonstration: tractors crawling along the road, preventing anyone from passing. *(The photo on the right is of Fran and me at the demonstration.)* The farmers are upset because their produce cannot compete in quality or variety with that of the West or the South; they can produce a limited range cheaply enough, but are now finding that few will buy, and in addition they are being threatened with the withdrawal of all subsidies. Of course, the protest massively irritated everyone affected. The farmers lose immediate friends, but hope that the irritation will cause protests to go to those who in fact have some responsibility for the farmers' problems—clearly not the ones in the cars being delayed. It's the same problem public service workers have in the United States, or anywhere; when they strike, they hurt many innocent people, but how can they possibly not? I only lost sympathy with the farmers when I saw a West German flag on one of the tractors; that's exactly the cause of their problem! Who do they think they're protesting against? The DDR never wanted to subject them to the European Common Market's removal of subsidies and unsheltered competition!

The celebration of the meeting of U.S. and Soviet forces at the Elbe is a giant public relations game, played for the cameras: two flags approaching each other from opposite sides of the river, a joyous meeting at the middle of the bridge across it, hand shaking, speeches. But the only Americans we saw were from Growing Awareness through Experience, a Christian Peace Fellowship-affiliated group, maybe twenty people. We were asked to carry the  U.S. flag, two little ones on sticks, and did; I think it's the first time I've ever carried a United States flag in my life. The United States had refused to send a delegation or representatives from the Mission, despite a formal request (we were told) from Merkel, the foreign secretary. Because of Lithuania? Old ways? Maybe the request was barely made, Merkel has other things on his mind?

The Association of Professional Soldiers (Berufsverband Bundeswehr) was invited for the first time, and a representative spoke, very much appreciating the invitation. It sounded like he was being admitted to an international club of professional soldiers, to which the United States and the Soviet Union already belonged; no recognition that soldiering and peace were just a little bit contradictory. Pastor Schorlemmer picked up on it a little, in the best speech of the day, saying he hoped the Soviet soldiers, there in uniform, would soon not have to wear them, that no fear of Germany would exist that would necessitate them. (As if that was why they were there!)

After the formalities and the speeches, they attempted to make the event more "participatory" by having a festival on the large grassy area along the river, with four different bands, permitting private booths and stands along the paths. We didn't stay for the bands; they seemed to us a little excessive for the number of participants. The booths and stands made a somewhat sad impression: it was nice to be able to buy ice cream or, at one spot, slices of roast pig turning on a gas spit, but a lot of the booths were simply people selling their old unwanted bric-a-brac or peddlers similar to those at Pragerstrasse in Dresden, the Polish market in Berlin, or the subway entrance in Hamburg: people at the edge of the economy, trying to make some money in ways that could hardly be satisfying to them.

The advocates of high culture are offended by scenes like this, and even more by the fare that's being broadcast daily on radio and television. The comment is that forty years of SED rule didn't do half as much harm to the culture of the people as one year of the private market!

Which is saying quite a lot:

> "What's the difference between naturalism, realism, expressionism, and socialist realism?"
>
> "Naturalism is when the painter paints what he sees, realism is when he paints what he knows is there, expressionism is when he paints what he feels, and socialist realism is when he paints what he may."

April 30

Unter den Linden opened up to a street fair this morning. Booths for every West German beer company, fast food counters, knick-knacks and souvenirs, a few DDR publishers with books, black marketeers still trying to change money for people but catching only the unknowing tourists (quite a few of whom were present). A lively, crowded scene; unimaginable under the SED. Atmosphere? For the West Germans, still somewhat gawking at their poor relatives; for the DDR people, pleasure at the life and color, but shock at the prices; for families, just a good time. Pretty commercialized, everything, but much better than the grey desolate official buildings standing unloved along the edge of the wide street.

There is supposed to be a nationwide election campaign going on, to fill local offices. The election will be May 6 (the date originally fixed for the national elections, set aside for the local ones when the national were moved up to March 18). Only one piece of party propaganda lying around, from the Bündnis 90/Greens. The election campaigns are the most desultory I've ever seen. In the big street bazaar at Unter den Linden even the camera teams covering it were surprised that none of the parties showed up. They're not used to mixing politics with commerce with pleasure? Or they don't have the energy left? Or don't think it matters?

Candidates in any event seem to be in short supply. That's another result of forty years of SED: all those with experience, or almost all, were in the SED and are now discredited. Others simply aren't around. I haven't seen statistics, but I doubt if any party has been able to field candidates equal to the number of positions open. The PDS, I understand, only put up candidates for 40 percent of the spots in Cottbus, 20 percent in Erfurt, although they are important cities; not even the CDU had candidates for every post.

May 1

Three public events today: the big May Day parade and rally, a protest against the planning for Potsdamer Platz, and a PDS festival at Köpenick, a suburban part of Berlin. May Day has a special significance for us; it's the day Fran and I first met, forty-two years ago, at the May Day parade in New York City. We've looked around for other May Day parades to go to since then; although the holiday started as an American one, in memory of the Haymarket martyrs in Chicago, it's always been considered a radical holiday in the United States, a holiday many even think is imported from the Soviet Union! So parades in the United States have become fewer and farther between.

The May Day parades and rallies here are full of ambiguities. The one we went to was the big one in Berlin and was joint East-West. Others, e.g., Potsdam, were separate: the trade unions of the two sides

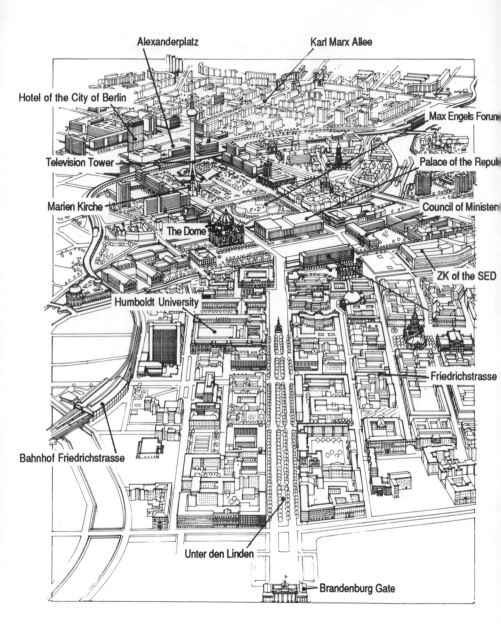

Alexanderplatz

Karl Marx Allee

Hotel of the City of Berlin

Max Engels Forum

Television Tower

Palace of the Republic

Marien Kirche

Council of Ministers

The Dome

ZK of the SED

Humboldt University

Friedrichstrasse

Bahnhof Friedrichstrasse

Unter den Linden

Brandenburg Gate

couldn't agree to work together. The big issue is, on the surface, working with the Free German Trade Union Federation (FDGB), the central trade union organization in the East, because of its Stalinist past. That carries over to its PDS-linked present. But the objection is a beautiful example of the ambivalence of anticommunism: it's in part against an organization that consistently sold out the workers' interests to a Stalinist state; but it's also against a union that, having now "reformed" and changed its leadership, put through a trade union law under Modrow that is far stronger than what the West German unions are asking, and frightens them with the specter of real socialism. The togetherness today must have been carefully negotiated; the new head of the federation spoke at an East German rally at the Lustgarten in downtown Berlin, then the East German contingent marched off to join the Western contingent for a big rally in front of the Reichstag, which was clearly a West German Trade Union Federation rally. When the line of march passed through the Brandenburg Gate and the border station, no one even bothered to show their identity papers; the guards just read the newspapers. At the Reichstag, all political signs were declared unwelcome; a large number of SPD signs and a small number of PDS ones were nevertheless in evidence. The only East German speaker was a member of a Berlin construction union. But the head of the West German federation said, as did other speakers, that no one should be excluded from the future united unions because of their past affiliations, everyone should be judged by their present positions.

The one thing all the speakers were proud of was that this was not an "official" celebration, as it had been in the East for the last forty years. Only the independent little Marxist Group, in an overlong leaflet handed out at the rally, called attention to the fact that Hitler had first made May Day an official holiday, which it is in both East and West Germany now, and suggested that it was a co-opted celebration.

The rally at Potsdamer Platz in West Berlin was supposed to protest the construction plans, but almost no one showed up: perhaps one hundred people. Poorly publicized, poorly organized, the speakers only had a portable megaphone, a few nice big banners. Kids and good feelings, but very chaotic.

Then to a PDS rally at Köpenick, where we met Fred and Ushi Staufenbiel. The Köpenick castle, where the rally was held, is on a promontory that sticks out into the conjuncture of the Spree and the Dahm rivers, a beautiful site, now a park, grass and flowers and the castle's yard and a cafe. A platform had been built near the entrance, where a band was playing as we arrived. Maybe the speakers had already come and gone, or maybe the speeches were interspersed between the musical numbers, and there were little flags and whirligigs to be seen, but no one seemed interested in the politics; kids ran around, people sat and drank beer or coffee or ate ice cream, stands sold trinkets, couples walked around the park. This is really the most desultory political campaign we've seen in a long time. The liberals seem to have the most posters, the CDU has practically none, PDS few, SPD many and in very good spots; their links with the prevailing party in West Berlin should help them a great deal in East Berlin. Bündnis 90 is occasionally visible in posters too. But almost nothing on TV, little in the papers, no sidewalk stands or leafleting and few posters. Most people must feel everything has already been decided anyway. Our friend from the Tenants' Union told us that their official founding will be May 19, but also that people aren't really excited—yet, he says.

We walked along the river to the streetcar stop. A pleasant path, only low bushes separating us from the water, buildings on the other side set back behind shrubbery and public lawn. It was not always thus, Ushi explained. Once the properties on the landward side extended down to the water's edge, and there were either buildings or private gardens. We could see how it was on the opposite shore. But, after the destruction of the war, the new government decided to clear what remained from the shore and make it a park. Eminent domain was not a problem; they just did it!

We took a streetcar back home, although it was the long and slow way around, to see more of the city. Three sights particularly typical of real existing socialism struck us: (1) Bus and trolley stops often have concrete sheds over the waiting areas, painted inside with all kinds of motifs: an underwater scene, a living room, animals, abstractions. And they're an old institution. We didn't have shelters at bus stops in New York City until someone figured out you could sell advertising space on the sides of them and make enough money to pay for putting them up. (2) An ambulatory health center for the state-owned electric utility's workers. The idea of providing health care at the workplace, for anything other than work-related injuries, doesn't exist with us. (3) More old factories with smokestacks billowing than you'd care to see. That's because there's been no investment in modernization; the DDR has been using up its invested capital for the last twenty years, achieving an artificially high standard of living by shifting money from replacement accounts of industry to consumption purposes.

May 2

The details of the currency union were announced today. Classic electoral politics; there is really no reason for the kind of partial announcement that was made, which leaves many questions open, except one: there is an election coming up. The CDU wants credit for bringing in the West German mark and assumes (correctly) that it will get more pluses than minuses for what it has negotiated. The difficulties will show later, as prices rise when subsidies are cut and wages stay low, when unemployment hits in a big way, when plants shut down and rents rise and West Germans take over. But even the spokesperson from Radio Stern, a major electronics producer where massive layoffs are pending, complained that few people showed up to protest at the May Day rally. I think the CDU strategy is correct; in this election people are concerned with national issues, and will vote for national parties. And everyone is clear that local issues in the DDR will be resolved by national, not local, events.

May 3

Steffi Knopp, the reporter who's spoken to us several times about a longer interview, says *Wochenpost*, the DDR's most popular weekly newspaper, is in danger of going under, despite a circulation of over 400,000, because it is part of Berliner Publishing House and the management wants to continue all of the enterprises, both losing and profitable (or potentially profitable). But without subsidies, the losers will pull the profitmakers under. So they are trying to sell the whole publishing house as a package. But that makes no sense, from either a capitalist or a socialist perspective. Capitalist: if the whole enterprise is sold, the buyer will undoubtedly close the losers anyway; nothing is gained by keeping them open now. Socialist: if the losers serve a public purpose, they must be subsidized publicly, and that possibility can be explored separately. Either way, the two types of businesses must be separated. It sounds to me more like a paralysis of decision-making and inexperience than an insoluble problem.

What's worse is that Steffi doesn't know what's happening, ordinary employees aren't consulted, every now and then there's an employee meeting called by management but they are only informed in a sketchy way about the negotiations. Democracy is hard to learn, for those who have to give up power for it.

Spoke in the evening at a meeting of the Jewish Cultural Association, in a large meeting room in the old ZK building which the PDS had made available to them for the occasion (landlord-tenant relations seem to be pretty good here!). I told some of our personal history: my grandfather and his refusal to believe that the Nazis would really implement their rhetoric against the Jews until he was denied his normal summer holiday reservation at Baden-Baden; our emigration, via Switzerland and France, to the United States; my first encounter with racial discrimination in trying to rent a summer house on Cape Cod for my parents; our activities in the civil rights movement, and black-Jewish tensions; joining our Temple as a statement of ethnic identity (I should have spoken of New Jewish Agenda, but forgot). For slides I did segregation in New York. Then I raised questions about DDR history and anti-Semitism and hostility to foreigners, and didn't have to say anything more for the next hour—a very un-DDR-like meeting, with everyone talking at once, heatedly, sometimes too fast for us to follow. They explained the rise of anti-foreign actions by pointing to increasing tensions caused by worry about jobs, housing, income, prices, general insecurity, finding an outlet in group hostility. It's the scapegoat theory of race prejudice. The news report on Frankfurt/Oder, at the DDR-Polish border (everyone got along fine for forty years, now Poles must go if there are lay-offs) supports the idea. Right after that someone spoke of the importance of overcoming prejudice against foreigners, saying how useful community festivals were but how few people they reached. Of course, if the scapegoat explanation is right, neighborhood festivals won't do a thing; attention has to be focused on the real problems, the real causes.

Fred Kempe, a reporter for the *Wall Street Journal*, is doing a piece on Jews in East Germany. He was at the meeting, and took us aside afterward to get some impressions. He said he'll be quoting Irene Runge's comment that "she has never encountered anti-Semitism in the DDR," I gather with incredulity. A Jewish woman at the meeting had told of marrying a non-Jewish German, meeting his family, and encountering all kinds of pre(mis)-conceptions about Jews.

Kempe asked whether we saw a difference between the handling of the Jewish question in East and West Germany. A big difference, I said: while strong elements of anti-Semitism survive in various places within various groups in both countries, the issue had been publicly debated and worked over (again, among some groups in some places) in the West, but not in the East. This was what I objected to in the strong punishment of anti-Semitic or pro-fascist activities in the DDR—five years in jail for painting a swastika on a wall. Such extreme penalties suppressed any open discussion of the issue, I suggested. The whole political interpretation of the history of the DDR as a clean break with fascism goes the same way: no one in the DDR had any responsibility for National Socialism, those were only the other Germans, the "Nazi-Germans," as one newspaper story had it. Any dealing with anti-Semitism or fascism has to deal with its roots, roots which we saw in a very different way in the American leadership and among American soldiers in Vietnam or Panama and in the widespread jingoistic support for them at home in the United States. Questions such as these were at least raised in West Germany; they were never even discussed in the East. That's why the PDS speaker at the election rally on March 11 could not even understand how anyone could see any trace of anti-Semitic prejudice in his comment; *of course* he wasn't anti-Semitic, why, he was a good DDR citizen and PDS member.

Kempe agreed. He told us he had family in Dresden, ordinary DDR people, and had raised with them the question of anti-Semitism, telling them he was doing a story on East German Jews. They became indignant, told him there was no anti-Semitism here, never had been, that it had nothing to do with them, they had more important things to think about, why didn't he write about something else. They got into a big fight about it (good for the *Wall Street Journal!*), and the next morning his hosts told him they had half expected him to leave; he said no, disagreements were a normal part of life, no reason for personal antagonisms.

In Wittemberg, the Round Table decided to remove a Soviet T-34 tank from a monument to the Soviet liberators because it symbolized Stalinism. Another case of not working through the past, of oversimplification or suppression of history, intolerance of ambiguity.

Miscellany: Kempe says his relatives in Dresden told him the old SED people were still where they always had been, running things in the big factories, broadcasting for DDR television. Very likely; anyone who was anyone (almost!) belonged to the party, few outside the party had (or could get) the competency. The question is, what role they played. I'd almost reverse the generally accepted rule of thumb that makes current membership the test: the opportunists have left the party, they have nothing to gain by staying, anyone in today is most likely in on principle.

Christian Fahrenholz tells me on the telephone from Hamburg that an architect in Schwerin told him he was anxious to open his own office, start his own practice, but if he did, he didn't understand, who would pay his salary?

May 4

We went shopping this morning at Anton Saefgow (Anton Safeway, we call it). It's one of the best developments I've seen so far in the DDR. The commercial space is laid out along a wide L, the leg of which is a plaza leading from the stores to the street, with streetcar and bus stops and a large wall/fountain providing shade and coolness in the summer, protection in the winter. Along the middle of the vertical of the L are grass and trees, along one side is a six-story building block with apartments above, stores below, on the other the large supermarket and other stores. At the top of the L is another open plaza with a large stone abstract statue. Behind the L are the apartment blocks. All laid out on a generous scale, but not overpowering, with attention lavished on the public spaces, with the commercial playing a quiet and supporting role, not being the purpose of the development. Nor, as in Leipzig, for instance, is the whole thing out of scale so as to show the heroic socialist way of life. A politically and socially, as well as architecturally, well-balanced development.

And the stores have plenty in them, West goods at higher prices, East at lower. Hardly a bankrupt economy. Why can't they stay exactly the way they are now? Or why couldn't they have done all this during the last forty years? How does it contradict socialism to sell capitalist goods in socialist stores in a socialist housing development?

On the way back, we passed the recreation center that Eric Honecker provided as his "gift" to the young people of Berlin. A proud building and a good social construct *(see photo facing page)*.

May 5

A walk through downtown to the German Historical Museum, with Wilfried Kaib, now in charge of housing for the city of Offenbach, near Frankfurt in the West, with John Doling, of Birmingham University, and Hans Harms, from Hamburg, all here to visit; East Berlin is really an attraction these days! I complained about Marx-Engels Forum and Marx-Engels Platz as overscale. The forum is a large open space between the Palace of the Republic and the commercial center of Berlin, starting with the TV tower that is East Berlin's trademark, and stands next to Alexanderplatz, the planned center of activity for the city. So the Palace of the Republic and the center of downtown are separated by a large, formal, geometrically laid-out and landscaped open space that few people ever use. The whole composition is monumental and, to my sense, out of scale. By contrast, across the twelve-lane boulevard that borders the composition is the old Lustgarten, the royal pleasure garden, now surfaced with small stones and lined with trees, all on a much more human scale and potentially much more attractive. Marx-Engels Forum is poorly planned and well executed; the Lustgarten was well planned and is now poorly executed.

A statue of Karl Marx and Friedrich Engels stands on one side of the space overlooking it. Engels is standing, Marx sitting. Why those positions? The joke goes:

> Engels says to Marx: "Well, how do you like it?"
> "Not bad," says Marx, "not bad. How much did it cost?"
> "You better sit down," says Engels, "while I tell you!"

Hans felt large open spaces in the city's heart were much needed; I agreed, but not to this scale. The Forum was virtually empty, and generally is. The scale is a tribute to the desire of the SED to demonstrate its power, a representation of pure might that, both in the Forum and in the broad parade boulevards like Karl Liebknecht Strasse and Karl-Marx Allee *(see photo on page 226)*, are hostile to pedestrians and to urban life in general. The same is true of the Marx-Engels Platz, on the other side of the Palace of the Republic, now simply a parking lot, not even with trees; there a park would have fit, with underground parking, but for that resources were simply not sufficient.

In general, Stalinism and socialism arguably can be differentiated in terms of their effects on city planning and building. Architecture and urban design have a long tradition of being used to represent power, in many different ways, from ostentatious displays of wealth (the palaces of France, the baroque of Vienna) to artistic quality (the doors of Florence) to sheer might (fascism) to ornate massiveness (the skyscrapers of Moscow) or to height and technical virtuosity (the skyscrapers of Manhattan and Chicago). The Stalinallees of the DDR, whatever their names (Stalinallee was the name of the major twelve-lane route laid out to Alexanderplatz from the east; it was renamed Karl-Marx Allee in 1956), represent the same thing, as do the inhuman scale of many city center plazas, Pragerstrasse in Dresden, etc. The uniquely socialist elements are at least three: the mix of uses, not centered around all those uses that can afford to pay the price, but all those uses that political values suggest should go together; the accompanying lack of commercialization, places organized to bring people together or give them joy, not to put them in the mood to buy something; and the people who live there, not selected (self-selected, more insidious) by income but selected (bureaucratically, admittedly, and with exceptions) by need (some of these ideas were discussed in Excurs 3).

Charley Marx's 172nd birthday was celebrated this afternoon around the corner from us at Rosa Luxemburg Platz. Book stalls with left-wing books, Trotskyite, Dietz Verlag, some new independents; buttons, posters, some nonpolitical T-shirts, political records. A pleasant informal affair, many people knew each other, baby carriages and older folk. A cartoon:

> On a huge banner, a portrait of Marx, hands in pockets, eyes downcast, saying: "Sorry, kids, it was just an idea I had..."

At the panel discussion in a tent outdoors afterward the crowd was overwhelmingly young, e.g., under thirty-five. Gregor Gysi and Heinrich Finck, the new rector of Humboldt University (chosen through pressure of students over the establishment candidate), were the main speakers. Gysi spoke generally, along lines that might be expected: Marx said much good, not the last word, should be read but not as Bible, didn't give answers, just as well we have to learn to find our own. Later he quoted Marx's thesis that ownership was critical, reinterpreted it to say that private ownership had led to the development of harmful, antisocial material interests, so had state ownership, the search was now for a third way. Not a bad formulation, although not applicable on a small scale; a third form of ownership inside a dominantly private ownership system won't do much. He also defended the limited self-criticism within the PDS: he had just come back from Plauen, where party membership had dropped from 12,000 to

236, and they were beleaguered on all sides by the right and the conservatives. How could he tell them their top priority was now even more self-criticism? If their friends outside the party would ease up a bit, show a little more understanding, it would make self-criticism a lot easier.

The most interesting, and somewhat puzzling, comment came from Bettina Wegener. In response to a comment by Finck about the importance of holding fast to one's identity in this period of transition, she said her problem, and that of her generation, was to find an identity, to establish the "I" that they want to be.

We raised the question of identity that evening with Erika Planitza. We had supper at her apartment, on Leipzigerstrasse. It has a beautiful view over Berlin. Every city, Wilfried Kaib pointed out, is at its best at dusk, with the lights twinkling on, the buildings still visible, the shapes suggestive, the details shadowy. Cities aren't organisms, although it's popular to talk of them as if they are; but the people who live in them are all humans, and they have patterns of life in common. Those patterns also give cities much in common, overriding socialism, Stalinism, the market, the superimposed organizations of temporary control. A good thing, too. The Marienkirche, the Church of St. Mary, stands at an angle completely skewed from the main lines of the central city development, its architecture discordant with the representation of modernity attempted all around it, totally out of place ideologically—but an important presence. It represents survival, at the moment, since its use also is out of place; but given a new turn of events, people will be enormously pleased it is there. Those possibilities of change should not only be kept open but made more conscious.

Erika was in sympathy with Bettina's quandary. She spoke of her own experiences in going to West Berlin for additional courses and seeing how it's done there, and using their hypodermic needles. They were simply so much better than what they had in the East that it now hurt her to have to give an injection to a child here, thinking how much safer and more painless it would be had they the right needles. I argued that that was no identity crisis, that it should give rise to anger and criticism but not self-doubt. Perhaps, I suggested, the problem was with the uncertainty now created in people's daily lives by the unification, the currency union, the threat of job loss; but even that, I said, shouldn't be an identity crisis, it should lead people to react, to search, to do something. The year 1933, I suggested, was much worse; but no one spoke of an "identity crisis" then, they were only too aware of their identities.

It's not the uncertainty, she said, that bothered her; it was the shock of finding out that what she had known for a while about the hypodermic needles, and for much longer about the absurdities of the DDR health care system, but had always seen as failures of a system that was generally sensible and moving ahead, turned out to be characteristic of every part of the system. The loss (maybe "of identity" isn't the right word, but "loss" in any event is) came at the beginning of the *Wende*, not today; with revelations about the SED, not from actions of the CDU. If people don't know in which direction to go, the period to mourn over the loss hasn't been long enough. That, curiously enough, is exactly what someone, I think Finck, had said at the rally that afternoon.

May 7

It's interesting to get other people's fresher perceptions of East Berlin. Rhoda Karpatkin, executive director of Consumers' Union in the United States, stopped to visit on the way from an International Council of Consumers' Unions meeting in Amsterdam. She's traveled widely, and tells us that, having spent her first day here sightseeing, she was really impressed by the café at the opera, the museums, Unter den Linden, the streetcars, the new market hall, the shopping, the life on the streets. Of course she was focusing on the center of the city. She says she was surprised at how lively, pleasant, cared for the city was, not the drabness and pessimism of Warsaw. Contrast that with our initial impression of East Berlin: greyness, drabness, pompousness, coldness. We feel differently about it now too, but for other reasons.

The local elections are today. We walked around downtown looking in at the various parties' election headquarters. What a difference from March 18! The excitement simply isn't there. Neither is the international attention, but of course these are only local elections. The results, as they trickled in, paint a picture little different from that of March: roughly the same percentages all around. The percent of those eligible to vote who actually voted is still much higher than similar percentages in the United States, if lower than in March. Elections do make a difference here, at least for now.

The local elections represent a historical turning-point, not so much in what they produced as in what they didn't produce. This was the last opportunity the people of East Germany had to express themselves as to the future of their country; from here on out all elections will be done in a unified Germany, under unified laws. These were only local elections, true; but had there been serious afterthoughts about the CDU, or about unification, or about the impact of getting into bed with West Germany, this would have been the time to voice them. Had they been voiced now, there might have been some slowdown in the West German juggernaut of unification. But no hesitations were voiced, no resistance appeared.

These elections mark the end of the DDR's political independence; political unification has been achieved in substance, if details of implementation still have to be worked out. The next phase of unification will be the implementation of economic unification; that will start with the currency union, in all likelihood, and will be much more painful before it's over.

One of the major issues that remains unresolved is the future of Berlin. Excurs 5, which is an expanded version of a talk that I gave on April 22, takes what is undoubtedly a minority position on it.

excurs 5

THE FUTURE OF BERLIN:
THE IDEAL OF A MODEST CITY

The Question

The future of Berlin is very much in public discussion these days, understandably. The city has been artificially divided for forty years, along lines drawn with no relationship to uses, services, transportation patterns, or anything else: lines simply (and hurriedly) drawn to solve a problem in international relations. No one, in 1945, when the four sectors of Berlin were laid out by the victorious Allies, ever expected any sectors or group of sectors to want to become a city unto themselves. But, whether they wanted to or not, both halves of Berlin—the three Western sectors in one half and the Soviet in the other—have had to struggle mightily to make themselves into independent cities: in the West, with the aid of massive subsidies, far over and above what any other city in West Germany ever received, because the country had its national prestige (as well as that of the Americans) invested in the survival of Berlin, uneconomic as it might be; and in the East, with similar preferences accorded the new "capital city," to the dismay of other cities throughout the DDR, whose construction crews, allocations of supplies, and funds were ruthlessly shifted to "Berlin, Hauptstadt der DDR," "Berlin, Capital City of the DDR," as it was officially called.

Yet neither half worked well. The old central city had been cut in half, relations of residential areas to jobs were in disarray, local rail routes crossed borders and went through areas where no one was allowed to disembark, long-distance train stations had no lines entering them from their own territories, old well-established neighborhoods were suddenly cut in two. For many years West Berlin, as a matter of national policy, kept planning as if the division were only temporary; in the DDR, after a few years, an aggressive effort was made to show that the capital city of the DDR could in fact survive very well by itself.

But everybody knew it made no urban sense at all. No city wants to be cut in two. Who would even consider separating Brooklyn from Manhattan, Buda from Pest, or the Stare Mesta from the Nueva Mesta in Prague, even though a river separates two formerly independent cities? And in Berlin the river had nothing to do with the boundary, but flowed through both halves equally. Even more: Berlin had a strong self-identity before the war—Berliners were Berliners, just as Saxons were Saxons and Bavarians were Bavarians. Their accent was different, their humor was different, they cooked differently and ate differently, they bargained with each other differently—Berlin was as different from the rest of Germany as New York City is from the United States. Yet the city has been divided for forty years, the residents of one-half barely allowed to visit the other, a huge concrete Wall stood between them, a symbol of competition, hostility, estrangement, involuntary division, subjugation.

So everybody, but everybody, that lived in the city was delighted for the city when the Wall opened, and the euphoria of that first pouring through the border on November 9 was easy to understand. *(The photo on the left shows sidewalk vendors selling pieces of the Wall to tourists.)* Not so easy, six months later, contemplating a single government, a single territory, to decide what to do with the consequences of the forty years of division. All kinds of proposals have flourished:

- Keep the Wall as a monument.
- Keep some pieces of it, but move them out of the way.
- Run a superhighway through the *todes-streifen*, the "death alley" between the two Walls that the DDR had built.
- Make the location of the Wall a green strip running the full length of the former border.
- Sell it off for development .

And what to do with the new unified city of Berlin?

- Make it the new capital city of the united Germany.
- Make it the cultural center, but not the political center.
- Lure industry and commerce, and make it an economic center.
- Restrict industry, protect its environment, make it a university city.

And, most pressing:

- Should Daimler-Benz, the second largest industrial concern in the West (the result of a merger between the firm that builds the Mercedes automobiles and the firm that built the Messerschmidt airplane of World War II fame), be allowed to develop a choice piece of empty property at Potsdamer Platz to build a high-rise center for its service business, at what was once the transportation hub of central Berlin, cut off by the adjacent Wall, barren for more than forty years, but now a symbol of what unification could mean and produce?

It is not easy to see who is on what side of these issues: are there really broad lines of principle, or real conflicts of interest, or simply different technical evaluations, different personal preferences?

I suggest three fundamental questions underlie the debates: the handling of history, whom a city serves, and the significance of power.

The Representation of History in the City

The Wall is certainly a part of history, symbolic not only of the division of Berlin but also of the division of Germany, of the Cold War, of the unfriendly competition of ideologies and systems in a hostile and suspicious world. It must be remembered. It is a part of the identity of several generations, and its memory should be a spur to a different solution of problems, a different way of dealing with differences, a past failure and a problem for the future. The reminders of the Wall should be reminders of problems still unsolved; the question here is not to commemorate a great victory or, certainly, to memorialize a noble deed, but rather to raise questions, spur thinking as to whose responsibilities, whose interests, whose ideologies, what combination of causes, past and present, lead to such a history.

That suggests a memorial that is not pretty, that is not comfortable, that gets in the way and jolts, that is large and symbolically oppressive: A large length of the Wall, something that still interferes with the easiest movement, the greatest efficiency. Something central, in the area of the Brandenburger Tor or Potsdamer-Leipziger Platz. Perhaps a piece of the Wall, perhaps something even bigger than the Wall was, with the Wall within it. But the exact line of demarcation between the two parts of Berlin seems to me to have little historic significance. It had no logic, as to its precise location, when it was drawn on a map; it should not retroactively be given a meaning it never had. A greenbelt through the middle of a city, dividing parts that had been organically together, separating neighbors, impeding contact, is not useful; more green space certainly belongs in most cities, Berlin not excluded, but their location should be integral to the form and uses of the city, not a creature of historical chance. And certainly a super-highway through the dead center of a city is a concept no one who cares about urban life would today endorse; such highways have been stopped, and their approaches even ripped down, in city after city throughout the world. Such highways serve commuters, people driving through the city, visitors. Cities should be designed, first and foremost, for those living in them.

Who Is the City For?

But is that really who cities are for: those living in them? How about Daimler-Benz; does it not also have an interest in the city, is it not entitled to a location useful to it, just as other residents are entitled to locations they like? I think not. Let me leave aside for the moment the question of the particular concern that Daimler-Benz is, what placing this particular enterprise in the new heart of Berlin represents, and deal only with the question of whom a city is to serve, what the priorities of urban development should be.

The general answer seems clear to me, and is not the truism it looks: cities are for the people who live in them. That does not mean that housing and residential amenities take precedence over all other uses, of course. People need jobs, education, goods and services, transportation, utilities. Some of these may get in the way of residences, and residences must then sometimes give way. But the purpose is still the service of the residents. Daimler-Benz and the people of Berlin do not have equal rights to the city; the city should belong to its people, present and future, and Daimler-Benz's needs should be respected by the city only to the extent that they advance the interests of residents. If no one from the city worked there, for instance, and if Daimler's profits were all spent elsewhere, then Daimler's "rights" to the use of the city should, I would think, be subordinated to the rights of those who do live there. Daimler's rights are derivative, residents' rights primary.

In any given case, interests will likely mesh in some ways, conflict in others, and general principle won't resolve all individual cases; but it should set the priorities. Thus the question is what benefits will Daimler's presence in Berlin bring the residents of the city (jobs, taxes, beauty, pride) at what cost to them (exploitation, fiscal burdens for services, ugliness, environmental degradation, shame). And, of course, what alternate locations might produce a better mix of benefit against cost for the residents of the city. Not knowing the answer to the latter question, I cannot come to a final conclusion, but all the evidence suggests to me that Daimler should not be at Potsdamer Platz.

Berlin and German Power

The third question, the significance of power, is directly involved here. Daimler-Benz is after all no ordinary concern; it represents the power of German industry, of German capital, of German technology, indeed, of German supremacy, as does no other. The questions involved with its locating at Potsdamer Platz are related to the questions of Berlin being the capital of a united Germany. Both have to do with power. And with German power in particular.

Let me tell a story:

At the first discussion of the future of Berlin which I attended, a member of the regional committee appointed by the governments of East and West Berlin spoke of the committee's long-term perspective (indicating that he was describing the committee's thinking, not his own, for reasons that will become obvious). He said their view was of a Greater Berlin: the metropolis, not the arbitrary legal boundaries. Greater Berlin had an outstanding location, seen in its European context, sitting as it did at the intersection of the axis running from Stockholm to Rome, from Paris to Moscow. With the opening up of Eastern Europe (I am quoting directly in all this, if from memory), Greater Berlin was the closest major Western center to Eastern Europe, the logical point of entry for all those wanting to expand their business or interests in the East. It could be the "turntable" for East-West trade and commerce, as for North-South. Berlin could thus once again become a great world city, in a world this time at peace; it had of course forever renounced military might and committed itself to peace, and should be a center of peace, but it could be that on an international basis, a key city in a united Europe. As the capital of a united and prosperous Germany, it could hardly avoid that role. It was likely to add over a million residents in the next ten years, going from 4.3 to 5.5 million inhabitants. It could and should be a mighty city.

The presentation made not only my but others' hair stand on end. If city planning can be enlisted in the service of national might, this was it. For those concerned with the history of Nazism, for those for whom the connection between German national history and culture and the rise of Hitler remain a troublesome question, such an open pursuit of power was particularly unsettling. The very use of the word "axis" is eerie: does this generation really not know that Nazi Germany and Fascist Italy formed the Axis that unleashed World War II? But, even leaving all that aside, the question of who such a quest for city status and power served was troublesome enough.

For the might of a city, the power it represents, does not necessarily serve its own residents. On the contrary: it could well be argued that the mightier Daimler-Benz is, the more its power dominates the city of Berlin, the worse it is for the residents of that city. No one should be subject to another's power, and the relative weight given Daimler-Benz by wooing the concern and giving it pride of place in the city's center is a disparity of power that is unpleasant enough, just in abstract contemplation. But more concretely: Daimler's presence, its domination of the city, will benefit some but injure others, many more.

Daimler-Benz proposes to build a center for its service activities, high-tech knowhow, technically trained people, top staff and professionals. They, and the owners of the firm, will be well served by a central location; so may those doing business with it (although of course not its competitors). But for the those not trained in the technical skills Daimler uses and sells, those not able or wishing to work for it or its clients, those more interested in Berlin as a place to live than a place to work, or those whose work is not benefitted by Daimler's presence, that presence can be a real disadvantage. The U.S. has had experience with the trickle-down theory of economic development: help the top firms and their top personnel, and the benefits will ultimately flow to the poor, to minorities, to the homeless or the helpless or the outcasts. The results of that experience have been clear: feeding the sparrows by feeding the horse so it will leave droppings for the sparrows to feed on is neither efficient nor effective nor humane.

Further: the greater the power of those at the top of the economic pyramid, the greater their separation from the rest of the city, from the middle classes, from the poor, from the unemployed. We can speak of New York as a quartered city, a city pulled apart, in which the leaders of industry, finance, and commerce, and the gentry, the top-level professional, technical, administrative people, live in a different city from the middle classes, skilled workers, white-collar workers, who in turn are separated from the lowest paid, the irregularly employed, the service workers earning minimum wages—who in turn fear the totally unemployed, the marginalized, the criminalized, the excluded. We can no longer talk about "the" city; New York is at least four cities, four separate quarters of a quartered city.

The more international one quarter becomes, the less its concern for the purely local quarters around it; while one depends on the other, their interests are in conflict in countless ways. Since many of the top echelons in the power structures of most cities do not actually live in the city, but see it only as a place in which to work and from which to make money, there is a sharp dividing line between the city as source of profit and the city as source of residential, cultural, social life; but the lines of division are not by use but by user. Daimler-Benz as user of Berlin will have quite different interests from Gertrude or Hans Berliner, who simply live and work and raise their children and try to live out a peaceable life with their neighbors there.

Nor does a mighty Berlin bode well for other cities in Germany, or in Europe either for that matter. Inter-city competition, again, is a phenomenon well enough known to us in the United States. And we know that the more cities compete with each other, the more are business firms benefitted and residents hurt: business firms benefitted, because the tax breaks, the economies of scale, the public investment in infrastructure serving private interests, escalate as one city tries to outdo the other in creating a "favorable business climate"; and residents hurt, because their taxes pay for the incentives to businesses, and the jobs created in one community, generally already the more prosperous, are at the expense of jobs in others, generally the poorer. Inequalities are heightened, both inter-city and intra-city.

These are all problems known in the West but not solved in the DDR either, of course. The slogan about the "unity between economic and social policy," which Honecker and his cohorts used time and again, was a recognition that there should be such a unity, but it was a statement of an aspiration, not an achievement or even a policy. For the first twenty-five years of the DDR's existence, economic policy had priority: cities were built for industries, housing was to make sure factories had workers nearby. In the last fifteen years, arguably, social policy had priority: investment was made in housing at the expense of investment in industry, production stagnated, innovation disappeared. No balance between the two was ever achieved. And the idea of Berlin as a showplace of the power of the nation was as prevalent on the East side of the Wall as it was on the West. No model for the solution of the Berlin question can be found in the actual experience of the DDR.

A Proposal for a Modest City

Modesty is not often put forward as a goal for a city or a nation, but it seems to me a desirable one, for Berlin and for Germany. I would say the same thing about Washington, D.C.: a less self-consciously imposing capital might lower a slight bit the inclination to arrogance displayed in one war or invasion or international game of pressure politics after another. One of the things we responded to most positively, intuitively, in the DDR was precisely the absence of arrogance: the knowledge of limitations, of smallness, of deficiencies, so that the declamations of achievement, superficially so similar to those of the West, were universally—really universally—taken with humor, disbelief, and dismay; it really came as a surprise to many people when, after the beginning of the *Wende*, they found that Erich Honecker really believed what he had been saying. We felt, on the other hand, that in West Germany the boastfulness was unconscious, the arrogance second nature, the belief in superiority unalloyed.

Modesty would certainly be becoming to a unified Germany. Both in terms of the centuries-old German past and in terms of promises about how a united Germany would live in the House of Europe, the display of might is, to say the least, inappropriate. Does the same logic not apply to Berlin? Could not Berlin perhaps be content to try to achieve a humane environment in which its many residents could live, a model of tolerance and mutual respect, of acknowledgment of limits and the priority of social goals over economic or political might, a city in which people of widely divergent pasts—from the East as well as the West, for instance—could live in harmony and equality? Such a demonstration might indeed earn Berlin international respect, make it a model on a world scale. It would be a quest, not to attain power in one way rather than another, not to achieve economically what fifty years ago it failed to achieve militarily, not to cover with a public relations of peace a striving for domination and superiority over others, but rather a new turn in the city's development, combining some of the East's voiced commitment to equality and social concern with some of the West's commitment to technical progress and efficiency in planning.

A modest Berlin—is such a thing thinkable?

journal

THE SECOND PHASE: PREPARING THE ECONOMIC GROUNDWORK

From the Local Elections to the Currency Union

May 8

Met Fred Staufenbiel at the Tierpark, both a zoo and a park. We wanted to talk about our collective book. The weather is beautiful (nothing to do with socialism!), warm and dry, and it would be a shame to be indoors; but Fred doesn't have a dacha or a suburban house with a garden, just a large apartment in a new development. I suppose his balcony would have been all right, but it would be like sitting in a concrete box ten stories up in the air, looking out at other concrete masses, with green way below. At the Tierpark, at the Terrace Café, we got ourselves a pleasant table in the shade on a large terrace, surrounded by booths for snacks. The place was only half full (even later, at lunch time), and we could spread out papers on the table and talk uninterruptedly. Families with noisy children took tables near us from time to time, but in that environment it didn't bother us; it becomes part of the psychologically accepted background, not an intrusion.

The combination of a large apartment in a high-rise and a nearby pleasant park is also a decent alternative to a suburban single-family house with garden, with some advantages: no lawn to mow in the summer, no walks to shovel in the winter, and when outside, food prepared by someone else, human contact without human intrusion, more beautiful grounds and space to walk in than at home. The only disadvantage is that you can't "garden" yourself, can't get your hands dirty, can't have the pride of individual accomplishment in having produced beauty yourself. But presumably that could be worked out collectively too. And certainly, for the environment, denser compact housing and larger collective green spaces are sensible.

May 9

Disagreement with Andrée Fischer about title of our book in German. Dietz Verlag would still like to see it be *An American Looks at the DDR* or something similar. They want a title that will sell. We want a title that will reflect the contents of the book more directly and honestly, something like: *The Wende in the DDR: An Outsider's Perspective.* We don't see us as having an "American" perspective, if there is such a thing, certainly not a "United States" perspective; probably only 2 percent of the U.S. population would see things as we do.

We discussed the matter at lunch, around the corner from their office. The restaurant was in a building that used to provide housing for SED functionaries when they came to Berlin for conferences, meetings, etc.: a modern, relatively plush building, organized like a hotel with a lobby, dining facilities, a view of the Spree, etc. Now it has to pay its own way, and is indeed a hotel, open to the public, called the House on the Spree, and seems quite busy.

I don't like ruling classes, and the restaurant was ruling class. The service was good, too good, almost obsequious. And it wasn't done for tips, it was to please the masters. Here of course it's been a political ruling class, and its status was formal; we're used to an economic ruling class, with its power mediated through (and cloaked by) the market. And our ruling class is richer and more powerful; compare a luxury French restaurant in New York with the House on the Spree. But both reek of status.

In the evening, Bruno tells us that one could define socialism by what's repealed in the draft of the contract between the West and the East, formally the "Contract for the Creation of a Currency, Economic, and Social Union." It was a contract, not a treaty; this was a business deal. The key provisions were clear and simple:

> Art. 2 (1) The parties recognize a free, democratic, federal, lawful, and social order. To protect rights grounded in this contract, the freedom of contract, freedom to do business, establish firms, and engage in professional activities, the freedom for Germans to travel in the entire territory of the currency union, the ownership of real estate by private investors as well as the ownership of the means of production and the freedom to establish associations for the protection and advancement of working and economic conditions, are to be established.
>
> (2) Contrary provisions of the constitution of the DDR about the foundations of its previous socialist society and state will no longer be applicable.

In a protocol-memorandum attached to the contract, it is provided that:

> Requirements imposed on public agencies based on or referring to socialist legality, the socialist organization of the state and society, the obligations and goals of central guidance and planning of the public economy, socialist legal structures, socialist perspectives, the perspectives of the working class, or socialist morality, or comparable concepts, will no longer be applicable.

And then follow, as appendices, lists of West German laws to be adopted by the DDR, lists of DDR laws to be repealed, and lists of new laws to be adopted by the DDR.

May 10

The Real Property Office showed me the system they use for registering titles to real property. It differs from that in the United States, and is basically a cadastre system. We find things alphabetically by the names of the parties to a transaction; not the location of the physical land, but the private parties to the private transactions affecting it, determine where it is recorded. Under the cadastre system, the registration is by parcel, although parcel boundaries are in turn defined by the owners of the neighboring properties. What's amazing is that the system here is unchanged from before 1945—indeed, little changed from the original Prussian system of the nineteenth century. A modification of Marx's comment that ownership forms are critical to the characterization of a social system: not the formal legal handling, but the substantive legal rights. For what happens here is that state control is simply represented by an entry, "under state administration," on the second card of the three kept by the office. That represents a change of all legal rights; the earlier owner is out, socialist "ownership" takes over. The changes in legal rights really are based on a legal system entirely different from the prior one, in which legal title, as represented by entries in the cadastre, were controlling. In the DDR, such legal niceties as title on the cadastre cards were essentially irrelevant; the law regulated rights of use, transfer, etc., independently of the formalities of ownership. Now, however, those formalities will become important again: a new law wipes out the state's rights of administration and we're back to the old system. The DDR would have made it harder for the transition if it had either changed the legal forms entirely, i.e., eliminated the cadastre and title systems, or if it had consistently adapted them to the new content of socialist law and reflected the new substantive rules in changes in formal title. But they did neither the one nor the other consistently, and I assume many individuals using property they thought they had full "ownership" of will now be disappointed at the legal situation they meet when West German laws are applied to the DDR's inconsistent records.

That afternoon a long talk with Bernd Grönwald, a most interesting man and in many way representative of many in the DDR. He started off in the SED responsible for youth activities in one city, marked as an up-and-coming party member, behaving himself but very competently pushing causes that didn't follow the party line, convincing the party hierarchy that building up the Bauhaus would be an asset to the reputation of the DDR, opposed in the Bauakademie by the "concrete-heads" (the name given dyed-in-the-wool party members who refused to accept the changes produced by the *Wende*) before the *Wende*, but now isolated from his natural associates in the West because of his former party position.

May 11

The *Berliner Zeitung* carries a straight-faced account of a meeting of doctors from East and West. Four hundred doctors were invited by a private firm, a bank providing loans to doctors, on a boat trip from Tegel to Wannsee. The West speaker is quoted as telling his East German (woman) counterpart, "Stop acting like an ordinary worker in an ordinary trade, you're not a baker or a shoemaker, you're a professional. For heaven's sake get out of the trade union, you should have a professional association. Stop considering the health insurance program as your partner; start figuring out how to make money out of each injection. Then the new equipment you need will take care of itself."

Classic: in other words, change what's best in the system now.

May 12

Visit to Uli Hedtke at his summer house south of Berlin, near a beautiful lake, with Elke Judersleben. We asked how he came to have it. He said he saw the piece of land, it was a private garden, pretty run down, between fields now owned by a farm in the next town that raised cattle. When the decision was made nationally to separate the production of meat from that of plants (in retrospect a decision almost everyone admits was simply a mistake, made because of a mania for specialization), those who had owned this piece didn't need it for meat production, so it was not included in the new plant-producing cooperative. So it remained in the hands of a private owner, who sold it to Uli, who now rents half of it back to the former owner. The agreement with the former owner was until 2010, but the official who recorded it stamped it "unlimited duration," and no one now knows what the length of the term will actually be. Uli knows that under the prevailing rules for the area he can't build on the land, but there is a bungalow on it. How come? He bought it from the mayor of the town in which it is located, so nothing was said!

Uli is a trained philosopher, working at the Academy of Sciences. Since he insisted on dealing with the nature of work under socialism, raising awkward questions about it as a central concept of socialist ideology, they expelled him from the party in 1980 and barred him from giving lectures or publishing, but kept him on full pay at the Academy!

We knew Elke had been a candidate for the Berlin city council, but didn't know how she had done in the election. She had come in sixth on the SPD list, which had received only enough votes to place five candidates; but one of the five ahead of her might take a full-time position with the city administration and then she would be in. She has not been consulted, or been involved, in any of the decisions the SPD has made since the election: whether to enter a red-green or a red-black coalition, work with the PDS, etc.

Elke is also unhappy with her job and looking around for alternatives. She works for a governmental office responsible for international cultural exchanges, and is enthusiastic about her work. But her boss is incompetent, and only got the job through her SED connections. Now that the *Wende* has come, her boss has quit the party, since it can't help her anymore, but still has her job, and is buttering up her opposite numbers in the West in an effort to guarantee her position.

May 13

To Frankfurt/Oder, just on the DDR side of the Polish border, for a talk at a building conference. The city's chief architect (the term means a combination of development director, head of city planning, and director of urban design), Manfred Vogeler, met us and we walked around the center of the city and talked. He told us the story of the building of the single dominant high-rise in the city, decided on as matter of policy by the Politburo—every city had to have one, and symbolically it had to be taller than the tallest church. It was originally intended as an office building, but with no particular offices in mind; then, in 1969, funds for its construction were abruptly cut by the Politburo to save money, even though the foundation and some of the superstructure were already in place; funding was subsequently reinstated by the chief architect through support of the first secretary of the party in Frankfurt/Oder, out of local pride. But when the building was finished no one wanted to use it, only Jugendtourist, the official Youth Travel Agency, had money, so they got it and it became essentially a youth hostel (it wasn't suitable for a normal hotel because the bathrooms were centralized on the floor). Bruno calls the building representative of "architecture in the service of the class war," because of its visual antagonism to the main church in the city. Now it will presumably be converted back to offices; it's much too good a location for Jugendtourist, either by market or social standards. The chief architect doesn't get along with the citizens' movements in town, because they don't trust him as an old SED-cooperator, and he in turn doesn't like their critical attitude toward efforts to control development. He likes panel construction if sensitively undertaken, has done a decent job with it if the elegant pedestrian zone leading from the center of the city to the river is any indication. In my eyes, a typical decent, competent but technocratically somewhat arrogant architect.

We walked through the pedestrian zone. It was indeed well done, with attention to variations in facades, views down side streets, awkward open spaces pleasantly defined, automotive access for deliveries out of sight, careful and discreet signs. All of a sudden, a bright yellow Eduscho (West German coffee producer) sign, bolted on at right angles to a building, jarring and even potentially dangerous. We asked the chief architect about it. It's illegal, he said, and he's lodged a complaint with the town attorney. But the citizens' groups attacked him for doing it: "Interfering with the establishment of private business in the city," they said. Of course, in a year they will be the ones complaining about unregulated signs, interference with the aesthetics, etc., but right now they don't differentiate what he does that's good from what he does that's bad.

May 15

To Czechoslovakia, and a day in Bratislava. The most prominent party in Czechoslovakia is also called "Forum"; did New Forum begin the vogue in the use of the name? Probably not; reciprocal influence of different East European revolutions is probably slight as to such detailed matters, the real outside influence was the clear recognition that the Soviet Union would not intervene; but each country took its own road.

From discussions: the Czech revolution, which came after the DDR's, differed in three significant ways: the domination of the party had not been effectuated with the same Prussian thoroughness (the security apparatus was not as pervasive, the planning system not as stultifying, the ideological line not as rigidly and slavishly imposed); after the revolution there was no West Germany to introduce capitalism through pressure, seduction, and direct political intervention; and the citizens' protest movement had a leader, Vaclav Havel, who had national stature, was almost unanimously elected president, and could continue some of the original reform ideas after the overturn of the party. The euphoria that I described as the first stage of the *Wende* in the DDR is also to a large extent still in effect in Czechoslovakia, at least as far as we could tell. We deduce all this in part from conversations with Peter Mikhailovich, head of a section of an urban research institute in Bratislava, who is excited at being involved in a discussion with the minister for housing next Tuesday on new policy proposals—an equivalent feeling to ours when we were drafting policy proposals for rent reform in Weimar in November-December.

May 21

Back in Berlin, called Steffi Knopp to tell her of our planned symposium the next day on the book Fred and I are doing. She told me of the sale of *Wochenpost*, presumably by the PDS, to the Maxwell group. I asked if the workers had been consulted; she said no way. A sad reflection on the new turn of the PDS!

The Academy of Social Science, "attached to the Central Committee of the SED," is now a stock corporation, owned by those who work there. Does it have its old real estate? Apparently. Is the change legal? No one knows, but who will challenge it? Andreas Schubert called it theft of state property, and he's right; but morality doesn't seem to play much of a role, when existential anxieties are involved.

May 22

At the symposium on the book Fred and I are editing, exactly the right number of people for a good discussion came. Nothing strikingly new in the discussions; the only general impression was that, in the energetic debate on whether publicly owned land should be made available for private speculative purchase, the Wessies were well to the left of the Ossies in the audience, consistently warning of the dangers of the market economy, while the Ossies insisted land and real estate had to be available for sale if the DDR wanted to attract any investors to do business. But the issue wasn't easy to debate in the abstract; everyone agrees a blanket prohibition on sale makes no sense, some land should be sold because it will never be wanted for public purposes, and everyone agrees that not all land should be sold, and that price should not be the only consideration; the hot question is where to draw the line between the two. The devil lies in the details, as always.

The report I found most interesting was from Heinz Schwartzbach, from Dresden. He related that, the local elections being over, the new city council members feel themselves legitimated and no longer see a need for the grassroots citizens' movements, the Round Tables, etc. He suggested the new constitutional provisions for municipal government should try to merge the achievements of grassroots democracy with the forms of representative government. Helmut Meltzer, who worked on the new constitutional provisions, nodded in agreement, but nothing he said successfully grappled with the problem. The "bureaucratization of democracy" seems well under way.

Fred thinks we shouldn't try to put any final recommendations in the book because they'll be too quickly outdated. In the past, he says, there would have been no problem; one knew what next year would bring, very much the same as this year. No, says Wolfgang

Schumann; one could indeed be sure, but the certainty was that next year would be like this year, except a little worse. Did anyone ever support the old regime in the DDR?

May 25

Second conference of university teachers at the Academy of the Arts in West Berlin, with practitioners from East and West, about the future of city planning in the two Germanies. Again a mixed bag: some solid academics, some left practitioners, some right, some defensive and against citizens' initiatives as blocking their professional self-fulfillment, some innocent. They reject some of the most effective legislation we've had in the United States, viewing environmental impact statements as too inhibiting of new projects (including, of course, their own ideas), but also circulate an editorial from *Die Welt* under the title "First Thing: Block It!" calling for a moratorium on new projects until at least crude planning is in place. "Capital is a timid doe," one person at the conference said, apparently quoting Graf Lamsdorff, the liberal West German party leader, arguing that investment won't take place unless capital is carefully sheltered, and in particular allowed to buy real property too. That concerns Attachment IX to the proposed contract between East and West, the one that requires that West Germans (and others) be given the right to buy real property in DDR cities. By implication, they argued, no roadblocks should be put in the way of using such real property—not even in the name of environmental protection.

Discussion of the same issue with a teacher at an elementary school in Berlin that evening at a party held by the Liga, now renamed the Society for Friendship with the United States. She says her school administration is still the same old people, acknowledged incompetents, universally detested, formerly hard-line party members. Everyone knows all this, but no one is acting to remove them. She never joined the party and rather sees herself as a citizens' movement supporter. But her husband works at an old and respected left-wing cultural magazine, *Weltbühne*; there the editors are long-time party members, but were constantly in confrontations with the ZK about what they could print, were always on the side of their writers in trying to get material in. They also remain in their positions, but with the full support of their staffs.

In city planning terms, I see the citizens' movements as critically important for at least two reasons: they permit an ongoing participation in planning and decision-making, through possible mechanisms like the Round Table, rather than the once-every-four-years kind of participation that exclusively representative parliamentary democracy provides; and they permit representation of the intensity, as well as the numerical extent, of citizen interests, something representative government does not do well.

May 26

Tenant demonstration at Alexanderplatz in defense of tenants' rights. Curious mix of old-time politics and new, both "progressive," i.e., tenant/user-oriented. Two SPD speakers (one from here, one representing Momper, the SPD mayor of West Berlin) got booed, partly by old-time types, with "Shut up!" and "I wonder where *he* lives?" and partly by others who listened to what they were saying and booed when they called for rent increases or the private market to take over. Gysi, from the PDS, and Ullman, from Democracy Now, were the only principals from the parties who spoke, both good, Ullman a little academic, Gysi right on point: against housing allowances (income supplements shouldn't be needed, raise wages, pensions directly; applying for allowances is degrading), against cost-covering rents (how do you control costs?). But still a rather passive form of protest; the idea of protest marches, more confrontational styles, sit-ins, etc., hasn't hit yet. A good coalition of owners and tenants, though: a housing users' association, maybe? We could learn from that.

Walking with Bruno is like walking through living history. On the way to the Palace of the Republic: a part of the phony facade on the building of the Council of State *(see photo on page 250)* is from the old palace, which stood nearby. Ulbricht didn't want the old palace restored; why keep a monument to feudalism? Only the facade was kept, from the balcony of which Liebknecht announced the founding of a new popular republic in 1918! But who knows that now? Is there even a tablet there? Architecturally, it strikes me as surprisingly successful. The foreign ministry next to it *(see photo on facing page)*, by contrast, is huge, brutal; it was deliberately built to impress, to support Ulbricht's efforts to get the DDR recognized internationally and into the UN. But then he insisted it be lowered several stories from what the architects suggested, so as not to overpower the planned (but not built) central governmental structure. The little turrets and spike-like crosses on top of the cupolas of the big Protestant cathedral *(see photo on page 252)* used to look like the tops of Prussian helmets, so in the restoration they decided: not again! Instead, no turret, just a

wishy-washy little thing sticking up, with a ball on top, for the four smaller cupolas, a cross on top for the main dome. It took a very conscious sense of history to be concerned with such things; in the United States it would never occur to anyone to worry about histori-cal meanings such as these. But once they're brought to consciousness, wouldn't it be better to deal with them than to try to obliterate them?

When the foreign ministry was built, it was (and still is) too big for its prime tenant; the ministry of higher education is there now too. Another example of ideology overriding or dictating architecture: the building was designed, not primarily for those going in and out of it, or even for the joy of those going by, but for how its appearance served the interests of the regime. In the United States, the demand for space (contractually expressed, or guessed at) comes first, the building second. The reverse in the DDR. And here it's public money, money that is supposed to be used to meet social needs; redefining social needs to mean representing power is ugly.

The Palace itself (originally, a Moscow-style huge high-rise thing was planned, but the enthusiasm ran out after Khrushchev canceled

Stalin's plans for further monsters in Moscow) is a cold, glitzy, chrome and marble building which we first saw in a depressing rain a year after it opened, in 1977. Then we couldn't even tell what it was, either from the outside or after we got in, and its overwhelming scale intimidated; it struck us as an example of Stalinist architecture at its worst. Today the inside architecture is still harsh and pretentious, the chrome flashy, attempting unsuccessfully to be stylish, the imitation of a five-star hotel painfully evident; yet the building works. It has cafés, bars, restaurants, snack bars, theaters (three of them), movies, exhibition space, meeting halls. In the old days, when the side housing the Chamber of Deputies was in use for one of its sessions, they closed the rest of the building down; no longer. The building is in fact available for all kinds of uses, from rock music performances to alternative theater to charity sales to television coverage of election

returns. Many of the activities that come together in an organically grown city center are housed here, temporarily and often incongruously, but nevertheless they *are* here: in a central publicly provided indoor space, in the middle of town, where they can best do their thing. Life triumphs over even bad art!

It's a saving grace that at least the monstrous high-rise that could have been built there was not built—the dominant structure in Berlin thus ends up being the Television Tower, a much more politically neutral structure more expressive of technological than of political power.

June 1

A tour on the Spree and its connecting channels through the center of Berlin and its outskirts. Great. What that landscape had to put up with, and survived: Weimar, depression, Nazis, SED. A river's edge really reflects the values of its society. Here the giant cable works, hogging huge spaces along the shore; desirable for the works, for ease of transportation, but in a setting that would have brought great joy to many people—as residents, not as producers. Under socialism, the river's edge becomes industry; under capitalism, first industry (in raw

capitalism), then luxury housing (in refined capitalism). In a civilized society over a minimum threshold of development, it should be a public park, with guest houses and public facilities along it. In some spots the DDR isn't so far from it; vacation homes for trade union members at 35 marks for two weeks, with boats available along the shore.

Bruno and Lily have thought of leaving the DDR; it no longer feels like "theirs." (A friend had commented to us earlier: "This CDU/West German regime has no connection with us.") But they wouldn't go to West Germany; Bruno would rather go to France. A "voluntary" choice of nationality—nationality is imposed by birth?

Again a discussion of identity. My identity includes a long nose, but that doesn't give it value. Identity is a fact, undebatable, including the history of the person, culture, etc. Whether you like it or not is another matter. It can't be changed as identity, as past, but a different culture, set of values, landscape, can be chosen voluntarily. Or parts of one's identity can be weakened, thrown off: the formality of the Germans under the influence of the democracy of the United States, for instance, for German immigrants in the 1930s. Nationalism has more to do with resistance to external forces, versus anti-Semites, invading Russians, unpopular rulers, etc., than with identity or positive pride; pride, identity, become national in the service of resistance to national oppression.

Saw *Mein Kampf*, by a Hungarian playwright, Tabori, with cards bought at the last minute at the box office; this time the worst seats in the house, but at 3.50 marks each we can hardly complain. An outspokenly friendly piece about Jews, which I was very pleased to see, with two very sympathetic Jewish characters as protagonists, plus the early Adolf Hitler, clearly made fun of, but to my taste not taken seriously enough. On the other hand, the pogroms and the context of anti-Semitism were portrayed starkly. And with Jewish humor:

> What did Michelangelo ask the Pope, when the Pope hired him to do the ceiling of the Sistine Chapel?
> "What color do you want it?"

The typical de-mystifying, de-inflating everyday Jewish wit. I assume Tabori is Jewish; who else would write a play called *Sigmund's Freude* ("Sigmund's Joy," literally)?

June 4

Visit to Sabine Nobel, on Merkelstrasse in Prenzlauer Berg. On the outside, a decaying building. Mixed occupancy, some "social problem" types, enough solid people so that the minimum gets done, but no community. They tried but couldn't get a cooperative together to take it over from the KWV; only one or two other tenants were interested. The dining table is in the living room; almost no one we know has a separate dining room. A result of the housing shortage, but it seems to us not so terrible.

The new politicians, Sabine says, know from nothing; at a neighborhood meeting the SPD candidate for one of the city council seats, when asked about his program, said he'd have to assess the situation, see what the problems were, then decide; they said, shouldn't you have done that before you decided to run for office? The New Forum candidate did much better; he was an old neighborhood activist.

June 5

Privatization proceeds apace. Siegfried Lassak, who teaches law in Leipzig and had invited us there, is opening his own law office, together with two West German colleagues. Michael Bruckner's wife is starting her own taxi business, having been in charge of transportation for a state-owned enterprise. Bruckner, newly elected mayor of Treptow, a community along the river in Berlin, is an interesting character. We met him and his wife for coffee at Alexanderplatz. He was a member of an engineering group that helped set up new factories, from start to finish; what in the West would have been an eight-person consulting firm. They tried to go private but couldn't get all the necessary permissions, space, etc. Now they've split up, some going private, some with firms they helped get off the ground. He's convinced that specialization is the answer, no firm can transport its own goods as efficiently as a transportation firm. I tried to suggest the danger of such overgeneralizations; many, many firms in the United States do their own transportation. But never mind; such things get settled in the concrete, not in the abstract. We discussed the idea of a city (or community) exchange between Treptow and West Harlem; a fascinating idea.

Call from an architect from New York City, now in West Berlin, who wants to do pre-fab panel construction in East Berlin. Who should he talk to? God, go home, I thought (to myself), they've got enough pre-fabs here already. He isn't working with West German architects but with developers he wants to bring from the United States. He's seen great spots for development just walking through East Berlin twice; who would he have to convince to get the land? I sometimes feel ashamed of both my profession and my country!

The niceties of politics, such as fair play, due process, minimal courtesy to opponents, seem to be getting lost here (or maybe they have yet to be learned). The CDU-SPD coalition introduces into the legislature and passes, with its two-thirds-plus majority, a law confiscating a large part of the assets of the PDS. The law provides for no hearings, no appeals, no investigation, no deliberation. It is put on the agenda fifteen minutes before the opening of the session; so no chance to read it carefully, let alone prepare a defense. And the small parties, the citizens' movements, approve, not realizing that if a majority can do this to a minority, they are vulnerable too.

The same mean-spiritedness in the handling of the results of the local elections in Berlin. The rule had always been that the largest party in a district gets to name the mayor of that district, whether it has a majority or a plurality. Now they have changed the rules to permit coalitions and the election of a mayor by majority vote. So of course, where the PDS has the plurality, the CDU and the SPD gang up, form a coalition, and prevent the PDS from naming a mayor.

June 6

Unlimited confusion over the proposed currency union, which is to become effective July 1. A front-page story on loaves of bread fresh out of the oven being fed to pigs because the stores don't want to stock them, or any DDR goods, since they get 20 percent commission on Western goods, under 12 percent on those from the DDR. Nobody has the sense to change the rates and/or the prices on DDR goods, which people would love to buy. Firms have to pay out wages and salaries in West marks at 1:1, but only get 1:2 for their East mark bank accounts; the more liquid they are, the more they lose. No wonder so many DDR firms are facing bankruptcy; it's not only their inefficiency, but also the halving of their liquid assets. People continue to leave the East for the West at a rate of over 2,000 a week; no one cries now that it's a desperate situation or the government is ineffective, as they did when it happened under Modrow. And of course the migration will continue; since the jobs there pay twice what they pay here, what else would you expect? And joblessness has already hit 100,000 here. Long lines at all the banks, to open or make deposits to accounts; money will only be changed that is in bank accounts, no DDR currency will be honored after July 8. They even ran out of forms to apply for exchange at the banks yesterday, the first day they were announced as available! Careful long-range planning it's not.

Finally, someone said it directly: invasion. The head of the German Chamber of Industry and Commerce, Hans Peter Stihl, said, according to today's *taz*, that there will be "an invasion by West German entrepreneurs" into the DDR. "With its low wages and its

43-hour working week, the DDR offers a very good location.... The opening of the East is a real economic boost for the West... In order to fulfill its potential, the economy of the DDR must be opened to merciless competition. Stihl complained in this context about the hesitations of both workers and leaders of industry in the DDR." At the same time, the president of the Kiel Institute for International Economics said, again according to *taz*, that "a transitional period is necessary, in which the structure, but not the level of benefits, of the West German system of social security should be taken over in the East."

"Responsibility for the past": a constant theme these days, whether it's in debates with Gysi about whether the PDS has responsibility for the SED (and whether it is entitled to keep any of the SED's assets, a somewhat different question), or whether it's in criticism of Christa Wolf, the DDR's leading writer, in the forefront of the reform movement within the SED (and a speaker at the November 4 rally). Why didn't she leave the DDR? Westerners, DDR dissidents who left for the West, involuntary expatriates, make it much too easy for themselves, I think, when they say that anyone who is here now and who had any opportunity to leave should have, and is "responsible" for the SED if they didn't.

If people are "responsible" for the society in which they live, then we all have a large burden to bear. Anyone in the United States not wholly committed, and wholly active, in the protest against the war in Nicaragua, against racism and sexism, against armaments, against homelessness and poverty, against chauvinism and religious bigotry, is then "responsible" for these things. Everyone in West Germany not daily involved in the struggles around atomic power, South Africa, unemployment and social housing, political tests for public employment, and anti-Semitism is "responsible" for those things too. And if they are really "responsible," but feel that they can't affect the results, they should leave and go somewhere else. If they don't, they share the responsibility. That seems to me the logic of the argument being applied to DDR stayers. But where should we all go?

June 12

An extended trip to Hungary and Bulgaria before a final return to Germany. In Budapest, conversations with people in ministries, at the Academy of Sciences, with journalists, later at an urban historians conference at Lake Balaton. What stands out about the difference between the Hungarian and the DDR experience are two related things: first, the pervasive and arbitrary control of the party was never as absolute in Hungary, and second, the central plan never dominated the economy as completely, economic reforms started much earlier, both the legal and the nonlegal market and private enterprise were further developed in Hungary. Hungary is closer to Czechoslovakia than to the DDR.

Socialism, on the Stalinist model, had fewer indigenous roots in Hungary; in the DDR socialism, including aspects of the Stalinist model, drew on some historical traditions—on the one hand, Marxist, on the other hand, modern centralist and authoritarian—neither of which existed in Hungary; there, it has always been something of an alien intrusion on an underlying and continuing different way of life.

Kadar, waiting a decent interval after the invasion of Hungary in 1956, permitted, not a thousand flowers to bloom, but at least a few dozen. The history of the DDR shows a similar, if much weaker, pattern: protest, an increase in repression, after an interval gestures to recapture the allegiance of the protestors. In any event, the changes connected with the reform, then the retreat, then the defeat, of the party in Hungary were much more gradual than in the DDR. The absence of West Germany as a ready, willing, and anxious buyer/occupying power also make a vast difference. In terms of everyday life, the changes in Budapest are much less visible than those in East Berlin, and their direction seems much less determined.

June 15

In everyday life here, the hostility to the Soviet Union is palpable. In the DDR, people tend generally to make a separation between Stalin and Russia; here they take Stalin simply to be a recent embodiment of the fundamental Russian character. The evidence from jokes is everywhere:

> A man rescues an old woman from drowning. She tells him she is a fairy, and will grant him three wishes for his good deed.
> "I wish the Chinese would invade Poland, and then go back home," he says.
> "And what is your second wish?"
> "I wish the Chinese would invade Poland again," he says, "and then go home again."
> "And what is your third wish?"
> "Well, I wish the Chinese would do it all once again."
> "What do you have against Poland, that you make such wishes?" the fairy asks.
> "Nothing," the man answers. "It's just that this way they'll have to go through the Soviet Union three times with their armies!"

June 22

What did we learn after four days in Bulgaria, three of them in Sofia in a series of intensive meetings with ministry people, researchers, friends, and one day in Plovdiv, the second-largest city, meeting with city officials and planners, and seeing the city?

Besides many details, we learned some humility about generalizing about Eastern Europe or real existing socialism. Of course, everything has to be seen in its concrete historical and national context; everyone knows that. But the tendency instinctively, thoughtlessly, to generalize, is hard to overcome; it keeps cropping up in conversations we have all the time, when we think we've figured something out about how the system works, and find the same "system" in a different place or time works differently. In Bulgaria, for instance, the old Party (a generalization again: in some places it was called Communist, some Socialist, some Socialist Workers', some Socialist Unity—the common thread was a claim to a Marxist-Leninist ideology, political ties at the international level, and internalized Stalinism, but the differences were substantial), after a change in leadership and reforms whose depth we are not able to judge, won a procedurally fairly free election, has mass support in the countryside, and the *Wende* that led to change has not (yet?) eaten its children. Many other differences from the DDR too: less anti-Soviet feeling, more private property in housing, even less knowledge of the West. But the World Bank is sending a mission, the government is very anxious for foreign advice and investment, and economic pressures may make it virtually irrelevant whether the government is "Marxist" or private market-oriented in ideology.

To summarize our experiences in Hungary, Bulgaria, Czechoslovakia (and earlier trips to Poland):

Three factors came together to explain the changes in Eastern Europe: internal disintegration, external disintegration, and external pressures. Internal disintegration seems a common element: after a period of general economic growth in the late 1960s and early 1970s, each country's economy began to stagnate; whether out of mistaken planning, payment for earlier policies of forced growth, or inevitable limits to tightly centralized planning, standards of living stopped improving and in most countries declined absolutely. When Gorbachev released a reform movement in the Soviet Union, the political means to control the dissatisfaction resulting both from economic stagnation and continued political repression erupted. Thus internal disintegration.

External disintegration refers to the reciprocal effects of internal changes in each country on the others. It is particularly apparent in the difficulties caused within the Council for Mutual Economic Co-operation, the socialist analog to the European Economic Community. With markets drying up in other countries, with payment in non-hard currency being ever more difficult if not fruitless, the economies of each individual country also suffered seriously.

External pressures were the major difference between the DDR and its "brother" countries to the East, and, it seems to me, explain why its evolution is and will be different. In the other countries, the consensus was that the centralized economy should be disbanded, but, since no obvious model presented itself to replace it, the disbanding went slowly, much behind the rhetoric. This is true even in Poland, where the political crisis accelerated economic change even where the direction of such change was clear only on what was not wanted. In the DDR, by contrast, the direction of change was clear: toward West Germany and its system. Realistically speaking, the precise ways of changing from a centralized economy to a private market were just as obscure as everywhere else, but the impression—deliberately conveyed by the West German leadership—was that it would be easy. Thus there was no inhibition in dismantling the old system, and change was rapid. For the foreseeable future, then, I would predict that the territory of the DDR will become a seriously backward and blighted part of Germany, with problems more serious in many ways than those that will be faced, comparatively, in Czechoslovakia or Hungary.

July 14

After a week in West Germany, we flew back from Frankfurt/Main this evening and didn't notice until after we were out of the airport in Berlin that no one had asked to see our passports. Of course, it's a single country now, for most purposes. The whole passport and visa thing was absurd from the beginning, but it's very nice to have it over with.

We've been away from the DDR since before the currency union and are now curious to see the results at first hand. Immediately obvious: taxi prices have risen substantially. Instead of people waiting for taxis at Friedrichstrasse, a perennial annoyance, taxis are waiting for people. It will take a while for demand and supply to balance, but there's no reason to think they won't. The same is true of the price of groceries in the stores: the closer to the border, the cheaper are West goods. The prices are much higher in Leipzig, for instance, than in East Berlin; people only put up with that if they can't go West and buy. Thus prices are supposed to be cheapest, in all of the DDR, in East Berlin. I'm sure that too will work itself out. So will the preference for fancy packed West goods over comparable cheaper but less attractively wrapped East goods—unless, of course, there are "non-free market" pressures from the West on stores or distributors to stock only West goods, a practice U.S. anti-trust laws would prohibit but against which DDR retailers and consumers do not yet have weapons. In East Berlin the CDU administration's answer seems to be to encourage more Western export to the East, not to support better production and marketing there.

July 15

Catching up on DDR news. West Germany won the World Cup Soccer championship, and apparently the whole DDR celebrated as well. German nationalism has taken over; the DDR is gone as an independent state, only the administrative complications remain. DDR identity is no longer a topic of significant interest; the early instigators of the *Wende* are no longer interviewed or quoted in the news. The SPD may allow some of them to run as candidates on the SPD lists, for old times' sake, in the next all-German national election. New Forum so far doesn't want to; other individuals from Bündnis 90 seem to be interested, as a way of getting into parliament, since the 5 percent minimum threshold would otherwise exclude them. The PDS is still isolated. In the East German parliament, all the opposition is ignored, laughed at, or heckled; the "political culture" is worse than in the West. Fear of the skinheads is widespread. There is talk of modifying the Buchenwald monuments to reflect the incarceration of Germans by the Soviets after the war (thus relativizing the Nazi acts, of course). Prices are rising, wages aren't, little strikes are breaking out all over, everybody expects problems during the transition, everybody figures after the transition everything will be all right again; no one seems to doubt the wisdom of unification itself. No more big questions being discussed, just prices and wages, the problems of day-to-day life. What a change from nine months ago!

We discuss this, eating croissants, now sold from a booth at the U-Bahnhof Alexanderplatz. Our friends haven't had croissants before—also hard for us to imagine. And they try to serve them German-style: neatly cut open and buttered. Ever try to cut open a croissant neatly? French culture defeats German order!

July 16

We had, through our friend Wolfgang Schumann at Humboldt University, arranged for two weeks at a summer vacation home in order to finish writing the German version of this book. It was legit: under the Fulbright program, we were officially attached to the university and entitled to be treated as any other of its employees. The various writers' clubs and clubs of the cultural workers have vacation spots specifically designed for people to work in peace on their own projects, but they are in disarray: either all booked up or not available because they were rented from some municipality that isn't able to decide whether to rent them this year, or from some organization that no longer exists or can't decide either. Many of the old SED places, for instance, are simply empty, in a paralysis of indecision.

But this place of Humboldt's sounded fine: two and one-half hours from Berlin, two kilometers from a peaceful little lake, owned by a cooperative farm (LPG) and developed as a source of side income, sharing toilet, showers also shared and on only one floor, but with all meals—it sounded like just what we wanted. And dirt cheap, by West standards; subsidized by the university as one of the obligations employers have to care for their employees. Someone from the ministry of higher education drove us out. His map didn't have the Autobahn on it yet; the ministry is frugal! The shortest road would seem to lie along the east shore of the lake and then to Dahmen, but the road abruptly stops at the lake. Why? That's where Willi Stoph, the former head of the Council of Ministers, had his summer home, in the middle of a protected nature reserve, in which they simply forbade traffic. The vacation home is in a village called Dahmen: one grocery store, a part-time post office, a youth hostel, a camping place, two unassuming restaurants, a cooperative farm, and you're out of the town again. The sign at the grocery store gives the minutes of the last meeting of the town council. The town council elected the mayor: the 9 CDU members voted for the victor, the 4 PDS and 4 Farmers Party/Women's Federation members voted for the loser. A little bit of the old regime surviving, in unexpected corners of the country; the candidates thanked each other after the vote, national politics are a little less hostile, more human, here.

July 17

We've been given two rooms, one to live in and one to work in. The place isn't full (the uncertainties of life, and its not being available—yet?—to Wessies), so the extra room doesn't cost the university anything and we can have it for nothing. Classic DDR: the priority isn't maximizing income, it's maximizing service, presumably with some level of income as a constraint. Of course they could aim to increase income and use some of it to add a shower on our floor, or a common refrigerator for after-hours use (both of which had been planned but shelved for lack of money), but that would take a major psychological reorientation. Right now, the two decisions are taken entirely separately, by separate criteria: how much should be charged is in accordance with what university employees can or should pay; how much should be invested is in accordance with what the plan provides, in competition with other claims on investment. The unity of social and economic policy? It seems strange to us, but has its own logic.

Certainly in the present context the arrangement is inefficient. For the university, the more people use the vacation home, the more money they lose, since, although they rent the whole place, they pay extra for meals but charge less than they pay. For the LPG, the more people use the home, the more work they have. So everyone, from a straight self-interest point of view, is better off if the home isn't used. After dealing with hotels in Paris and Madrid, where every penny is counted and every possible service charged for, it's strange. The system really does rely on different incentives than the West!

Strangeness also in the conversation about bicycle repairs. We can use the place's bicycles for free (even the youth hostel down the road charges 5 marks a day); it's part of the service. The manager of the vacation home had just picked up three bicycles that had to be repaired and was astonished at what he was charged by the newly opened private bicycle shop. (Last year, he had to pay much less but had to ride around for three days to every neighboring town before he could put together the parts and the repairman to fix them!) The shop only wants to sell bikes, our fellow guests say, not get their hands dirty; so they charge exorbitantly for repairs, not caring if they do them or not. But, says the manager, they'll see: when everybody has a bike, they won't be able to sell any more and will be back doing repairs, and for more reasonable prices too! The concept that "when everyone has a bike, they won't sell any more" is again classic DDR. If people stopped buying things when they had enough, the whole capitalist economy would collapse. But the world view of the DDR has been static—like "solving the housing problem by 1990," when everyone has a place to live. It's not only a difference in economic systems, but also in world views. And nobody has yet seen any of their hopes realized. On the joint ventures that are talked about so much, the story goes:

> A chicken from Hamburg approaches a pig from Mecklenburg and asks if it wants to participate in a joint venture.
> "What shall we produce?" asks the pig.
> "Why, ham and eggs, I thought," answers the chicken. "You produce the ham and I'll produce the eggs."

July 21

Working on the last few pages of this book, looking back over the text and the attempt to see what it all means, we find it's not easy. Our attempt to sum up is in the Excurs that follows. Whether our assessment for the future is correct or not, we cannot of course know. We hope to come back and see for ourselves. Till then: Goodbye, DDR.

excurs 6

SUMMING IT UP:
WHAT WAS THE DDR?
WHAT DID IT HAVE TO DO WITH
SOCIALISM?

Summing up a year's experience in a different country, in the midst of dramatic historical events, is difficult; doing it briefly is even more so; separating out personal and necessarily random impressions from the opinions of friends, media, writers, separating fact from rumor, the accidental from the inevitable, almost impossible. And it all is colored by the experiences and values with which we came. Given these limitations, let me try to summarize by addressing two questions: (1) What were the key characteristics of society in the DDR, the characteristics that differentiated it from West Germany in particular during the same period? (2) What did the DDR experience have to do with socialism?

What Was the DDR?

What were the key characteristics of society in the DDR, the characteristics that differentiated it from West Germany during the same period?

We tried to describe some of the major differences that we ourselves experienced in Excurs 1, and those dealing with housing and city life in Excurs 3. To catalogue the differences in more general terms:

** **Scarcity:** the different standard of living. That's the easy part of the answer, and the most obvious one at first sight. There's no doubt people are materially better off, in the sense of having more goods and services available to them, in the West than in the East. Whether you accept Kornai's argument that scarcity is an essential and functional element of socialism, or the conventional U.S. view that planning is inherently an inefficient alternative to a private market, or the SED view that other benefits offset the disadvantages of shortages, or the untestable argument that it was deformations in socialism, not socialism itself, that produced scarcity, or the view that historically the Cold War, reparations to the Soviet Union, and other external conditions played a major role in the process—the conclusion that there *was* scarcity is not debatable.

** **Stalinism:** a repressive political state. That's also obvious, and has been obvious for a long time. We had details long before we came, and books like *Nachruf* named names and dates and events. The revelations about the extent of Stasi surveillance were perhaps a shock, but only in degree not in quality. The reactions of people to Stalinism was also pretty evident from the outside, from accounts of *übersiedler*, those leaving the DDR for the West, from journalistic accounts published outside the country, and from literature in the DDR itself: in part an internalization, in part passive resistance, withdrawal, privatization of the important parts of personal lives, the exact opposite of what the Central Committee used to call the "socialist way of life."

"Stalinism" is only figuratively the right word for the phenomenon; Stalin was certainly the leading and historically dominant figure in its development, but its existence in so many countries thirty-five years after Stalin's death suggests that it had to do with essential characteristics of the systems of the countries in which it existed, and wasn't simply some practice imposed from the outside by a single individual.

In comparing the lack of freedom in the DDR with the situation in the West, it's easy to exaggerate the degree of substantive freedom in the West. How much news actually gets communicated through the media, to what extent are decisions about national or even local policies actually made by citizens or with their involvement, what range of choices do those with limited means actually have, etc. But the procedural freedoms of the West, despite their occasional limitations (*Berufsverbot*, the exclusion of Communist Party members from public jobs, in West Germany, McCarthyism in the United States, for example), were without any doubt vastly greater than in the DDR. One was a *Rechtsstaat*, a "country of law," the other wasn't, to put it simply.

** **Centralized planning:** governmental economic planning centralized at the national level. Whether it's called socialist or not, it clearly wasn't capitalist planning. It involved a complex central planning apparatus that followed bureaucratically established priorities. While it produced, if in quantity rather than in quality (e.g., industrialized housing), it failed to innovate or even modernize (e.g., in the chemical industry) and thus increasingly fell behind its Western neighbor on the international market and in the satisfaction of domestic demand. Because distribution as well as production was planned, the difference between rich and poor was much much less than in the West; the greater equality meant less poverty, but also less wealth, less insecurity about not working but also less motivation to work.

** **An anti-market ideology:** a rejection of the use of the market in the distribution of goods on ideological grounds. To some extent shadow prices were utilized in the productive processes, with estimates of the "real" costs of factor inputs being used in the preparation of plans, but a complete rejection of such estimates of costs, let alone market-established prices, in the distribution of consumption goods. Without going into the debates about market socialism, it seems clear that it was not economic logic but presumed political consistency that led to this approach (just as, to draw an exact parallel, it was political

and not economic logic that led Ronald Reagan to espouse deregula-
tion even where private producers benefitted from regulation). Thus
even the information-providing functions of prices in the supply of
goods in everyday life was lacking, and a high and visible sense of the
irrationality of many planning decisions resulted.

** **The priority of the workplace:** the workplace played a much
more important role in the DDR than in the West. The larger employers (and the tendency was to largeness) provided their own health
clinics, kindergartens and child care centers, recreation halls, meeting
rooms, club houses, senior citizens' centers, and often shopping facilities, things that in the West would be considered quite separate from
the workplace and best provided in connection with the home, or
independent both of home and workplace. When we were staying in
the country to write the last pages of the German edition of this book,
we bicycled every morning to the village post office past signs an-
nouncing: "Vacation home of the Rostock Electrical Works" or
"Children's Vacation Home of the Mecklenburg Postal Workers'
Union." Such facilities are the rule, not the exception; if we see the
equivalent now and then in the United States, it is exceptional, and
most likely to be for the higher paid or management employees of a
company, not because the system is structured around companies or
unions taking on such responsibilities.

The difference seems to me related to the whole question of the
social role of work in the DDR, if exaggerated and perhaps distorted
through the ideological quest for legitimacy: if work is not only
economically necessary but also socially central, not only done for an
alien market but also for personal satisfaction, if work is where the
private and the public come together, the economic and the social
meet, then much of what in the West is separated out as the private
and dealt with at home can be left as social and dealt with at the
workplace. Marilyn Rueschemeyer's research on organizational life
in the DDR (see bibliography) shows that workplace organizations
engendered much closer and more enduring personal ties than did
residential ones. That's probably true, to a lesser degree, in the West
too; the desire to have work be productive, creative, useful, central in
life, is a *human* desire. It is reflected more directly (if ineffectively;
reality and public theory rarely coincided here) in the noncapitalist

system of the DDR. What it has to do with socialism I want to take up a little later.

And that leads us to a more subtle, more difficult to define, aspect of the society of the DDR:

** A different relationship between economic and social policy: economic policy is to serve social goals as well as vice versa. This is the point that it is hardest to come to grips with. The "as well as" fudges the question of priorities. A recent Yugoslav comment has it that there is no such thing as a separate "social policy" in the countries of real existing socialism: economic policy *is* social policy there. SED statements always, at least after 1971, spoke of the "unity of social and economic policy." In the sense that two sets of goals were brought into unity, the statement is factually wrong; no such debates took place, no balancing of conflicting goals was ever undertaken. But in the sense that economic goals were seen as *being* social goals, the statement may be, even if ironically (economic goals were supposed to serve social ends, whereas the opposite happened), correct.

In the capitalist countries, social and economic goals are deliberately separated. The idea is that a nation should ruthlessly pursue economic growth by nonsocial market principles, and that, *after* wealth is economically and efficiently produced, it should *then* be redistributed, or its production modified, by social policy. Time after time West German pundits told their East German audience to produce first, then worry about the social consequences; if there's nothing to divide, equal division won't bring much, they said. The DDR system, whatever it is called, took an opposite tack: not only production targets, but methods of production, conditions of work, the distribution of what was produced, was in theory to be controlled by those who did the production, as part of a single social as well as economic policy.

In fact, it wasn't that way, no more in the DDR than here. But there is a significant difference. No auto worker in Detroit or tractor driver in an Iowa wheat field or engineer at Boeing feels that the Ford, the loaf of Wonder Bread, or the 747 jumbo jet is *his* or *her* product; at most, there may be some (more or less induced) loyalty to the company that produces the product. According to Marx, the alienation of the producer from the results of his or her efforts was a characteristic of the capitalist mode of production. It was not supposed to be a characteristic of socialist production. In reality, it was; but the expectation, the ideology, the proclaimed social values, emphasized the producer determining the product. When, on top of all the other problems of the society, that officially proclaimed value is directly contradicted, the psychological result can be devastating.

An example: the farm crisis in the summer of 1990. In July, De Maizière had to call his minister of agriculture back from vacation to deal with what was officially called a "complete breakdown of the agricultural system"; farmers were dumping milk and cabbages in the streets, bringing cows to protests at the Volkskammer, blocking traffic with tractors. They were confronted, for the first time, with the possibility that they would have to plow their produce under, that the fruits of their labor were not wanted, were not socially useful.

Consider what that does to the people involved. Ideally, a farmer farms. It is a prototypical productive activity; the sight of a well-tended field of bright green corn, or potatoes, or flowers, or even cabbages, is a pleasure in itself, a tribute to hard work and attention to nature. Producing a crop is something in which a man or woman can take pride, something at the same time socially useful and personally satisfying. A farmer who farms well should be able to be satisfied with what he or she does, and be rewarded with a decent life by what he or she produces for society; if a decent life means money to buy goods on the market, a good farmer should have a decent income. Within the limits of the overall level of development, by and large DDR farmers were in that position. There were lots of things wrong with DDR agricultural policy—the striving for autarky, excessive specialization and collectivization, lack of response to consumer preferences, inefficiency, environmentally damaging practices—but they could still be seen in the context of an overall system that functioned socially.

That ended in the summer of 1990. Farmers must organize, must protest, must market, must at the least worry about their income and at the worst do without, negotiate and agitate and speculate with their produce, see this as commodities to be bought and sold, not as something directly useful to be grown, eaten, and enjoyed. That's a whole other attitude toward work, toward production, toward life.

Farming becomes a job; its purpose is to make money, and if plowing under makes more money than growing, so what. A cabbage is no different from a bomb, producing shoddy products no different from producing quality, packaging airplane food no different from cooking a good meal; if somebody will pay for it and the producer gets a good wage, that's what counts. Such a system may have its advantages, of course, but clearly something is also lost in the process, something the DDR's system at least claimed to have or to want.

A thirty-four-year-old trained agronomist who runs a LPG in Thuringia was interviewed by *Spiegel* about making her large farm competitive. She knew what she needed: money for new equipment, more efficient buildings, focused marketing—and to lay off one-half the members of the farm. But how could she do that, she asked *Spiegel*? The ones she would have to lay off were the older workers, good people, productive, willing, competent farmers who had devoted their lives to their work. And there's the point: in a capitalist system, their interests are secondary. Efficient production comes first; theoretically, the result is a total of more jobs, but in the process those laid off can get badly hurt. In the DDR, the concern with the workers intuitively came first; efficiency was a means to their end, not vice versa. In that sense, social goals generally dictated economic actions at the individual or local level. At the national level, the distinction between social goals and the interests of legitimation of the ruling structure became shadowy. And at both levels the costs in economic efficiency are obvious.

Whether one system is better or worse than the other is a matter of enormous debate; certainly the private market, despite the drawbacks in the relation of the worker to his/her work—alienation, in classic terms—has proven advantages in levels of production and consumer choice, and a longer term view of the DDR's economy would—indeed, did—suggest that its priorities were short-sighted, under all circumstances. The point here is only that it *is* in fact a different system. And perhaps there is some other alternative that would combine the benefits of both systems.

** **Class structure:** different roles for the party leadership, state bureaucrats, and the working class. This is one of the thorniest problems of all: how was the class structure of the DDR different from that of traditional capitalist countries? It seems to be beyond doubt that it was. The privileged were the top of the party and state apparatus (largely identical), artists and cultural leaders, and outstanding athletes; they got the housing reserved for "those with special needs," access to Intershops where they could buy Western goods, were paid more than others, could travel more widely. They drove Volvos. Below them, in terms of privilege, were the ranks of the trusted party members, the Stasi, employees of some ministries and some party organizations; they were able to move ahead on waiting lists, got larger housing units, were paid something more than average workers. They drove Ladas.

Legal rights: women's rights, in particular to abortion, child care, and parenting leaves and time off, were stronger than in West Germany. The right to publicly paid abortions without question in the first twelve weeks of pregnancy was recognized, in West Germany as well as in the DDR, as an important gain for women, and after major battles it was agreed that it would be continued in substantially the same form for at least two years after unification. Rights to housing, nonspeculative land ownership, controls on city development, in the DDR in the past looked very attractive to many Westerners: housing at 3 percent of income instead of 18 percent in West Germany (or 30 percent in the United States), provided through massive public housing and strictly controlled private rents, city planning tools providing real public (and potentially, although not actually) democratic control by citizens of their own communities, including widespread municipal ownership of land; security of tenure with evictions virtually unknown and homelessness an alien concept; bureaucratic errors and lack of resources for city development aplenty, but not speculation and exploitation for private profit. The results: on the good side, a level of social mixing unthinkable in the West; on the bad, a monotony and backwardness compared to what was happening elsewhere, have been discussed in Excurs 3.

** Social ideals: a stated commitment to egalitarianism and social justice. Whether the social net was in fact much better in the DDR than in, say, Western Europe, is open to some question. As the joke has it:

A Frenchman, an Englishman, and a DDR citizen, all over 65, meet and discuss how they pass the time.

"I sleep late," says the Frenchman. "When I get up I drink my aperitif with my coffee, then go visit my mistress and we spend the afternoon together."

"I get up early in the morning," says the Englishman, "have my kippers for breakfast, and then I'm off to the racetrack for the day."

"I get up early too," says the man from the DDR. "I take my heart medicine, and then I'm off to work on the early shift."

But at least he has a job. Unemployment was virtually unknown in the DDR (not counting, as another joke has it, people on the job), there were no homeless, medical care was free, etc. The shortcomings in the social net had to do with scarcity and inefficiency not with intent; the system itself produced only limited inequalities and avoided the concentrations of hardships we are familiar with at home.

What might have been the fullest expression of the social ideals of the DDR was in fact a product of the *Wende*, of the revolt against the prevailing system of the DDR, not of the system itself. It was perhaps born from the early aspirations of the DDR, and might be considered a fulfillment of one part of its otherwise aborted potential. It was the draft constitution, completed by the Round Table on April 4, 1990, after the national elections and never even considered by the Volkskammer, whose agreement to incorporate the DDR within the West German legal system was already certain. It would have been the most humane fundamental document on earth for the governance of a state. But it was stillborn in the midst of the unification process. It reflects the best the *Wende* produced, and, perhaps paradoxically, the best the DDR produced in the process of its negation.

The preamble to the draft constitution (written by Christa Wolf) is worth quoting in full:

> Coming from the humanistic tradition to which the best women and men of all strata of our people have contributed;
> in awareness of the responsibility of all Germans for their history and its consequences;
> committed to live as a free and equal partner in the community of all peoples and to take part in the unification process of Europe, in the course of which the German people will also achieve its own unity as a state;
> convinced that the highest freedom is the possibility of self-determinant responsible action;

founded on a revolutionary renewal;
determined to develop a community of democracy and solidarity, that
guarantees the dignity and freedom of the individual,
provides for equal rights for all, ensures the equality of the
sexes, and protects our natural environment;
the citizens of the DDR give themselves this constitution.

The rights explicitly recognized are extensive. Freedom from
discrimination is guaranteed (as part of the obligations all individuals
owe each other, i.e., freedom from private as well as public discrimination) on account of race, origin, nationality, language, sex, sexual
orientation, social status, age, handicap, or religious or political conviction or world-view. Government has the obligation to work toward the equality of women. Life and freedom from bodily harm are
protected, as is the right to die with dignity. Abortion is a right; "the
state will protect unborn life through the offer of social support."
There are rights to engage in business activity, subject to legislative
regulation; rights to move, enter, and leave the country, to maintain
citizenship, for rights of asylum for foreigners, privacy, the right of
access to all public information concerning a person, protection of the
sanctity of the home and freedom from invasions of privacy, freedom
of conscience, with an ancillary right to alternative service if conscience forbids otherwise mandatory service, strict rights of due
process in criminal proceedings, freedom from self-incrimination or
the obligation to incriminate others, protection for communications
with advisors on law or social issues, freedom of speech, the press,
the other media, freedom of assembly, of forming associations, of
practicing religion—and so forth.

The catalogue of course draws heavily on the rights in fact invaded by the old DDR state, but extends them significantly beyond
what is in practice in the West, spells them out, and adds new ones.
The protection for the family, for instance, is provided for, but "other
arrangements for living in common," which are made permanent, are
protected against discrimination; a right to housing is provided for,
and protection against eviction, with a concomitant obligation to
provide public resources for housing, a right to a job, equal pay for
equal work.

The provisions affecting property ownership and economic activities are particularly interesting. Ownership is protected, per se, but property that is personally used or cooperatively owned, and claims to income based on personal performance, are particularly protected. The right of eminent domain is provided for, but property that is personally used may only be condemned in case of dire necessity. Property condemned or specially burdened must be paid for, but compensation is to be determined by taking into account both the interests of the community and those of the owner; only with personally used property is full compensation required. Cartels and monopolies are prohibited, but state monopolies may be established if necessary for the provision of essential goods or services or for the maintenance of order. The use of land is subordinated to the public interest; only public or cooperative bodies may own more than 100 hectares, and the sale of land, or the transfer of rights of use to foreigners, requires public permission. Increases in the value of raw land brought about by reclassification is to be recaptured, up to one-half, by the state. Owners are responsible for any environmental damage they cause.

And more in similar vein. How this would all have worked out in practice we will never know, but the thinking that went into its drafting, and the overall conception of the type of society such a constitution provides for, was a major accomplishment of the *Wende*, and suggests how great a loss was its premature end.

What Did It Have to Do with Socialism?

This is the other question which, in a summing up, I want to address; it is the one with which we began, which motivated us to come to the DDR to begin with.

In fact, the DDR experience had nothing at all to do with socialism, as to a large part of it. That realization is missing from a great deal of the current discussion about events there, but it is an important point to make. The DDR's forty-year history was the product of some factors having nothing to do with an attempt to build socialism. The politics of the Soviet Union as a nation-state, for instance (rather than as a "socialist" economy), exerted a dominating influence on what happened in the DDR. The Soviet Union demanded and obtained control over developments in the eastern part of Germany in the four-power accords at the end of the war, and it used that control to make certain that it had a subservient state at the western edge of its sphere of influence, and that the Germany that had twice invaded it would not do so again. It had, in the early years, no interest in a vital or prosperous East Germany; on the contrary, it extracted reparations and imposed conditions and terms of trade that bled the territory of its former enemy. The contrast with the Marshall Plan and the treatment of the nascent West German state by the Western allies is striking. It is the starting point for the history of the DDR.

The Western allies, and then West Germany itself, contributed their bit to shaping DDR policies and to creating difficulties for it. Adenauer's hostility to the East German state was never concealed; several recent pre-*Wende* West German studies document the extent to which East-West tensions dominated thinking about DDR policies. The Cold War between the United States and its allies and the Soviet Union and its bloc made victory in the competition between East and West Germany not just an economic but also a political goal. At some point the constant SED talk of the "class enemy next door" lost touch with reality; nevertheless it began with a basis in fact.

Within the DDR, the system Stalin established, and which continued long after his death under pressure from the Soviet rulers and then in the self-interest of the SED top hierarchy, was more a consequence of these developments than of any economic or social theory. Counter-tendencies to the police state mentality that generally characterized the SED leadership were constantly cropping up, and interesting research suggests that, immediately after the war, there were deliberate efforts to establish a political model in East Germany different from—more democratic than—that in the Soviet Union. Those efforts went aground not because they were inherently implausible, but because conditions both in the East and West militated against them.

What then of socialism in the history of the DDR? I take socialism to consist of two elements: a moral critique of capitalism (recognizing, however, the major contributions it has made), and an analysis of modern history that suggests that an alternative form of social organization can, and may, evolve from it, one that is morally superior and based on differentiations of classes and individuals in the processes of production. From these two elements have come much speculation, and some experiments, as to what these alternative forms might be; central planning has played a conspicuous role in most, and an alternative to private market mechanisms in production and distribution play a role in all, but their precise form seems to me not central to the concept of socialism, and certainly today a matter much more for thought and experimentation than for dogmatic assertion.

The moral critique of capitalism in turn has two parts, and both are directly relevant to the DDR experience. The first is that many are excluded from the benefits of capitalism: not only a minority in the developed capitalist countries (at least a minority in periods of prosperity; the inevitability of crisis has long been a part of the Marxist analysis, and is still a possibility today), but also the residents of the third world, certainly a majority of the world's people. For countries like Germany, that was the problem of equality, of social justice. The other part of the critique of capitalism is the effect it has had, not on the minority excluded from its benefits but on the majority for whom it appears to work well. And that has to do with the relations among people: that they have become commodified, market-determined, one-dimensional. Even those who do well under capitalism have undergone a distortion of their motivation, have had to focus on making money and negotiating with their fellow humans, rather than exercising their creative abilities and loving their fellows. That may sound flowery, but is evident in what happens to the successful and prosperous people one sees about one every day in the West. It accounts for a good bit of support the DDR had even in the last years. One friend tells the story of meeting a couple, just returned from their first visit to West Berlin, waxing enthusiastic about all there is to buy, how modern, how new, how nice. He asked them if they'd like to live there. After a pause: no, they said, they had seen their friend there come home from work utterly exhausted, having to rest for half an hour before he can talk to another person decently again—their friend needed all those material possessions just to get over what he had to put up with at work. They wouldn't want to live like that.

Capitalism, or those who believe in capitalism and work within it, are by no means insensitive to these concerns. In my own area of work, urban development and housing, I see them frequently expressed, if more often in theory than in practice, in housing policies, planning practices, aspirations for residential and community life. But they are completely separated from the area of work, from production. There, the assumption is, the first priority is to produce, efficiently, competitively, more and more and better and better. Having produced, we will deal with the question of equality by redistributing, the question of social relations by constructing nonwork communities where people can interact on a human basis with each other.

This attempt to overcome the separation of work and production, on the one hand, from concerns for equality and social relations, on the other, is what I would consider the most important socialist component of the actual DDR experience. Let me put the matter concretely, from our own experience. In the United States, and even more in the more social welfare-oriented countries of Western Europe, cities are supposed to be treated differently from factories. Cities are designed (so we say, at least, and let us take us at our best intentions) for the benefit of the people who live in them. They are directly to be used, to be enjoyed, to provide protection and communication and enrich life. Whether a city is a good city or not is judged by whether people like to live there, whether it enhances or restricts their lives. A city's past is of value; when cities get old, they should be renewed, with due respect for tradition, not discarded. If they become inefficient, they should be modernized, but their survival should not be put in doubt. Ultimately, the society as a whole is responsible for the condition of our cities, for residential life. The individual has a right, as a member of society, to a decent place to live, in decent surroundings. Some minimal level of equality is guaranteed. It is part of the function of society to provide for the quality of life in its cities. It does that in part by regulation, in part by direct provision; if private provision serves the interests of the residents of the city, fine, if not, it has no place. The decision, in any event, is to be made by the people who live in the city, democratically, publicly, with full information. That is the theory in the best of our urban tradition.

Not so with factories. Factories are there to serve their owners, not those who work in them. If something can be produced more profitably elsewhere, the factory is closed, or converted to some other use. The worker gets no immediate benefit from working in the factory; the benefit he or she gets is the paycheck, to be spent elsewhere. Whether workers enjoy their work or not is irrelevant (except to the extent that it influences how well they do what they do); pleasure in work is not the purpose of the enterprise. Factories are built, not to serve those who work in them but to make money for their owners. No person has a right to a job; whether he or she works or not is a private decision, generally beyond the immediate control of the individual. Decisions as to what is produced, how, when, for whom, at what price, and for how long are not made by the workers; that isn't their business. Workers are expected to separate themselves from their work, to be alienated from it, in precisely the opposite way from that in which citizens are expected to be at home in their cities.

In the DDR, work has played a different role in society. As a direct outgrowth of socialist theory and ideology, and rigidified and deformed though it may have been by other purposes and other pressures, the workplace has played a more human role in living in the DDR than it does in West Germany or the United States today. People form friendships at work, rather than compete with each other; they stay with their employers, rather than shop around for better jobs; they look to the company they work for for long-term protection and support. They have a right to a job, not only in theory but in practice. Both the good and the bad aspects of this difference cropped up throughout our stay; on the good side, kindergartens, health centers, coffee breaks, job security, lack of tension; on the bad side, inefficiency, make-work, waste, lack of innovation. It is a drastically different approach to the relation between work and production, on the one side, and "living," on the other side, than we had been exposed to before.

Some of this experience of the DDR is consistent with the best values of socialism; some is not. Creativity, innovation, self-expression, have been absent from most of DDR production (the creative arts, drama, are a conspicuous exception); very few workers would say their jobs have contributed to the free unfolding of their personalities. Nor has democratic self-determination ever characterized work processes in the DDR, despite official propaganda to the contrary. Whether decisions by freely associated producers should in any event be made at the workplace seems to me open to question; the interests of producers and consumers both must somehow be brought into play. However that may be, decisions as to production have been made democratically neither there nor any place else in the DDR. But that should not blind us to what was in fact done.

I hardly want to suggest that the DDR was successful in the way it dealt with work, or that it proved even the potential of socialism. But it contributed valuable evidence that seems to me to tend in this direction. What occurred in certain spheres in the DDR was different from that of other, more technically advanced, even socially oriented, market economies. And in many parts it worked, in ways that deserve to be studied and analyzed very carefully. For the Western private market model does not work very well either, and its problems become daily more severe: problems of inequality, of human unhappiness, of ecological damage (where the DDR has only bad experience to offer). The private market system is good at maximizing production, and may then deal with the unwanted effects of that process afterward. But that hasn't worked, and the failures have been more and more apparent in the capitalist countries. The DDR experience, incomplete and contradictory as it was, and particularly the potential abortively pursued in the *Wende*, have something to offer here. Neither blanket labeling nor blanket judgments of the experience will do.

postscript

THE THIRD PHASE:
TOTAL TAKEOVER
AND ITS CONSEQUENCES

After our return to the United States in August 1990, we kept in close touch with our friends in what was at first called "the territory of the former DDR" and is now called "the five new states of the German Federal Republic." We have read reports both in German and in United States newspapers and magazines; we returned for a visit in December 1990 and have hosted visitors from the DDR here since then. Since much of what happened took place before we ourselves learned of it, the particular dates things came into our knowledge do not seem important; thus I will now drop the journal dates and simply describe what has happened in narrative form.

On the issue I came to the DDR to study—housing and urban development—it is still too early to tell what will happen. Rents have already doubled for most units and are supposed to increase to market levels, going up by a multiple of about five in the fall of 1991. If economic conditions remain as bad as they are now, people will simply be unable to pay such rents; the housing allowances paid under West German provisions will have to be liberalized to cover them, the drain on government budgets will be substantial, and the net result will be a confused, insecure, and unstable preservation of the status quo for the immediate future. Simply to keep things from getting worse, Kohl has already committed himself to an additional 30 billion marks over two years to deal with problems in the five new federal states; his pledges of no new taxes to cover the costs of unification are not considered binding by the CDU under the new circumstances. Confusion, controversy, and litigation have slowed down the sale of city land, and the pressure of buyers and new investors has not yet reached major proportions (somewhat contrary to expectations), so little change is as yet visible on the urban front.

The Palace of the Republic is closed, ostensibly because asbestos was used in parts of its construction, even though the readings on asbestos in the air are well within otherwise permissible levels. The Volkskammer of course does not have to meet there anymore; it no longer exists, East German representatives sit in the Bundestag in Bonn. Lothar De Maizière was briefly a minister in the all-German government; but right after the CDU victory in the general election in December, allegations that he had been an informant for the Stasi surfaced and prompted his resignation. The allegations have until now neither been proven nor disproven; he is back in the party but not in the government. Theater performances are empty. Prices on the S-Bahn have risen to West German levels. A few quixotic institutions resist the adaptation to the West; one local savings and loan association, for instance, simply refused to raise its interest rates, saying they had an obligation to their customers to be of service. Such forms of resistance can't last. Salaries are still way below West German levels— in the universities they may go to 60 percent of what they are in the Western states by the end of 1991.

On the consumption side, tastes seem to have changed, offerings have changed, and what has been bought has changed. It used to be that there were many things in the stores, at very reasonable prices, but not particularly what people wanted and not of good quality. As one of the many jokes has it:

A man walks into a clothing store and says, "This jacket that I bought yesterday; it's junk! The buttons have come off, the sleeves unraveled, it doesn't fit well, the colors ran in the rain, and I can't wear it anymore!"

"Listen, fella," says the salesman, "don't get so excited over one lousy jacket. Just think, we have three thousand of them we have to get rid of!"

The joke seems bittersweet now, when the stores are full of things that people do want and they can't afford to buy them. At the same time, if they did want to buy the cheap old goods, with all their deficiencies, they can't. Those factories, considered "uncompetitive"—as indeed they are on the world market—have been closed. An old-established chocolate factory in Leipzig, for instance, that made cheap chocolate very popular with children in the DDR, is now out of business; the chocolate that is available in the stores is much better, but out of range of many people who could have afforded, and would have bought, the older kind. That what they produce would be bought at a lower price than the imported, and that it could often have been exported at a profit, does not matter; if sold in the East, the nonconvertible currency is not desired in the new Germany, and no business in the West seems to have wanted to invest in second-grade production facilities in the East.

Unemployment, likewise, has appeared for the first time in the East, and on a scale that would frighten people in the West also. Again, it wasn't perfect before; by many measures, there was indeed unemployment, but all of the unemployed had jobs. A recent joke has it:

"Why do you always go to work so early," a wife asks her husband, a manager at a local factory, "do you think they can't get along without you?"

"No, I think they could; but I'm afraid someone will notice it!"

Again, the story is more bitter than funny today. The latest figures I have are as of March 1991; they show part-time employment going from just over 600,000 in July of last year to over 1.8 million today, and totally unemployed going from just over 250,000 in July 1990 to almost 800,000 today. Those figures must soon be combined, for many were guaranteed at least part-time work until July 1, 1991, and will then move over into the totally unemployed column. The current prediction is for as high as 3 million unemployed by the summer of 1991. And street demonstrations are beginning again in Leipzig, but this time against the CDU!

For those that are working, conditions are not good. Pay scales are less than 50 percent of those in the West (the prices of goods are of course the same). Insecurity is prevalent. In the city government of Berlin, Ossies may not be supervisors of Wessies. Whatever was done in the old DDR is consistently denigrated; Professor Ralf Dahrendorf, a prominent sociologist, says, for instance, that "Nothing, absolutely nothing, is worth saving of the old DDR social science." Moderniza- tion of DDR industry is lagging; with one or two major exceptions, investors find they get better returns elsewhere. Trade with the former "brother socialist countries" has dissipated, as those countries face their own problems, lack the hard currency now required by DDR firms; the DDR's well-established trade relations with the East are largely dead.

That the economic situation in the DDR is disastrous is by now acknowledged all over Germany. The Kohl government, despite its earlier assurances about being able to finance unification within its existing budget, has been forced to appropriate additional amounts, in billions of marks, to finance a minimal safety net and to put in infrastructure improvements; normal tax revenues for municipalities and states in the five new states have, with the economic collapse, plummeted, they have no resources of their own to use. The Leipzig trade fair, in March, was a disaster; the old market in the East is no longer interesting, the West now has other access to eastern German firms if they want something, and the eastern firms are almost all in such a state of uncertainty about their future ownership and direction that they are incapable of making firm commitments on contracts.

For academics and researchers, writers and artists and intellectu- als, the problem is also unemployment, but not because of economic inefficiency. Under the unification agreement, all DDR institutions in these fields were to be evaluated, with a view to either simple closure or merger with corresponding West German institutions or continued separate existence, with or without major reform, all as the evaluation would indicate. Where structures or policies were found that suggested improvements in the corresponding system in use in the West, they were to be incorporated into the Western practice.

The implementation of these provisions has caused turmoil in East Germany and raised major charges of unfairness, lack of due process, and political witch-hunts against former SED members and against those with views unpopular with the members of the evaluation commissions, overwhelmingly West Germans. In the atmosphere created by views such as Dahrendorf's, commissions have begun work with an arrogance based on such views, treating their colleagues in the East with discourtesy if not contempt, often more interested in opening opportunities for the expansion of West German institutions than in the fair judgment of East German ones. Many East German personnel have been terminated as of July 1, 1991, whatever their status, from "tenured" professors to civil servants to clerical workers and research assistants; all may reapply for their own jobs, but so may outsiders. Those from the West clearly have an advantage in such a competition, particularly if it is judged by the West German standards on the bodies that will make the decisions on new appointments; West Germans are more familiar with the current technology, the state of Western social science, the vocabulary of the establishment West.

The situation is not all bad or unfair, of course. Many university departments of "Marxism-Leninism" deserve to be closed; they were often simply propagating dogma, doing "research" to prove pre-established conclusions, repeating, and teaching, words and phrases and slogans whose meanings had long since been suppressed. In many cases, on the other hand, social science research and teaching was done within departments labeled "Marxism-Leninism" simply because that phrase was taken as synonymous with social science; the label does not necessarily identify the content. Both good and bad, competent and incompetent, people will be fired in the dismantling of everything known as M-L. And there has been protest, most notably at Humboldt University in East Berlin, whose rector, a theologian we had met at Charley Marx's birthday party during the *Wende*, joined with his students and faculty in mounting a massive demonstration against the blind implementation of the new policies, with significant success. Things will go more slowly, more carefully, at Humboldt, and some jobs will be protected, research continued, that would otherwise have been lost. Many, pressured into early retirement, the least painful way of dealing with what seems an inevitable outcome, will find scope for continued involvement in their fields, if only because West Germans have a real need for people familiar with East German traditions, circumstances, ways, to find out what is happening there. Fred Staufenbiel, for instance, while taking early retirement from Weimar at 63, will be collaborating on a research project with people from the Technical University of Berlin (West) looking at city planning practices throughout the united Germany. Peter Voigt, having been elected dean during the *Wende*, will probably keep his job, and research will continue to go forward under his leadership at Rostock University (the new name for Wilhelm-Pieck University after the *Wende*). Bernd Hunger has left the Institute for City Development and Architecture of the Building Academy of the DDR, which has been disbanded, and is working in Berlin for the corresponding West German institution. Bruno Flierl continues to get his pension, and is more in demand for articles, comments, talks, lectures, than ever before. Many will find their way in the new circumstances.

But many will not, for various reasons. Ushi Staufenbiel was asked to resign her position with the Berlin city planning office at the beginning of the year, because the West Berlin administration wanted all its own people in positions of importance, and she did. The policy has been, we are told, that no West German official is ever to work under a former DDR person. Over one-third of all East German civil servants have been laid off; particularly those with experience, in key departments, are not wanted, since they might interfere with a smooth takeover. So Ushi is doing what she calls "grandmother-service," taking care of her grandchildren while her own children work. Their daughter, who had made a decent living as an independent potter, selling her own wares, has now taken up the study of taxation, and will provide tax advice for a living instead of potting, where she can no longer compete with the great variety of imported factory-made goods. Katya Remple, the teaching assistant in Weimar responsible for dealing with the social aspects of urban development and an early proponent of the *Wende* both inside and outside the SED, is unemployed. It is no accident that those having the most difficulty today are women.

For some, as for Bernd Grönwald, to whom this book is dedicated, the problems were too much to bear. Grönwald committed suicide—the German term is *wählte den Freitod*, "chose a voluntary death"—out of despair for the future on January 28, 1991. He had worked long and hard, within the structure of the prevailing order, to build up islands of independence, of professional competence and integrity. He was, on the one hand, a loyal party functionary, helping to implement a rigid and authoritarian system. But he also got the Bauhaus in Dessau reestablished and gave it a new, progressive role, both in the DDR and internationally; he built up the Institute for City Planning and Architecture within the Building Academy, making it a center for research on the human impact of DDR housing and planning policies, including exposure of short-comings few others had dared point the finger at. Throughout his life, from his early days teaching at the HAB in Weimar, he had given opportunities for development to many younger people and sheltered them from the pressures of the surrounding official environment. But he found himself, after unification, blacklisted from any positions of significance because of his participation in the SED structures of his day. He could see no value salvageable from what he had accomplished in the past, and no future for himself in the new Germany. He felt, and many others to whom we have spoken since also feel, as if they are living in an occupied country. Grönwald took the most desperate of all measures to escape his impasse.

Bruno Flierl's tribute to Grönwald echoes our feelings:

> Bernd Grönwald experienced the contradiction between power and knowledge that was typical of the DDR, without being able to resolve it in favor of the socialist ideal against the Stalinist practice.... He had wanted the *Wende* in the DDR, he had helped prepare it. He could not endure what it in fact became. Prisoner of his own past, he could not achieve his own freedom. He, who had given hope to so many others, in the end had no hope left for himself.

A chapter in history has closed. But the experiences gained during the time that chapter was open have yet to be soberly read and evaluated. Both the good and the bad will leave their effects long after their causes have disappeared. There is still much to be learned from those experiences, and from the people that lived through them, and from those that did not survive them.

glossary

Allianz für Deutschland Alliance for Germany, the coalition of the East German CDU, DSU, and DA, engineered by Kohl before the March 18, 1989, election in the DDR

Ausweis Identity card, which includes key official information such as address, jobs, arrests, etc.

BRD Bundesrepublik Deutschland, the Federal Republic of Germany, or West Germany

Bauakademie Building Academy, the central research institution for building and architecture in the DDR; the Institute for City Development and Architecture is situated within it

Bundestag The lower house of the West German legislature

Bündnis 90 Coalition 90, consisting of the New Forum, the Initiative for Peace and Human Rights, and Democracy Now

CDU Christlich-Demokratische Union, Christian Democratic Union: member of the National Front in East Germany; largest West Germany party

CSU Christliche Soziale Union, Christian Social Union, the conservative analog party of the West CDU in Bavaria, West Germany

DA Demokratischer Aufbruch, Democratic Opening, one of the new groupings appearing during the *Wende*

DBD Demokratische Bauernpartei Deutschlands, Democratic Farmers' Party of (East) Germany, member of the National Front

DDR Deutsche Demokratische Republik, the German Democratic Republic, or East Germany

Demokratie Jetzt Democracy Now, one of the citizens' movements that first raised the call for the *Wende*

DFD Demokratischer Frauenbund Deutschlands, Democratic Womens' Federation of (East) Germany, member of the National Front

DGB Deutscher Gewerkschaftsbund, German Trade Union Federation, the central body of the West German trade unions

DSU Deutsche Soziale Union, German Social Union, the East German party modeled after the CSU in Bavaria

FDGB Freier Deutscher Gewerkschaftsbund, Free German Trade Union Federation, the central body of the East German trade unions

FDJ Freie Deutsche Jugend, Free German Youth, the SED-controlled mass organization for young people up to age twenty-five, member of the National Front

FDP Freie Demokratische Partei, Free Democratic Party, in West Germany; LDP merged into it after the *Wende*

HAB Hochschule für Architektur und Bauwesen, College for Architecture and Building, in Weimar

Haus der Demokratie House of Democracy, a building in the center of East Berlin owned by the SED and turned over after the *Wende* to the citizens' movements to use as their offices

Humboldt Humboldt-Universität, Humboldt University, the most important East German university, in Berlin

ISA Institut für Städtebau und Architektur, Institute for Urban Development and Architecture, situated within the Building Academy

Initiative für Frieden und Menschenrechte Initiative for Peace and Human Rights, the oldest (formed in 1985) of the East German citizens' movements to raise the call for reform

Jüdischer Kulturverband Jewish Cultural Association, for secular Jewish activities in the DDR

KWV Kommunale Wohnungsverwaltung, Municipal Housing Administration

Kombinat Large state-owned business organization that centralizes operations within whole sectors of the economy, sometimes on a national basis, sometimes by *Länder*

KPD Kommunistische Partei Deutschlands, the pre-World War II Communist Party of Germany

Länder The twelve states that made up the DDR, a revision of the state structure established by the Nazis, then converted to five states plus Berlin in the unification agreement with the West

LDP Liberal-Demokratische Partei, Liberal Democratic Party, successor to the LDPD

LDPD Liberal-Demokratische Partei Deutschlands, Liberal Democratic Party of (East) Germany, founded 1945, member of the National Front, later changed its name to LDP

Liga für Völkerfreundschaft League for Friendship Among Peoples

LPG Ländlicher Produktiongenossenschaft, agricultural cooperative

Ministerrat Council of Ministers, the leadership of the government; its chairman (minister-president) is analogous to a prime minister

Nationale Front National Front, entity comprising the organizations represented in the Volkskammer; prepared nominations for that body before the *Wende*

NDPD National-Demokratische Partei Deutschlands, National Democratic Party of Germany, member of the National Front

Neues Deutschland New Germany, formerly the official newspaper of the SED, now connected with the PDS

Neues Forum New Forum, one of the early, and the largest, of the citizens' movements during the *Wende*

Ossies People from Ost Deutschland, East Germany

PDS Partei Deutschlands Sozialdemokratische, formerly the SED

Politburo Executive committee of the ZK

SBZ Sowjetische Besatzungszone, Soviet Occupation Zone

SDP Sozialdemokratische Partei, Social Democratic Party, original name of the party formed in the fall of 1989 and renamed SPD in January 1990

SED Sozialistische Einheitspartei Deutschlands, Socialist Unity Party of (East) Germany; formed from a merger of KPD and SPD in 1946; changed named to SED-PDS in December 1989 and then to PDS in February 1990

SPD Sozialdemokratische Partei Deutschlands, Social Democratic Party of Germany

Staatsrat Council of State, elected by the Volkskammer, with largely honorific functions; its chairman is analogous to the largely ceremonial president in a parliamentary system

Stasi Staatssicherheitsdienst, State Security Service, the East German internal security police

taz *Tageszeitung,* or *Daily Newspaper,* a lively alternative/left newspaper published in regional editions throughout Germany, with good coverage of the DDR

Trabant Name of the most widely owned car in the DDR, the equivalent of the Volkswagen in the West

UFV Unabhängiger Frauenverband, the Independent Women's Federation, of East Germany

VL Vereinigte Linke, United Left, of East Germany

Volkskammer The parliament, or highest legislative body, of the DDR

Wende Turn, the name given to the political change from SED rule to parliamentary democracy during the fall of 1989

Wessies People from West Germany

ZK Zentral Komitee, Central Committee (of the SED)

chronology

1985 - 1990

1985

Election of Gorbachev as general secretary of Communist Party of the Soviet Union

1986

February 6 The Ministry of State Security (the Stasi) is honored with the Order of Karl Marx

February 19 The president of the DDR parliament meets with West German leaders, invited by the West German SPD

June 8 Elections to ninth session of parliament; 99.74 percent of eligible voters reported as voting and 99.94 percent reported as voting for candidates of the National Front

1987

June 7 Altercation between DDR police and youths wanting to hear rock concert near Wall in West Berlin

June 9 About 3,000 people demonstrate in East Berlin, demanding demolition of the Wall and supporting Gorbachev

July 17 Abolition of the death penalty

August 26 West Germany increases the "welcome money" paid to visitors from the DDR to 100 marks per visitor per year

September 7-11 Honecker visits Bonn
October 12 Broad amnesty, 24,612 prisoners reported released
November 1 Easing of restrictions on bringing in records, technical publications, stamps, calendars

1988

January 17 Over one hundred people arrested at demonstration during the official commemoration of Rosa Luxemburg and Karl Liebknecht's murders; others, from the Church of Zion in East Berlin, protest restrictions on speech and travel, and are given choice of facing charges or emigrating
March 1 Residents of West Berlin are allowed to stay overnight on one visit a year to East Berlin
May 9 West German Chancellor Helmut Kohl embarks on private three-day visit to the DDR
December *Sputnik,* popular Soviet news magazine, banned

1989

January 1 New travel regulations permit appeals by those denied permission to emigrate; regulations further expanded after protests on April 1
January 15 Eighty people arrested in Leipzig while demonstrating for freedom of expression during commemoration of Luxemburg-Liebknecht murders
March 12 Six hundred people in Leipzig demonstrate for right to emigrate
May 2 Hungary begins demolition of fences at border with Austria
May 17 In local elections, 98.85 percent reported as voting for the candidates of the National Front; widespread allegations of vote fraud by opposition and church leaders monitoring elections
June 5 *Neues Deutschland,* the SED newspaper, defends massacre at Tiananmen Square in China; parliament does same three days later
July 6 Agreement between environmental ministers of East and West Germany about West German investment in East German projects
July 15 First reports of DDR citizens who want to emigrate taking refuge in West German embassies in Budapest, Prague, and East Berlin
August 7 DDR protests that West Germany is supporting the emigration, giving DDR citizens automatic citizenship and entitlements
August 8 Building housing the West German Permanent Representation in East Berlin is closed; over one hundred DDR citizens have taken sanctuary there
August 10 Beginning of direct West German-East German air travel

August 13 Closing of West German embassy in Budapest; 181 DDR citizens have sought sanctuary there

August 19 During a Pan-European Picnic in Hungary near Austrian border several hundred DDR citizens lift barrier at border and cross over

August 22 Closing of West German embassy in Prague; 140 DDR citizens have taken sanctuary there

August 24 Hungary permits 108 DDR citizens to leave West German embassy for Vienna; others informally not prevented from leaving

September 4 Hundreds demonstrate in Leipzig for freedom of travel

September 7 Some eighty people arrested at Alexanderplatz in East Berlin in demonstration against election fraud during local elections

September 10 First public call for reforms by New Forum

September 11 Hungary voids agreement with DDR to enforce visa restrictions regarding DDR citizens, opens border to Austria; within three days approximately 15,000 DDR citizens cross

September 12 Democracy Now founded, issues call for citizen action for reforms

September 18 Some one hundred people arrested at a demonstration in Leipzig

September 19 West Germany embassy in Warsaw closed; one hundred DDR citizens are in sanctuary there. New Forum applies to register as a legal association, with Gysi providing legal advice; denied September 21; appeal filed

September 24 Eighty representatives of various reform groups meet in Leipzig

September 25 About 8,000 people demonstrate in Leipzig for legalization of New Forum and freedom to travel; a dozen arrested

September 27 West German Foreign Minister Hans-Dietrich Genscher negotiates an agreement with his counterparts from Czechoslovakia and the DDR to permit the more than 3,000 people in various West German embassies to leave for West Germany; the DDR insists they leave on DDR trains and travel through DDR territory

October 1 Democratic Opening (DA) founded

October 2 Demonstration of between 10,000 and 25,000 in Leipzig broken up by the police

October 3 An additional 7,600 DDR citizens seek sanctuary in the West German embassy in Prague; they receive permission to leave, again traveling by train through the DDR, but visa-free travel between the DDR and Czechoslovakia is stopped

October 4 As the train carrying the DDR emigres from Prague goes through the Dresden railroad station, an estimated 3,000 Dresden residents try to climb aboard; violent clashes with the security forces; the trains are sealed for the rest of the trip

October 5 All DDR citizens in the West German embassy in Warsaw are given permission to leave for West Germany

October 6 Gorbachev arrives in East Berlin for the celebration of fortieth anniversary of the founding of the DDR; meeting of about 2,500 people approves the declaration of New Forum and other reform groups asking for free supervised elections

October 7 Fortieth anniversary of the founding of the DDR; protests, suppressed by police, mass arrests; founding meeting of the Social Democratic Party (SDP) in the DDR

October 9 Massive street demonstrations in Leipzig; no police interference

October 10 Five hundred demonstrators, arrested in Dresden, are released after discussions between opposition groups and Mayor Wolfgang Berghofer

October 11 The executive committee of the Writers' Union adopts a resolution calling for "revolutionary reforms"; published October 16, in LPDP paper

October 12 Meetings of church officials with mayor of East Berlin; promises of liberalization

October 13 One hundred delegates from New Forum meet in East Berlin

October 16 Demonstration of over 100,000 people in Leipzig, 10,000 in Dresden; no police interference

October 18 Meeting of Politburo of the SED; resignation of Honecker from key positions in party and government; others resign as well; election of Krenz as general secretary of SED; he declares SED has initiated a change—the *Wende*

October 21 Demonstrations in Leipzig, Dresden, East Berlin, Plauen, Potsdam, and Karl-Marx-Stadt; SED officials appear at several and debate with crowds

October 21 The "Monday demonstrations" continue in Leipzig and many other cities; officials promise to investigate excessive use of force in dealing with earlier protests

October 24 Election of Krenz as head of Council of State; the Politburo recommends that all DDR citizens be permitted to travel to the West

October 26 Mass meeting in Dresden with Hans Modrow, head of county SED, and Mayor Berghofer; they answer questions, declare that a "revolutionary change" is in progress

October 28 East German CDU newspaper calls for free elections

November 1 Krenz meets with Gorbachev; unification of Germany, says Krenz, "is not on the agenda of history"

November 2 Margot Honecker resigns as education minister; Harry Tisch resigns as head of Free German Trade Union League (FDGB); other SED leaders also resign; Krenz confers with vice-president of European Community about trade agreements

November 3 Visa requirement for travel to Czechoslovakia suspended; some 19,500 DDR citizens leave for West Germany via Czechoslovakia within the next four days

November 4 Demonstration of 1 million in Berlin organized by Union of Artists, for freedom of expression, travel, association, and free elections; Stefan Heym, Christa Wolf speak; SED extensively criticized

November 6 Government publishes draft of new travel law

November 7 Draft of travel law rejected by parliamentary committee as inadequate; the government, under Willi Stoph, resigns; agrees to stay in office until successors elected

November 8 Meeting of the Central Committee of the SED; massive demonstrations of SED members before Central Committee building; all 21 members of the Politburo resign; Central Committee elects a new 11-member Politburo, including Hans Modrow, who is recommended to Parliament as new minister president; New Forum is recognized as a legal association

November 9 Press spokesman for Central Committee announces that borders with West Germany will be opened; opening of Berlin Wall as tens of thousands cross over that night

November 10 Helmut Kohl interrupts visit to Poland to speak in West Berlin; chairman of DDR-CDU, accused of corruption, resigns, Lothar De Maizière elected new chairman

November 12 After numerous meetings of reform groupings in the SED, the Central Committee agrees to call an extraordinary party congress

November 13 Parliament elects Hans Modrow minister-president, Günther Maleuda of the DBD chairman; Restricted Zone along border is opened

November 17 Modrow announces comprehensive reforms

November 20 Demonstrations in many cities against leading role of SED; Krenz and Modrow meet with West German representatives to discuss economic and financial issues, travel

November 22 The SED offers to talk to other parties, citizens' movements at a Round Table

November 24 Green Party founded in the DDR; West German CDU leaders meet with their counterparts in the DDR-CDU

November 26 Leaders of West German Free Democratic Party meet with leaders of East German LDPD and Democratic Opening

November 28 Kohl releases 10-point plan for new all-German structure, a confederation leading to a federation; "Appeal for Our Country—for the

Preservation of the Independence of the DDR" is signed by Christa Wolf, Stefan Heym, and others; Krenz and Modrow sign following day

December 1 Parliament removes SED claim to leading role from the Constitution, apologizes to Czechoslovakia for participation in invasion of 1968

December 2 Thousands of SED members demonstrate before Central Committee, demanding resignation of Politburo and of Central Committee; Krenz shouted down

December 3 Central Committee, Politburo, and General Secretary Egon Krenz all resign; Working Committee appointed to prepare for extraordinary congress

December 4 Demonstrations in many cities; first calls for immediate reunification of Germany; the CDU withdraws from the Democratic Bloc of parties in the National Front

December 5 Attorney general resigns because of allegations of dilatory prosecution of those guilty of corruption or abuse of office

December 6 Krenz resigns as chairman of Council of State

December 7 On invitation of churches, government and opposition parties meet at Round Table; demand for dissolution of Stasi and free elections on May 6, 1990

December 8 Extraordinary Congress of the SED elects Gregor Gysi chairman, Modrow and Berghofer vice-chairmen

December 15 Congress of DDR-CDU confirms De Mazière as chairman, removes references to socialism from its constitution, and adds commitment to unification of Germany and market economy

December 16 SED Extraordinary Congress changes name of party to SED-PDS (Socialist Unity Party—Party of Democratic Socialism)

December 18 Second session of Round Table

December 19 Kohl comes to Dresden for two-day working visit, meets with Modrow; agreement on formation of a "contractual community"

December 27 Round Table warns against the rise of neo-fascist tendencies

December 31 - January 1, 1990 Giant New Year's celebration at the Brandenburg Gate

1990

January 2 Round Table protests decision of Modrow to create a Constitutional Protection Agency (Verfassungsschutz) and a Central Intelligence Agency (Nachrichtendienst); threatens to withdraw from Round Table unless satisfactory evidence of dismantling of Stasi is produced by January 8

January 3 SED-PDS cosponsors a mass demonstration to protest vandalism at the monument to the Soviet army at Treptow; rivalry with the cosponsoring SPD apparent; accusations that the SED-PDS (or the Stasi) did the vandalism generate wide ill-will

January 5 West German spokesman declares progress toward unification depends on free elections in the DDR; Walter Janka, editor sentenced to prison in 1957, is exonerated by the courts of any crime; declares his continuing commitment to socialism

January 8 Strongly pro-unification, anti-SED demonstration in Leipzig

January 11 Modrow withdraws proposal for Constitutional Protection Agency; parliament authorizes foreign firms to operate in the DDR

January 13 First Congress of the Social Democratic Party (SDP) changes its name to Social Democratic Party of Germany (SPD) like West German party

January 14 Modrow calls for social market economy

January 15 Modrow attends session of the Round Table, asks its members to help oversee dissolution of Stasi; mass pro-unification demonstrations in Leipzig, Dresden, Karl-Marx-Stadt

January 20 German Social Union (DSU) founded in Leipzig, splintering off from Democratic Opening, as Christian conservative party

January 21 Executive committee of the SED-PDS decides not to dissolve party, as many members had urged, but to change name; Berghofer and other leaders from Dresden resign

January 22 Modrow invites members of Round Table to participate in government

January 25 Council of Ministers agrees on freedom of operation for commercial, craft, and service businesses, up to 49 percent foreign ownership of DDR firms

January 27 Formal founding conference of New Forum agrees to remain citizens' movement, not become political party; calls for referendum on unification in both parts of Germany

January 28 Members of Round Table agree to participate in a Government of National Responsibility; parliamentary elections are moved to March 18

February 1 Modrow releases proposal for path to German unification; central points are a contractual confederation, European neutrality

February 2 SED-PDS changes name to PDS; three citizens' movements (New Forum, Democracy Now, and Initiative for Peace and Freedom) agree to form coalition for the March elections; Kohl and Genscher travel to Moscow; Gorbachev agrees German unity is a matter for German people to decide

February 5 Ministers without portfolio elected from opposition parties to serve in Modrow government; in meeting with Kohl in West Berlin, CDU, DSU, and DA form electoral coalition for the March elections

February 11 Three "liberal" parties in the DDR form electoral coalition

February 12 Round Table agrees to request a contribution of 10-15 billion marks from West Germany

February 13 Conferences in Bonn between Kohl, Modrow, and members of both cabinets; West Germany rejects contribution idea; both sides agree on commission to prepare plans for currency union and economic cooperation

February 14 Green Party and Independent Women's Federation form electoral coalition; in Ottawa, relevant foreign ministers agree on a two-plus-four (East and West Germany, the United States, Great Britain, France, and the Soviet Union) conference to resolve questions of unity

February 15 Founding congress of the Independent Women's Federation

February 25 Ibrahim Böhme elected SPD chair; PDS platform adopted calling for unification with protection for social benefits; Modrow elected honorary chair but relieved of party responsibility to permit service as independent minister-president

March 1 At meeting with Kohl in Bonn, CDU and its coalition parties agree on common election program; call for unification under Article 23 of the West German Fundamental Law

March 5 Round Table submits a social charter to Parliament, to protect DDR rights

March 12 Round Table approves first version of pre-unification draft constitution

March 18 Parliamentary elections; CDU largest number of votes while SPD trails unexpectedly

April 4 Round Table approves final draft of a new constitution

May 6 Local elections; CDU again largest winner

May 19 First contract between East and West Germany looking toward unification

July 1 West German mark becomes official currency in the DDR

September 6 Second contract between East and West Germany provides for unification under Article 23 of the West German Constitution

September 12 Two-plus-four meeting authorizes unification

October 3 Official incorporation of DDR states into West Germany

October 14 Elections for new state governments in the former DDR

December 2 All-German elections to the Bundestag; CDU victory

a note on sources

I have relied on a number of sources to check my facts after completing this book; although it is not intended as a scholarly study, I believe the facts are presented as accurately as is possible for an involved observer writing in the period of their occurrence. For newspaper accounts, I have found the *Tageszeitung* consistently informative and reliable, if often openly opinionated; we subscribed to its Berlin (West) edition, and, after it began publishing its DDR edition, we bought that as often as we could. We subscribed to *Neues Deutschland* early in our stay in Weimar, since we were starved for news and it was better than nothing, and have relied on it sporadically for official information and the party line, but did not find it particularly informative. Since the *Wende*, it has gotten much better. Similarly, East German television, deadly dull before the *Wende*, we found tremendously interesting afterward; because "Aktuelles Kamera" on the DDR channel and West German news came back-to-back in the evening, we watched both whenever we could.

For dates and for quotations, there are several good chronologies available. Two of these are: Zeno and Sabine Zimmerling, *Neue Chronik DDR, Berichte, Fotos, Dokumente* (Berlin: Verlag Tribüne, 1990); Frank Schumann, ed., *100 Tage die die DDR erschütterten* (Berlin: Verlag Neues Leben, 1990). The Deutsches Museum put out a catalogue, including the text of all of the speeches, covering the November 4 demonstration. A number of collections of documents for the period have appeared, and innumerable volumes of essays, special editions of magazines, journal articles, and so forth; I would only mention one that we found of particular value: *Nichts wird mehr so sein, wie es war* (Leipzig: Reclam Verlag, 1990). Frances, much more than I, read widely in East German literature, from Maxie Wander and Viktor Klemperer to Jürgen Kuczinski and Erwin Strittmatter; as indicated in our text, Stefan Heym's *Nachruf* (Bertelsmann, 1988), was in a sense our introduction to life as it was in the DDR. We found many of the jokes we already knew, plus many other good ones, in Rudi Geerts, ed., *Hier lacht das Volk, Witze aus der alten und neuen DDR* (Hamburg: Rowohlt Verlag, 1990). For both facts and interpretation of the physical and social history of Berlin, I have relied on Harald Bodenschatz, *Platz frei für das neue Berlin! Geschichte der Stadterneurerung seit 1871* (Berlin, Transit: Eine Publikation des Instituts für Stadt- und Regionalplanung der TU Berlin, 1987) and Bruno Flierl has been unfailingly helpful with his tremendous knowledge of the history of the city and its political background.

Several of my own papers are referred to or quoted in the text. The full versions may be found in: *Monthly Review* (Summer 1990), for "The Politics of the Turn"; Bengt Turner, ed., *Housing in Eastern Europe* (Gävle, Sweden: The Swedish Institute of Building Research, 1991), for "DDR Cities and Housing—Socialist?" and the *International Journal of Urban and Regional Research* 14, no. 3 (September 1990), for "Social, Political, and Urban Change in the GDR: Scarcely Existing Socialism." The Turner volume also includes a detailed history of DDR housing policy and practices I wrote with the help of Wolfgang Schumann of the Institute for Sociology of Humboldt University in Berlin. The book I co-edited with Fred Staufenbiel is called *Wohnen und Stadtpolitik im Umbruch: Perspektiven der Stadterneuerung nach 40 Jahre DDR*, and is due out in 1991. An interview dealing particularly with feelings of being Jewish appeared in *Sonntag*, which also published a column of mine on the Potsdamer Platz controversy; an expanded version of the latter (under the title "Die bescheidene Stadt") will be published in Austria shortly. A piece on the future of the PDS appeared in *In These Times*.

A number of published works available in English are recommended to readers wishing to pursue issues relating to the DDR. Among those we found most useful are: Marilyn Rueschemeyer, with Christiane Lemke, *Quality of Life in the German Democratic Republic: Changes and Developments in a State Socialist Society* (New York: M.E. Sharpe, 1989), which includes Marilyn Rueschemeyer's own article on "New Towns in the German Democratic Republic: The Neubaugebiete of Rostock" (I have reviewed the book in the *Journal of International Affairs*); David Childs, Thomas A. Baylis, and Marilyn Rueschemeyer, *East Germany in Comparative Perspective* (London: Routledge, 1989); Mike Dennis, *German Democratic Republic*

(London: Pinter, 1988); C. Bradley Scharf, *Politics and Change in East Germany: An Evaluation of Socialist Democracy* (Boulder: Westview Press, 1984); David Childs, *The GDR: Moscow's German Ally* (2nd ed.; London: Unwin and Hyman, 1988); Ivan Szelenyi, *Urban Inequalities under State Socialism* (Oxford: Oxford University Press, 1983) and "Housing Policy in the Emergent Socialist Mixed Economy of Eastern Europe," *Housing Affairs* 4, no. 3: 167-76.